# DIALOGUE,
# CONFLICT RESOLUTION,
# AND CHANGE

SUNY series in Israeli Studies
Russell Stone, editor

# DIALOGUE,
# CONFLICT RESOLUTION,
# AND CHANGE

## Arab-Jewish Encounters in Israel

Mohammed Abu-Nimer

STATE UNIVERSITY OF NEW YORK PRESS

Published by
State University of New York Press, Albany

For information, address State University of New York Press,
State University Plaza, Albany, N.Y., 12246

Production by Cathleen Collins
Marketing by Fran Keneston

**Library of Congress Cataloging in Publication Data**

Abu-Nimer, Mohammed, 1962–
    Dialogue, conflict resolution, and change : Arab-Jewish encounters
in Israel / Mohammed Abu-Nimer.
        p.    cm.—(SUNY series in Israeli studies)
    Includes bibliographical references and index.
    ISBN 0-7914-4153-9 (alk. paper).—ISBN 0-7914-4154-7 (pbk. :
alk. paper)
        1. Arab-Israeli conflict—1993–    —Peace.    2. Intergroup relations—
Israel.    3. Jews—Israel—Attitudes.    4. Palestinian Arabs—Israel—
Attitudes.    I. Title.    II. Series.
DS119.76.A35    1999
956.9405'4—dc21                                                               98-35837
                                                                                          CIP

10  9  8  7  6  5  4  3  2  1

For all the Arab and Jewish peacemakers who are
constantly battling stereotypes, prejudice, and
discrimination in their own ways

# Contents

# Figures

# Tables

# Acknowledgments

This book could not have been completed without the cooperation, willingness, and openness of the directors, facilitators, and participants of the various Arab-Jewish groups and organizations who agreed to be part of this project. I certainly hope that this research contributes to their efforts in bringing Arabs and Jews together. I am also thankful for all the Arab and Jewish politicians and community leaders who granted me their precious time, and spoke openly and frankly about Arab-Jewish relations in Israel.

There are so many colleagues and friends to acknowledge. However, I am most gracious to the directors and facilitators of Neve Shalom/Wahat El Salam, Giva'at Haviva, Beit Hagefen, Van Leer, Adam, Eshkolot project (Unit for Democracy), and Shutafut, who were open and courageous enough to share with me their experience, questions, and most important feelings. I am particularly thankful to Walid Mula, Elias Eidi, Elias Zidan, Edna Zaretsky, Hagiet Zaletsberg, Hagiet Gor Ziev, and Dr. Peter Lemish. I am also thankful to all the Arab and Jewish participants who granted me the privilege of observing their encounters and who accepted me in their houses and towns for the period of the field research. Also, to friends and colleagues who hosted me throughout the field research, particularly Amal Abu-Zidan.

I would like to extend my appreciation to and acknowledgment of the late Professor James Laue, Institute for Conflict Analysis and Resolution, George Mason University, who provided me with the support and stamina needed to complete this project, and provided consistent and constructive feedback for every draft; and to Professor Christopher Mitchell and Professor Kevin Avruch of the Institute for Conflict Analysis and Resolution, George Mason University, for their helpful remarks, notes, and suggestions.

Special thanks to Haviva Bar (Israeli Institute for Applied Research, Jerusalem), whose assistance gave me a sense of direction and focus in a complicated field research context. I also must recognize David Parson, director of the ESL program at Guilford College, for his thorough review of the manuscript; and Barbra Wien, training coordinator at the United States Institute for Peace (USIP), for her review of the manuscript too.

The funding and monitoring of several institutions was very instrumental in completing this project, especially the Ford Foundation, whose financial support was an essential factor that allowed me to concentrate my efforts in completing the field research and analysis; the United States Institute for Peace (USIP), whose "Peace Scholar fellowship" award also contributed to the completion of this project; and Guilford College's and School of International Service at American University dean's offices, whose research fund awards assisted me in updating and completing this research.

Finally, this research would not have been completed without the patience and support of my family: my wife, children, and parents, whose understanding and acceptance of my peacemaking efforts inspired this book.

# Introduction

If asked, many people are likely to say that dialogue is good. It has been linked to "motherhood and apple pie," something which no one would publicly reject. (Gordon & Gordon, 1991:2)

Attempts to establish dialogue and communication between conflicting parties are usually welcomed regardless of their content, structure, motivation, or outcome. Those who oppose these attempts are usually labeled "radicals" or "fanatics." Nevertheless, the assumption of this study is that there should be no immediate, naive acceptance or warm welcome of every dialogue setting. Thus, the following research is an in-depth examination of intergroup intervention programs whose aims are to promote peace through communication and dialogue. The conflict resolution framework utilized in the study focuses on the analysis and criticism of the parties' existing power relationship.

In some divided societies such attempts to bring conflicting groups into encounter proceed without either interference or support. In others, they are encouraged by the regimes since their main assumption is non-violence and communication, which is less threatening to the ruling regimes than demonstrating and organizing or other protest actions. These initiatives of encountering adversarial parties are usually considered to be an integral part of the forces that act for change in the relations between the conflicting parties or the different ethnic groups in the divided societies. In divided societies such as Northern Ireland, South Africa, Israel, and countries of Latin America, the attempts to establish dialogue and communication between communities have become institutionalized through youth, teachers, and professional encounters conducted by nonprofit organizations.

The concept for such encounter was imported from the interpersonal and intergroup relations approach that was popular in the United States in the late 1960s and early 1970s. The organizers of these encounters are not only inspired by the U.S. approaches, but also receive financial aid from Western countries (i.e., Europe or the United States).

Many of these encounters are implemented by organizers who rarely reexamine or question the applicability of these programs to the specific conflict or culture. A central question for this research is the extent to which these programs or intervention efforts are designed and implemented to contribute to the change process that operates to alter the social and political structure of dominance and control of one group over the others.

To address such issues this book examines the intervention models applied by six of the largest Arab-Jewish encounter programs in Israel: Neve Shalom/Wahat El Salam, Giva'at Haviva, Medreshet Adam, Beit Hagefen, the Arab-Jewish project in the Van Leer Institute, and the Eshkolot project in the Unit for Democracy and Coexistence in the Ministry of Education. These programs generally involve Arab and Jewish secondary and high school students and teachers. The encounters last from one to three days. They are led jointly by Arab and Jewish facilitators. In some cases the encounter is part of an annual intervention model that the organization implements in the schools, and in other cases the two or three encounters make up the model. These programs are aimed at improving Arab-Jewish relations in Israel and assisting in raising more tolerant, democratic, and culturally sensitive generations. Most of these types of programs—of which there are about forty in Israel—are supported by the Ministry of Education and other governmental offices.

This research examines critically the six intervention programs these organizations implement. It discusses four major concepts that were operationalized into the four following questions about each model:

1. How do intervenors and participants perceive Arab-Jewish relations in Israel?
2. What are the similarities and differences among the six intervention programs? Do they operate from the same assumptions, structure, process, content, and facilitator role?
3. How do intervenors and participants perceive the outcomes of their intervention programs?
4. How does the changing political environment impact the different programs' intervention models?

The findings are presented according to two main levels of analysis, reflected in the following questions: (1) Do organizational and national affiliations influence the participants' or intervenors' perception of the four concepts? (2) What is the influence of national affiliation (Arab or

Jewish) of the participants and intervenors on their perceptions of the four research concepts?

By analyzing the intervenors' and participants' responses to these questions and examining the nature and design of the six intervention programs, the findings will reflect the degree of professional integrity that intervenors have and the level of commitment and involvement among participants to change Arab-Jewish relations in Israel. Based on all the findings and the analysis of existing research, this study addresses the issue of whether these intervention programs are directed and implemented to promote political change or whether they support the existing status quo control system that characterizes Arab-Jewish relations in Israel.

One of the main purposes of this research is to identify and propose an alternative set of conflict resolution principles that can be applied in such dialogue groups and encounters. Such a proposition is based on the examination of the different approaches and intervention models in the emerging field of conflict resolution.

Obviously, there are many factors that motivated my interest in studying Arab-Jewish encounters in Israel. First, since the general thrust of these programs is nonviolence, communication, peace, and dialogue, they are hardly criticized, and are welcomed at least by the moderates in both adversarial communities. This research analyzes and identifies assumptions that underlie the work accomplished in some of these programs, specifically between Arabs and Jews in Israel. Second, although Arab-Jewish encounter programs have operated in Israel since the early 1960s, there has been no comprehensive systematic study that compares the work and the models implemented by different organizations. Third, this conflict has been neglected and avoided by both Palestinians and Jews, as well as politicians and scholars. Neither the Palestinian Liberation Organization (PLO) nor the Israeli delegates were interested in discussing the status of the Palestinian minority in Israel since the beginning of their negotiations in Madrid and Washington in 1991 and 1992. This conflict has been addressed less and has been overshadowed by the more violent conflict in the West Bank and Gaza. But there is the potential for escalation of the Arab-Jewish conflict in Israel in the aftermath of the agreement between Palestinians and Israelis. Fourth, most of the studies of the encounters between Arabs and Jews in Israel focus on a single organization or program. Most of them are also evaluative, quantitative studies, which were designed to evaluate and report on the actual impact that a specific program or encounter produced. None of the scholars have compared the models that are implemented by the different organizations. None of the studies explores the impact of the context on the design and implementation of the intervention models. Fifth, as in any other social science research,

researchers' personal and professional experiences as well as their backgrounds influence their priorities in selecting their research themes. In
addition, to being influenced by this conflict as a Palestinian resident of
Israel, I trained and worked as a facilitator in the Arab-Jewish programs in
Israel for fifteen years. During these years I witnessed and experienced the
different changes in this field, and was constantly challenged by political
events, which often made continuing and promoting Arab-Jewish encounters essential.

In designing and conducting the research that led to this book, the
major difficulty that is faced in comparing and evaluating the impact of
these specific intervention models in Israel and other models in general is
the identification of evaluation and measurement criteria. Another difficulty is the notion that it is impossible to isolate or control the impact of
the political and social context on the output of any intervention models.
The current research addresses these two major problems by eliciting the
criteria of success and impact as intervenors and participants perceive
them, and presenting them as the basis for any future evaluation of the
Arab-Jewish intervention programs. The context impact problem is treated
by considering the political context as part of the intervening factors that
have an impact on every stage of the intervention.

By addressing the two problems of (a) the criteria of evaluation or
success and (b) the impact of context on the intervention model, this
research aims to establish a foundation for further discussion of a third
dilemma in the conflict resolution field: the quest of every intervenor to
transfer the output of any intervention from the intergroup or interpersonal level to the political or decision-making level. In other words, how
can an intervenor be more effective in promoting change processes in a
conflict situation?

The encounter programs are important educational frameworks for
Arab and Jewish students and teachers who are segregated in most contexts
of their lives. However, there is a need to reexamine and redesign the
programs if they are to contribute directly and intentionally to political
change in Israel.

Finally, I should indicate that having worked fifteen years in leading
dialogue and encounter groups of Arabs and Jews in the Middle East, I feel
as if no book or text will be successful in capturing both the pain and
frustration and the joy and hope that filled these encounters. Words fail to
describe Palestinian teenagers or teachers when they truly, and for the first
time, realize that Jewish participants who are associated with dominance
and power, are sincerely scared of Arabs. Or the sudden awareness of a
Jewish participant who just finished his or her first personal encounter with
an Arab.

This book is an attempt to capture the experiences and perceptions of the Arab-Jewish encounters' participants. The book includes ten chapters. The first chapter is a review and critique of the different theories of intergroup relations and the contact hypothesis approach in terms of their contribution to change processes. The second chapter discusses the conflict resolution models and theories as an emerging field. It also addresses the problems and limitations of the different conflict resolution intervention models in relation to the political and social change processes. Chapter 3 presents several related aspects of Arab-Jewish relations in Israel as background to the case studies. It is a review of the historical, social, political, and educational relationship between Arabs and Jews in Israel on both micro and macro levels. Chapter 4 is a brief history of the field, "coexistence and dialogue between Arabs and Jews in Israel"; it also contains a comprehensive review of the major findings of the research conducted on Arab-Jewish encounter and education for democracy programs since the 1970s. Chapter 5 presents the four major research concepts of this study: the perception of conflict, the design of an intervention model, the success of intervention, and the impact of context on the intervention model. It also describes the major features of the six encounter programs in this study. The sixth chapter introduces results related to the design of the intervention models in each case study. The seventh chapter introduces the perception of conflict as it is presented by intervenors and participants. The eighth chapter is an analysis of the perceived impact and output of each model by intervenors and participants. The ninth chapter identifies the major impacts of the current peace process, the Intifada, the Gulf War, and the Soviet Jewish immigration on the design of intervention models and on the programs in general. Chapter 10 examines whether the Arab-Jewish intervention programs contribute to conflict resolution and change or to political control. It also includes an alternative approach to conflict resolution, a list of limitations and critique of Arab-Jewish programs, discussion of whether Arab-Jewish programs are conflict resolution models, and a list of recommendations to improve the design and implementation of Arab-Jewish programs in Israel in particular and conflict resolution programs in general.

# Abbreviations

| | |
|---|---|
| ADR | Alternative dispute resolution |
| AJP | Arab-Jewish programs |
| AJPE | Arab-Jewish program encounters |
| AJR | Arab-Jewish relations |
| APS | Analytical problem solving |
| BH | Beit Hagefen |
| DOP | Declaration of Principles |
| GH | Giva'at Haviva |
| IPJAC | Intervention programs in Jewish-Arab contacts |
| MA | Medrashat Adam |
| MO | Movement organization |
| NS/WAS | Neve Shalom/Wahat Al Salam |
| PLO | Palestinian Liberation Organization |
| PS | Problem solving |
| PSW | Problem-solving workshop |
| UFD | Unit for Democracy |
| VL | Van Leer |

# 1

# Intergroup Relations Approach

## CONTACT HYPOTHESIS THEORY

Contact hypothesis theory is a central part of theories of intergroup relations. Generally, the contact hypothesis theoretical propositions are used to explain prejudice reduction and discrimination in intergroup situations, which are subcategories of the larger arena of intergroup relations.

Contact hypothesis theory refers to the approach that brings members of different cultures together over a concentrated period of time. By using group techniques, these meetings seek to strengthen interpersonal relations and thereby change participants' attitudes and opinions toward one another. Hewstone and Brown define and criticize the contact hypothesis's main assumption:

> Increasing physical intergroup contact inevitably will lead to changes in the mutual attitudes of interacting members and improve their intergroup relations. It focuses on similarity and mechanical solidarity with scant attention to differences and organic solidarity. (Hewstone & Brown, 1986:172)

The classical contact hypothesis theory belongs to the extensive human relations movement that emerged after the Second World War. It attempts to combat all forms of intergroup prejudice: racial, religious, and ethnic. According to Allen (1986), it extended into other intergroup domains, including the industrial relations movement and the international arena from which conflict resolution approaches and theories emerged. The main belief in the 1950s was that intergroup contact would inevitably lead to a change in mutual attitudes of interacting members and improve their relations (Ben-Ari & Amir, 1986).

Several attempts have been made to conceptualize and classify the literature on intergroup relations: Lewin (1947, 1958); Allport (1954);

1

Sherif (1958); Ashmor (1970); Ehrlich (1973); Tajfel (1982); Peled and Bargal (1983); Amir (1976); Ben-Ari and Amir (1986, 1988b); and Hewstone and Brown (1986). These scholars constitute the main bulk of researchers who have attempted to classify the theoretical literature on intergroup relations, especially the contact hypothesis, which stood for many years as the main approach to solving intergroup conflict.

Although Tajfel (1982) and Amir (1976) argue that despite the substantial amount of literature on the contact hypothesis, theoretically, there is still little understanding of how contact processes operate as change agents.

Peled and Bargal (1983) classified the outcome of these processes of prejudice reduction into three sets of frameworks:

*(1) Cognitive processes:* In this approach, three main cognitive processes to explain intergroup discriminations were identified: (a) the old belief-congruence approach, which argues that forming attitudes between people is the congruence of their belief system; people are attracted more to others with a similar belief system than to their social group members (Rokeach, 1960, 1968); (b) the social identity and social comparison approach, which assumes that people need to protect their social identity and tend to favor ingroup behavior even when there is no explicit or institutionalized conflict between the groups (Tajfel, 1982); (c) the attribution processes approach, which is based on a social-psychological framework, and relies on attribution theory to explain principles and guidelines that people apply in order to understand, comprehend, and explain the behaviors and attitudes of others.[1]

*(2) Personality development and sociocultural influences:* This set of explanatory theories includes the psychodynamic and the sociocultural approaches. The psychoanalytical theory includes aggression and frustration hypotheses (Dollard et al., 1939) and the authoritarian personality hypothesis, which is the modern developed approach of psychodynamic theory.

The sociocultural approaches explain prejudice and discrimination behavior on the assumption that these behaviors are learned through the socialization learning processes of the individual interacting with his or her environment (Ashmor & Del Boca, 1976). In the socialization processes there are four major channels or agents: parents, peers, schools, and mass media.

*(3) Intergroup conflicts and competition:* This type of explanation of prejudice and discrimination stands for the societal level of analysis and explanation provided by Ashmor (1970) and Ashmor and Del Boca (1976). In comparison with the previous sets, this type of theory does not rely on individual personality or development but on intergroup relationships as a cause in shaping an individual's attitudes.

In a comprehensive study of prejudice and intergroup relations, Hewstone and Brown (1986) identified the main theoretical propositions of Allport (1954), Cook (1978, 1979), and Pettigrew (1971). They emphasize a very fundamental distinction between the contact hypothesis and the intergroup relations approach, and suggest the adoption of intergroup processes as the basis for a theoretical explanatory framework. Their argument is based on Tajfel's (1982) social categorization and Tejfel and Turner (1986).

In conclusion, the different theoretical bases of the contact hypothesis are divided into two sets of theoretical explanations. On the one hand, there are those scholars who rely on personality and individual development as causes and methods of changing an individual's attitudes. This group of scholars tends to rely on psychosociological or psychodynamic theories. On the other hand, there are scholars who stress intergroup relations as the focal cause of changing and shaping an individual's attitudes. This group mainly relies on social-psychological and sociological theories.

Based on these different theoretical explanations of the contact hypothesis, practitioners and scholars have developed various types of intervention models.

## INTERVENTION MODELS BASED ON THE CONTACT HYPOTHESIS AND INTERGROUP RELATIONS THEORIES

The literature on the practical approaches to reducing prejudice and changing stereotypes is more developed and conceptualized than the theories and philosophy that attempt to explain the processes. Thus, there have been many attempts to classify the various intervention actions and principles applied in intergroup relations. This part presents three types of classifications of intervention models: (1) Hewstone and Brown (1986); (2) Peled and Bargal (1983); and (3) Ben-Ari and Amir (1986, 1988a, b).

In a comprehensive study, Amir (1969, 1976), based on the work of Allport (1954) and Cook (1962), identifies and lists favorable and unfavorable conditions that can promote or prevent change in attitudes and prejudice reduction processes. Amir also develops several theoretical propositions in relation to the input, process, and output of the intergroup relations. Those conditions are basic requirements in any intervention program that aims to achieve change in intergroup relations.

The favorable conditions are:

(a) Equal status contact (i.e., symmetry).
(b) Positive perception of the other group as a result of the interaction.

(c) Contact between majority members and higher-status minority members.
(d) Contact situation includes cooperation, not competition.
(e) Contact situation involves interdependence activities, subordinate goals, or separate goals that can be achieved only by cooperation.
(f) Intimate, not casual, contact.
(g) An "authority" or social climate in supporting intergroup contact.
(h) A pleasant or rewarding contact.

The unfavorable conditions are:

(a) Intergroup competitive contact.
(b) Unpleasant, involuntary, tension-laden contact.
(c) Lowering prestige or status of one group as a result of the contact.
(d) Frustrated group or individuals through the contact.
(e) Moral or ethical standards in contact group that are objectionable to each other.
(f) Majority members are higher in status or other characteristics than minority members.

*(1) Hewstone and Brown's (1986) intergroup model:* Hewstone and Brown's comprehensive review suggests a new and expanded approach based on their fundamental distinction between interpersonal/intergroup interaction and similarities/differences as well as the components and processes of contacts. Their review establishes the case that interpersonal processes and contact are less effective and produce the problem of generalization of effects beyond the individual participants. Their review of "outputs' generalization" is that:

> As long as the individuals are interacting as individuals, rather than as group members, there is no basis either for expecting any attitudes change to be generalized through the group or for one person to extrapolate the positive attitudes towards one individual to other outgroup members. (Hewstone & Brown,1986:20)

Based on these distinctions, Hewstone and Brown (1986) suggest a model that, unlike Ben-Ari and Amir (1986, 1988b) and others, focuses on the contextual conditions of the contacts. They suggest an intergroup focus of contact, based on these four conditions:

1. Superordinate goals: goals that one group cannot attain without the other group; they are interdependent.

2. Cooperation, not competition, between the groups.
3. Multigroup membership and cross-cutting social categories.
4. Achieving equal status by the manipulation of "expectation state." ("expectations training" to overcome the negative feature and expectation as a result of each group's self-image.)

The consideration of these conditions and the favorable conditions suggested by Amir (1976) and Ben-Ari and Amir (1988a) is crucial to the application of the intergroup contact model.

*(2) Peled and Bargal (1983):* Based on Lewin's research, Peled and Bargal track the source of interventions that aim to change stereotypes and attitudes to three types originated from different disciplines:

1. Attitude change derived from social psychology (interpersonal influence). In order to change the attitudes and behavior of people, either a meaningful reference group (Sherif, 1958; Kelly, 1968) or an alternative culture (Lewin, 1958) needs to be created. Peled and Bargal focus on Lewin's approach, which assumes that the changes in a person who is undergoing processes of prejudice reduction can change one of the three main sectors of his or her personality: *the cognitive structure (perceptions), the values (preferences, attractions),* or *behavior.* To cause a change in the three sectors of the personality, different components in the intervention process need to be integrated. These components should address the different sectors. According to the Lewinian approach, there are three processes to change the individual's beliefs and values: (a) "unfreeze" the existing beliefs and values in a "cultural island" setting that secures the individual's environment for openness and cathartic processes; (b) "moving," in which the group of people adopts the new values, beliefs, and perceptions of the other group; and (c) "refreezing," which reinforces the newly adopted values and perceptions by supporting the person, thus ensuring retention of these values.

2. Behavioral change and psychotherapy that is derived from clinical psychology. In this approach, which is represented by Rogers (1957), Allport (1954), and Egan (1970, 1976), certain conditions and mechanisms should be provided in order to achieve a change in the behavior of the individual's trusting atmosphere, an empathetic understanding of the facilitator of change, openness in both groups, and public examination of feelings and biases by confronting them in a feedback-based process.

3. Social influence (socialization) and educational impacts that are derived from organizational behavior. The conditions in this process of prejudice reduction are similar to those conditions required in socializing a person through an institution or organization. According to Brim and Wheeler (1966) as well as Mortimer and Simons (1978), there are three

stages of socialization: (a) anticipatory socialization, which relates to preparatory conditions and readiness as listed by Amir (1969) and Cook (1962); (b) socialization processes, which are applied by the agents and include all types of educational programs and exercises; (c) disengagement stage, which is determined by the organizations and institutions that conduct the socialization process.

*(3) Ben-Ari and Amir (1988a):* A third attempt to classify the intervention models applied in intergroup relations was made by Ben-Ari and Amir, who identify three intervention approaches: *contact model, information model,* and *psychodynamic model.*

1. In describing the contact model, based on Allport (1954) and Cook (1962), Ben-Ari and Amir state:

> It is based on the belief that intergroup contact will lead to a change in mutual attitudes and relations of interacting members. Underlying this belief is the assumption that contact among individuals from diverse groups creates an opportunity for mutual acquaintance, enhances understanding and acceptance among the interacting group members, and consequently reduces intergroup conflicts, prejudice, and tension. (1988a:87).

2. Based on Brislin (1986) and Triandis (1975), the information model's main assumption is that ignorance and lack of information comprise the bases for the development of prejudice, stereotypes, and consequent tension between groups. To reduce prejudice, members of each group should understand the cultural characteristics of the other group. This enables people to understand and evaluate positively the other group's members. Such results can be achieved by recruiting the means of mass communication and/or the educational system for the dissemination of new information about the target culture (Ben Ari & Amir, 1988a, b).

Within this model there are two approaches. One focuses on the similarities in teaching the history and providing new information (Stephan, 1985; 1987; and Stephan & Stephan, 1984) to both groups. The second approach stresses differences and misperceptions as the basis of the conflict between the two groups. By legitimizing the differences, and not by ignoring them, the group can reach a better understanding and tolerance level (Triandis, 1975).

3. Based on Gudykunst, Hammer, and Wiserman (1977), the psychodynamic model is described as the implementation of T-groups and a "new culture group." According to Amir and Ben-Ari, this model assumes that treating the individual problems and conflicts produces positive reactions to the opponent group because the origins of negative reactions are in the individual's psychodynamic processes and not in the target group.

In 1986, Ben-Ari and Amir suggested an alternative approach, or intervention model, which relies heavily on the cognitive or informational approach, but they also stress the need for integration and interaction of components:

> An integrative program including, in addition to cognitive contents, some intergroup contact that will emphasize the social and emotional aspects of interpersonal and intergroup relations might be more effective. (1986:57)

Having reviewed the theoretical and practical aspects of the contact hypothesis approach, it is also important to address its critiques and limitations.

## CONTACT HYPOTHESIS INTERVENTION: SHORTCOMINGS AND ALTERNATIVES

Since the 1950s and 1960s, when the human relations approach, especially contact theory, was developed, a great deal of criticism has been made. The main critiques and limitations are described by different scholars in Hewstone and Brown (1986). In the ninth chapter, Reicher certainly makes the case against the traditional interpersonal contact model and even against limited intergroup contacts. She states:

> Racism will not be overcome by individual acts, which leaves the racist structure of British society intact, but only through action to change the nature of that society. It will not change by contact but by collective action. (1986:23).

The "collective action act" can have several effects that basically produce a common "enemy" for the encounter groups or for the graduate of the encounter. It can help reduce prejudice for a longer period, as in Reicher's example of the white and black riots in 1981 in London.

Another critique of the intergroup relations contact approach is presented by Pettigrew (1986), who argues that the traditional, and even the improved version of contact theory, does not consider the situation in-depth or at the macro level of analysis. It looks at the individual as cognition and avoids and neglects the affective side. Also, theoretically, the contact hypothesis is a relatively static middle-range theory of modest scope like any other social-psychological formulation. Pettigrew lists three main assumptions underlying the contact hypothesis:

> (a) The fundamental problem of intergroup conflict is individual prejudice. (b) In turn, prejudice is an educational and psychological problem. Most prejudice simply reflects gross ignorance

about outgroups. (c) The effective remedy is education. Attitudes must be changed first, followed by altered behavior. Group stereo-types must be combated with "Brotherhood Dinners," pamphlets and other information means which are used to correct inter-group misconceptions. (1986:172)

An alternative and parallel analysis is drawn by Pettigrew (1986:172):

(a) Prejudice is an important but not the fundamental com-ponent in intergroup relation. Institutionalized discrimination is the core of the problem. (b) Prejudice is not simply a "psycho-logical problem." Stereotypes and prejudice are part of the social adjustment which are adopted by individuals. (c) Education by itself is a woefully insufficient remedy. On the opposite the focus on contact (encounters) efforts away from the real task—the sys-tematic structural alteration necessary to eliminate intergroup separation and institutional discrimination.

Another critique of the three previous hypotheses was drawn by Taylor (1981) and described by Pettigrew (1986:177): "Much of this apparently frequent and friendly intergroup contact is subtly biased so that it is more "illusory than real." Pettigrew recommends emphasizing in the future: (a) balance between interpersonal and intergroup relations; (b) structural and context effect; (c) balance between the affective and motivational aspects using a strong focus on the cognition of social psychology; and (d) a careful exchange between the contact similarities and differences.

Another combined model is designed by Lemish, Mula, and Rubin (1989) to deal specifically with Arab-Jewish relations in Israel. They identify five models in intergroup relations, and criticize the first three models: (a) Commitment-aversion; (b) contact; (c) information; (d) critical education; and (e) critical-structural education.

In criticizing the contact model, Lemish et al. argue that it is a border-line case of domination, and even if all the conditions deemed necessary were met, this approach might at best accomplish modifications in attitudes of participants from the dominant group. Further, it is not likely that the contact approach would enable the participants to attain a substantive understanding of the conflict and their society. Thus, it contributes very little to achieving a structural resolution. More fundamentally, the decep-tions of the contact approach suggest that it is an approach that works to ensure continued control by the dominant group (Lemish et al., 1989:23).

In conclusion, contact hypothesis models remain vulnerable to criticism regarding their effectiveness at the macro or structural level. Particularly, because the contact hypothesis is based on individual and interpersonal encounter, it lacks the ability and potential to address inter-ethnic conflict and asymmetric power relations.

The numerous limitations of the contact hypothesis motivated researchers and practitioners to constantly modify and construct new models to address these limitations. Therefore, the following chapter proposes a set of principles of conflict resolution in a new attempt to contribute to the building of effective models of intervention that will assist in dealing with interethnic conflicts in an educational setting.

# 2

# Conflict Resolution Principles in Intergroup Conflicts

*An Alternative Approach to Contact Hypothesis*

In classifying the substantial amount of research on intergroup contact, Amir (1976:92) argued that "The theoretical understanding of intergroup contact processes and contact as a potential for change is very limited." The same case can be drawn in classifying conflict resolution theories, or more accurately, the theoretical propositions made by scholars in this emerging field. In addition, there are uncertain and different answers to the question: What does conflict resolution include? Therefore, it is essential to describe the emergence of this field prior to discussing its intervention models.

## THE EMERGENCE OF CONFLICT RESOLUTION

Relative to other social science disciplines conflict resolution has a short history. Kriesberg (1991) and Scimecca (1991) trace the modern development of conflict resolution to the creation of problem-solving techniques and cooperation that were introduced into industrial organizational theory and practice by Blake, Sheperd, and Mouton (1964) (i.e., which emerged from the human relations and intergroup relations).These techniques substituted for the power and coercive negotiation techniques.

The development of the field of conflict resolution occurred in several parallel disciplines, but they all originated from the industrial organizational arena, which was motivated by the human relation movement in the 1940s and 1950s. Thus, conflict resolution practice expanded to the international relations arena, particularly when Burton (1969) developed his controlled communication approach to problem solving and conducted

11

the first international workshop in Cyprus. Following Burton's initiative, Kelman (1972), De Reuck (1974), Bank (1984), Mitchell (1981), and Ronald Fisher (1981) initiated other types of problem-solving workshops in the international arena as alternatives to the game theories' intervention models, which produced the coercive negotiation models.[1]

Doob and Fotz (1973) from psychology, and Kelman (1972) from social psychology, also began developing their approaches to conflict resolution. From foreign service officers and diplomats, the second track diplomacy was adopted and taught by practitioners such as McDonald and Bendahmane (1987) and Montville (1987). This informal negotiation, when paralleled with the formal negotiation, provided support and alternative options without political pressure on the formal representatives.

## CONFLICT RESOLUTION: DEFINITIONS AND THEORY

Since there is no one single definition of what conflict resolution is, this section focuses on distinguishing conflict resolution from alternative dispute resolution (ADR), peace studies, and the contact hypothesis or human relations approach. In describing the theory in conflict resolution Scimecca states:

> Furthermore, the field of conflict resolution lacks a theoretical base that can undergird its practice. And although there are many comprehensive theories of conflict, theories of conflict resolution are few and far between. Indeed it can be argued that conflict resolution theories can be divided into two categories: game theoretical frameworks and human needs theory. (1991:33)

As the result of the lack of a defined conflict resolution theory, the parallel developments of the field have been motivated by different movements and disciplines. In fact, scholars and practitioners are still attempting to agree on the terminology and jargon used in this field. For example, the following two columns (Burton, 1986; Scimecca, 1987; Rubinstein, 1990; Fisher, 1989) illustrate the difficulties in defining this new field and its theoretical assumptions.

| Conflict Resolution | Conflict Management and ADR |
|---|---|
| Conflict | Disputes |
| Needs and values | Interests |
| Resolution | Settlement and management |
| Problem solving | Negotiation and mediation |

Burton's distinction amont resolution, settlement, and management is the clearest attempt to draw certain lines to mark the field's boundaries:

*Conflict resolution:* entails the use of collaborative problem solving in a situation where a neutral (i.e., impartial according to Laue and Cormick, 1978) third party helps the disputants engage in conciliation, facilitation, and/or mediation. The resolution contributes to the elimination of the sources of the conflict. *Conflict management:* implies that conflict is an organizational problem, one that can be managed by changing conditions within social institutions. No real structural changes occur in the conditions that produced the conflict. *Conflict settlement:* fosters an outcome which does not necessarily meet the needs of all concerned, but is accepted for the time being because of coercion by a stronger party. (1990a:3)

Based on these distinctions, conflict resolution is an interdisciplinary process of analysis and intervention that is concerned with solving problems that result in destructive conflict (Burton, 1990a). Support for this definition is also provided by Bercovitch (1994), who defines successful resolution of conflict as a change in symptoms and underlying causes, in behavior and perceptions. It demands abandoning power-oriented strategies that treat symptoms only, and embracing a participatory, analytical, and noncoercive approach that provides for the release of pent-up feelings and brings to the surface underlying values, motives, and perceptions (Scimecca, 1987:31).

Another major and essential distinction is made between ADR and conflict resolution. It is basically a distinction between disputes and conflicts. According to Scimecca (1991), ADR is best described as an attempt to reform the administration of justice in the United States. ADR started in the 1970s dealing with the crisis in the courts and the justice system, as an alternative to the adversarial confrontational methods. Eventually, mediation and arbitration were developed to reduce costs and time. There are over 350 ADR programs in the United States, of which approximately 30 percents are run in conjunction with the court system. Based on this distinction, Scimecca and Burton narrow their definition of ADR as processes which are alternatives to the formal legal or court system, in particular, Neighborhood Justice Centers or Community Mediation Centers. They argue that conflict resolution as theory and practice of collaborative problem-solving is different from the ADR movement, which is heavily criticized for functioning as a social control force. In supporting this argument, Scimecca (1991) presents six differences between ADR and conflict resolution:

1. There is no broad concept of conflict in the ADR practice. ADR only relies on how to deal with conflict rather than with

why and when, while Burton's theory of conflict resolution depends heavily on the need for social change.

2. ADR, as any formal law, is embedded in individualism. Behavior and perception of a person are the problem and not social inequality. Conflict resolution that depends on human needs theory considers culture, race, and gender.

3. ADR focuses on misunderstanding rather than on the power structure. It assumes that conflict can be settled by the third party who helps clarify the misunderstanding and miscommunication. Conflict resolution's third party assists the parties to understand and analyze origins, culture, institutional, and human needs of the conflict (Burton, 1986).

4. ADR neutrality is problematic; according to Laue (1982), the supposed neutrality of the third party favors compromise and conceals the fact that values which confirm the existing advantages between unequals are necessarily biased.

5. ADR has lost its original concern for the poor and all those who didn't have access to the law. Conflict resolution with its insistence on fulfilling basic human needs is concerned with the oppressed parties.

6. ADR reflects an alternative to politics and community organizing that lack any organic connection to communities.

Basically, Scimecca (1991) argues the case that ADR is a social control force and movement while conflict resolution through its "infancy" has the potential of functioning as a social change and peacemaking force, especially in deep-rooted conflicts. Therefore, the critiques of conflict resolution as social control forces (Able, 1982; Bayley, 1973; Harrington, 1982; Merry, 1989) do apply to ADR but not to the narrow definition of conflict resolution.

During the 1970s scholars and practitioners of conflict resolution began theorizing their activities. The most prominent theory in the field is the "human needs" theory of conflict resolution (Burton, 1990a), which assumes that there are universal, inviolable human needs which, when thwarted, result in deep-rooted conflicts. According to Burton, there can be no resolution of conflict without analyzing the underlying issues that generate the conflict. Therefore, a resolution should consider the political realities of those parties in conflict. One of Burton's basic assumptions is that no matter what form or degree of coercion is exercised, there will be no societal stability unless human needs of individuals and groups are satisfied.

Burton (1990a, 1990b, 1984) and Azar and Burton (1986) distinguish between interests, which are negotiable, and needs and values, which are not. Needs should be satisfied in order to resolve the conflict, but interests and values can be transformed, exchanged, or negotiated to settle the conflict.

Based on Maslow (1954), Sites (1973), and Lederer, Galtung, and Antal (1980), Burton identifies a list of needs—for response, security, recognition, stimulation, distributive justice, meaning, rationality, control, and a role. The need for a role was added and defined by Burton; the other needs were listed by Sites (1973). The first four needs, which emerged as a result of the necessary dynamic of the socialization process, cannot be immediately and constantly satisfied.

There are several critiques of Burton's theory (Avruch & Black, 1987; Avruch & Black, 1990; Mitchell, 1990; Laue, 1990). However, most of these scholars acknowledge that Burton's theory is the only attempt to support a method of conflict resolution practice by a structural and defined theoretical framework.

Scimecca (1991) lists several critiques of the human needs theory made by different scholars: (a) it emphasizes generic determinism; (b) it fails to consider cultural components and differences as influential factors in practice and theory (Avruch & Black, 1987); (c) the relationships among the different human needs identified by Burton are unclear: are they hierarchical or not? (Mitchell, 1990); (d) it considers power relationships irrelevant to the conflict resolution practice. Power becomes "nonvariable" when parties are engaged in analytical problem solving.

In short, today it is difficult to identify and define a specific and conceptualized conflict resolution theory except Burton's attempts to develop the human needs theory and its practical application to the analytical problem-solving (APS).

## BASIC ASSUMPTIONS AND PRINCIPLES OF CONFLICT RESOLUTION[2]

Although it is true that there is no defined and agreed-on single theory of conflict resolution, certainly there are several assumptions that underlie most conflict resolution intervention programs or processes.

1. Conflict is not necessarily evil, or a failure of an existing system. On the contrary, conflict is often a creative force that generates new options, alternatives, and solutions to existing problems.
2. Conflict is a natural process that can have constructive or destructive outcomes.
3. Conflict is an intrinsic part of all important relationships.

4. Conflict is caused by many different kinds of specific events.
5. People are not problems.
6. Having clear and explicit expectations is a very crucial and essential part of any resolution process for reaching an agreement or understanding the issues involved.
7. Conflict can be positive when:
   a. It increases communication and trust.
   b. We can solve the problem.
   c. It results in development and growth.
   d. It releases feelings that were stored.
   e. It improves our work and performance.
8. Conflict can be negative when it:
   a. Develops into war or violence.
   b. Prevents and blocks personal and group development.
   c. Prevents people from addressing the real issues.
   d. Motivates people to become uncooperative.
9. Conflict can be managed/settled constructively through communication. However, not all conflict can be resolved by improving communication.
10. Not all conflicts lend themselves to joint or negotiated endings. But when mutually satisfactory outcomes can be found, they tend to be more self-enforcing, efficient, and durable.
11. The conflict resolution process can be creative. It can lead to new or improved relationships and help identify new criteria, resources, and outcomes.
12. Although there are many types of conflicts and many types of processes to resolve them, most people tend to approach a conflict with some expectation in mind, often based on previous experience.
13. Conflict resolution skills include analyzing the conflict situation; bringing parties together; assisting parties to shift focus from win/lose competition to joint problem solving; building cooperation and trust; and communication skills of observing, listening, and speaking.
14. The basis of conflict resolution is collaborative problem solving, which attempts to move parties with genuine substantive differences toward a productive resolution.

The above list of assumptions reflects the uniqueness and shift or proposed new approach to deal with conflicts. These assumptions and others are the cornerstone of intervention models in various levels, such as labor management, international, community, and interpersonal conflicts. Most

**Table 2.1. Conflict Resolution Processes and Models of Intervention**

| Model of Intervention | Process of Intervention | Scholarly Research |
|---|---|---|
| 1. International & Interethnic | | |
| Doob's workshops | Facilitation & PS | Doob & Fotz ,1973 |
| APS | APS | Burton, 1986 |
| PSW | PSW | Kelman, 1972 |
| Consultant PSW | PS | Fisher, 1981 |
| Second Track Diplomacy | Negotiation & PS | Montville, 1987<br>Bendahmane, 1987 |
| Intercultural Learning | Contact, Facilitation Conciliation | Amir, 1976;<br>Hewstone, 1986 |
| 2. Community & Organizations | | |
| Labor & Industry Management | Mediation, Negotiation, Arbitrat., Mediat. | Blake, 1964;<br>Colosi and Brekly, 1986 |
| Community Dispute | Facilitation & Conciliation | Salem, 1982<br>Pompa, 1987 |
| Public Policy & Environment | Mediation, Negotiation, Arbitration | Bengham, 1985;<br>Laue, 1982; Bacow<br>& Wheeler, 1983 |
| 3. Interpersonal & Family Dispute | Mediation, & Facilitation | Coogler, 1978;<br>Haynes, 1981;<br>Walton, 1970 |

of these assumptions are derived from or based on social-psychological and sociological theoretical frameworks.

## CONFLICT RESOLUTION: INTERVENTION MODELS AND PROCESSES

As in other fields, the application and practical aspects of conflict resolution are more developed than the theoretical framework (see Figure 2.1). As shown in Figure 2.1 there are several intervention processes, and they

**Figure 2.1. Intervention Processes and Involvement of a Third Party**

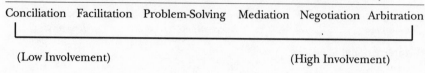

Conciliation   Facilitation   Problem-Solving   Mediation   Negotiation   Arbitration

(Low Involvement)                                    (High Involvement)

are being applied at different levels of intervention. Based on this classification, scholars distinguish the conflict resolution intervention models according to process or practice, intervention levels, and the role of the third party.

Moore (1987) argues that these processes differ according to the involvement and authority of the third party in settling the conflict. The arbitrator, who designs and shapes the agreement between the parties, is the most involved third party, while the conciliator only aids the process of conciliation, which is mainly dictated by the parties.

This research is focused on the educational models of intervention and on interethnic conflict and will present only the four models of intervention that are related to the concepts that the research addresses: negotiation, mediation, and problem-solving (PS), and conciliation.

*(1) Negotiation process:* Parties are directed toward reaching an agreement, or settlement, over issues in conflict (scarcity issues or other types of power components). This process is known as the classical and traditional strategy of conflict management. It is based on theories of coalition formation and game theory. Therefore, costs, benefits, and utility maximization are important elements in this strategy (Kriesberg, 1991).

*(2) Mediation process:* There are two types of mediation: content and process. In the content approach a third party in the process directs the parties to reach an agreement and build a package toward a settlement. It is very similar to the negotiation process. In fact, the negotiation process is an essential component in this approach, except parties receive the help of a third party who tries to motivate and even design the agreement for them. In general, the intervenor helps parties separate issues from people in order to establish a working relationship.

Krussel and Pruit (1989) define mediation as one of the main components of conflict resolution as a field. They also include the development of conflict resolution in international relations as part of the mediation approach development.

In the mediation process the focus is on relationship. The aim of the parties, as well as the third party, is to clarify perceptions, values, misunderstandings, and stereotypes. The product of this process is to establish a new channel of communication, create common bases for understanding, and educate the parties on each other's positions. This process produces change in the attitudes of the groups and individuals (see Kolb, 1983; Toval & Zartman, 1985; Fisher, 1981).

Based on these features, Kriesberg (1991) describes the mediator's role as: (a) providing information; (b) reducing the emotional tension and other interpersonal barriers to effective communication; (c) generating new options for the negotiators; (d) improving the negotiation procedures; (e) contributing resources to compensate for losses associated with an agreement; and (f) building support for the agreement among the negotiators and their constituencies.

*(3) Problem-solving:* This type of intervention process is basically an attempt to combine the two aspects of process and content. It focuses on issues (produces agreement) and attempts to establish new relationships and to educate the parties to a different decision-making process (interest-based bargaining in which the parties solve their problem jointly and look for alternative options) (see Laue, 1988; Moore, 1987; Bercovitch, 1984; Murray, 1984). As shown in table 2.1, there are several types of problem-solving approaches. Kelman summarizes the changes that result in applying his problem-solving approach to international relations: (a) Participants have learned that there is someone to talk to on the other side and something to talk about. (b) Participants have gained some insights into the perspective of the other party. (c) Participants have developed greater awareness of changes that have taken place in the adversary, and of ways of promoting such change in others through their own actions. (d) Participants have learned about the significance of gestures and symbolic acts and have become more aware of actions they could take that would be meaningful to the other and yet entail relatively little cost to themselves (1986:20).

Another type of problem-solving is the *analytical process*. This process is based on needs analysis. It is a relatively new approach to conflict resolution that is derived from "basic human needs" theory (Burton, 1990b). The underlying assumption in this process is that a conflict results from frustrated needs; therefore, the resolution of a conflict has to be through the satisfaction of these frustrated needs. The needs are ontological and universal. Value and interest disputes can be settled, but conflicts have to be resolved because the former are negotiable and tradable. To resolve a conflict, there must be a change within the system, and sometimes even a change of the system: "In resolving a social problem, either by resolution processes or by provention policies, we are, dealing in effect with changes within the system, and in some cases changes of the system" (Burton, 1990a:239).

However, to settle a dispute, there is no need for a change within or of the system because the settlement is mainly an arrangement over scarcity or a correction of misunderstanding. The resolution process is based on analysis and on costal approach for the satisfiers of ontological needs. Therefore, a cooperative and analytical problem-solving approach is more appropriate than the power framework that failed to resolve deep-rooted conflict (conflicts that involve needs, not scarcity or materialistic resources, and with a high level of intensity).

These types of problem-solving are implemented in: (a) interpersonal conflict (Wilmot and Hocker, 1978), (b) international conflict (Toval & Zartman, 1985; Kelman, 1986; Burton, 1969), and (c) labor management conflicts (Kolb, 1983).

In short, the APS process aims to create a change within and of the system and to achieve such a change by shifting the focus from a power framework into an analytical problem-solving approach (Burton & Dukes, 1990b).

*(4) Conciliation processes:* This type of intervention is focused on the relationship of the parties. It aims to improve communication and trust while reducing misperceptions and other psychological barriers. Curle (1971, 1986) describes its expected outcomes as a common task to work for harmony wherever we are, to strive to bring together whatever is sundered by fear, ignorance, or any of those conditions or attitudes of mind that separate us.

This type of intervention is often applied by the Friends Service Committee in different conflict areas (especially Africa and the Middle East). It also is considered sometimes as a subprocess that is used by mediators in public policy disputes (Carpenter & Kennedy, 1988).

Finally, in comparing Laue's, Curl's (which is based on conciliation approach), and Burton's approaches (a comparison among mediation, analytical problem solving, and conciliation techniques), the critical differences are in the areas of approaching the parties, process control, and attitude to asymmetrical conflict. However, they are similar in several aspects, such as face-to-face encounters, focus on relationship, need for extensive analysis, the concern and focus on individuals, identification of the base most appropriate for intervention, and the recognition of good in everyone. Based on the previous review of intervention models of contact hypothesis, this appears to be a similar model to those approaches that rely on the psychological aspects of the conflict concerned with the reduction of stereotypes and fears. Such processes of conciliation are also applied to build trust and confidence among adversarial parties.

## SELECT MODELS OF CONFLICT RESOLUTION

Since this study also focuses on the impacts of educational intervention models on political and social changes, it is necessary to review some of the basic principles of these models. For this purpose, three main models of intervention in conflict resolution were chosen: (1) Doob's intergroup inter-action (1970); (2) Burton's approach of problem-solving of deep-rooted conflict (1986); and (3) Kelman's problem-solving workshop (Kelman & Cohen, 1976).

*(1) Doob's Model:* Through his model, Doob applies the T-group techniques and other methods that were derived from the psychological approach, mainly group dynamics on interpersonal and intergroup levels. The workshop takes place in an isolated setting, a "cultural island." The third party is a group of social scientists who are presumably specialists in group processing. Participants are invited as individuals, not as repres entatives of their national groups. Emotional involvement and group solidarity cross national group boundaries during the interaction. Third-party interventions are generally aimed toward group and interpersonal process, agreement on the positive motivations of the parties, and pro-ducing an agreed-on solution. The products of the intervention would be some type of written agreement or document that would be used as an input into the policy debate.

*(2) Burton's Model:* Unlike Doob, Burton focuses on the analysis of the conflict; parties should be able to engage in an analytical (even academic) process that will enable them to understand better each other's positions, attitudes, and needs. Burton's approach is based on the theory of human needs; he assumes that conflicts can be resolved only by satisfying the basic human needs of the individuals and groups. The third party in his model is responsible for providing the appropriate analytical setting for the parties, and facilitating them in discovering each other's needs and interests. In his first few workshops, Burton stresses the necessity of involving participants in the workshops who have close ties to the decision-making level. Products of the workshop should be injected into the political system through the direct coordination of the participants with their politicians. Burton assumes that "the starting point in analysis and resolution of conflict is at the system level of the highest transaction" (Burton, 1986:13). This assump-tion indicates his idebt to the macro-structural approach and the primary international relations discipline.

In his paper, "Conflict Resolution as a Political System" (1988), Burton stresses his belief that conflict resolution models should be based on the assumption that human needs ought to be satisfied through the political system and that conflict resolution models have to provide the tools for satisfying these basic needs (1988:12). Conflict resolution in the longer term is a process of change in political, social, and economic systems. Burton distinguishes between settlement and resolution of conflict and argues that resolution of conflict involves a major change in the structural and social control system. Burton criticizes conflict management, especially through bargaining and negotiation (power-based bargaining), as being an inappropriate way of solving and satisfying an individual's human needs. Burton argues that the goal of conflict resolution theory and practice is problem solving, which means, ultimately, policy making. (1990a:23)

Burton summarizes his notion of change and conflict resolution in his latest book, *Conflict: Resolution and Provention* (1990), in which he argues that provention and conflict resolution are the answers to social problems and are the means and tools for future societies to achieve political stability within their systems. Burton lists and identifies the specific features and characteristics of conflicts that require *within* system changes and others that require *of* system changes.

Thus, Burton is concerned with creating conditions for transferring change from a group level to a policy-making level, while Doob is concerned with creating conditions for change (Kelman, 1972:182). Burton focuses on policy and structural change, while Doob focuses on individual and group level of change. Doob's model has less affiliation with the political process. Both approaches are designed to create conditions for effective problem solving and to revise distorted perceptions, moving from an antagonistic to a collaborative approach.

*(3) Kelman's Model:* This model is basically an integration of the two former approaches; Kelman selected some principles from each model to create and design his workshop model. In this workshop, the model emphasizes interpersonal interaction less than Doob does. On the other hand, Kelman focuses more on the intergroup interaction than Burton does. Kelman selected semiofficial participants and they were invited as representatives of their national groups. His model emphasizes the analysis and theoretical inputs in the setting less than Burton does. But, unlike Doob, he stresses the importance of the academic setting that the participants encounter.

Basically, as do Doob and Burton, Kelman presents the political change and the influences that his model should have at the policy-making level. Therefore, during the third-party intervention, parties should be encouraged to develop an initial agreement, which might be proposed to the official negotiators or to decision makers. Kelman summarizes the workshop products as the following:

1. Participants may acquire new information about the perceptions of the other side.
2. Workshops may introduce the participants to a new theoretical, empirical, and conceptual framework for analysis of conflict.

3. The interaction of group members might provide insights into the nature and course of the conflictual interaction they have in their real world.

Kelman stresses the importance of the influences that a workshop might create at the decision-making level since he believes that decision-making level units for each side of the conflictual parties are "Boxed in by a set of images of the other side, assumptions about the nature of the conflict, commitments to a national posture, and real or imagined constraints" (1986:10).

These factors prevent parties from exploring new options and alternatives for their interaction. Therefore, this type of workshop might assist during an impasse at the official negotiation level. It will help in generating options without the official political obligations. An additional function of Kelman's model is the *educational value*. By developing new ways of conceptualizing the conflict, the workshop is actually planting seeds among the elite segments of the population that will produce future change (1972:202). Kelman (1986:9) wrote that the primary goal of his workshop is educational, but it also has political effects.

Kelman has clarified, improved, and applied his model on several occasions during the past decade. He claims that resolution of conflict is a process conducive to structural and attitudinal change and eventually to reconciliation between the parties and to a transformation of their relationship (Kelman, 1986:3).

The direct changes are on an individual level but are directed toward changes in the larger system. Conflict resolution, as presented by Kelman, requires changes in individual attitudes and images as a vehicle for change and as an accompaniment of change in official policy and social action.

Kelman considers the debate about the *psychological versus political factors* and their relatively proportional influences to be beside the point. Psychological factors do not operate separately from political factors, but instead suffuse them. In interest and ideological protracted conflict the issues cannot be attributed simply to misunderstanding and misconceptions as social psychologists and psychologists did. A settlement of the conflict can take place on diplomatic and political levels, but overcoming the psychological barriers may help generate options and new possibilities for negotiations.

Finally, Kelman stresses the fact that his third-party intervention represents a political stance: it is "the search of solutions that are peaceful and just; it is win/win solution that requires compromise from both parties and at the same time it satisfies the parties' basic needs" (1986:20.) Kelman (1986) and Kelman and Cohen (1986) distinguish between political and psychological components of the conflict and argue that the workshop should address both aspects. The same principle is applied to educational versus political issues, goals, and outcomes. Therefore, in some of his workshops, Kelman had politically influential participants, whose primary goals were political. In another type of intervention, although participants were semi-influential, and the workshop did have political aspects and implications, the workshop's primary goal was educational.

## CRITIQUE OF CONFLICT RESOLUTION MODELS

As an emerging field, conflict resolution models still face many challenges and critiques. Some of the main critiques are stated by Avruch and Black (1991:7), who argue that "Emotions, in Fisher and Ury's world, compromise something that one must 'get past' (by allowing to 'ventilate,' for example) in order to get to underlying layers of interests."

According to Avruch, conflict resolution in Burton's and Fisher's approaches avoids emotions and focuses on the rationality of the persona. Avruch claims, and rightly so, that the rationality and emotions of the persons are not separable, but the conflict resolvers disagree.

Avruch and Black (1990) identify four major weaknesses with the emerging field of conflict resolution:

1. The characteristics of deep-rooted conflicts; the distinction between settlement, (management), and resolution.
2. The idea of empowerment; considering power differences or disparity between the parties.
3. The possibility for generic theory that is valid across all levels of conflict.
4. The analytical importance that should be ascribed to culture and class.

Another weakness of this emerging field is that it does not relate directly to the issues of social and political change, particularly in inter-ethnic conflict. Among the existing conflict resolution models, designs to be applied in intrastate conflict are lacking. The existing models relate for the most part to international or interstate conflicts, or to labor management and interpersonal conflict. Perhaps this explains the widespread application of intercultural sensitivity and learning models of contact hypothesis that mainly are developed to deal with interethnic, intrastate, and intercultural differences or conflicts.

Another set of critiques of the mediator's role in conflict resolution is presented by Kriesberg (1991). He argues that most of the mediator's functions do not relate to the substantive issues of the conflict, but are related more to procedures and communication problems. In fact, Kriesberg stated that the nature of the issues at stake was more important in deter-mining the outcome of the mediation effort than were the actions of the mediators.

In short, removing misunderstanding and misconceptions will improve individual relationships, but it does not directly aim at achieving social and political changes.

Similar to the critique of contact approach, the communication ap-proaches in conflict resolution:

> At best they cause the participants to sympathize with each other for a short period of time. At worst, they raise false hopes and endanger the participants who return to their communities with new-found and often deviant views. (Kelman & Warwick, 1973:10)

In addition to these critiques, there is a particular set of theories that relates to the problem-solving intervention models, particularly to Burton's and Kelman's designs. The ultimate goal of these models is to implement the changes and solutions that are generated in their workshops into the policy process. This remains the ultimate goal even though the workshops are designed to produce changes in their participants' attitudes and to generate options rather than transferring their products into policy processes. But, assuming that the workshop resulted in changes in indi-viduals' and small groups' attitudes, problem-solving models still have to face these two questions:

> (1) What is the likelihood that they will maintain these changes for a long period after they return to their hostile environments?
> (2) Assuming that the participants do maintain their changes, how can we assure that these changes will be injected and imple-mented, thus affecting the policy-making? (Kelman, 1972:195)

These two questions confronted Kelman, Doob, and Burton, as well as Ronald J. Fisher in his intervention and design of the "third party consultation model." He concluded his workshop by pointing out its impact and influence as a learning experience for the participants, but he did not make clear what its impact will be on the policy or behavioral level of the participants (1981:205).

These are serious questions, especially when considering the assump-tion that workshops might produce more individual and group changes when the participants are more isolated from their families, culture, and political reality. But, at the same time, this setting might produce more difficulties for participants' reentry into their communities and in main-taining the workshop's products. As Kelman points out, maintaining the changes after the workshop depends not only on the conditions of the workshop itself, but also on the nature of the setting and the reality to which participants will return. It is a problem because scholars, academics, and middle-class participants will not face the same reality that the working class and soldiers will.

In terms of transferring the workshop products, Kelman's conclusion confirms the traditional critiques of the psychological models of intervention. He argues that if the results of the workshops indicate that one side is more positive in attending negotiations or exploring negotiable compromise, then participants will feel more comfortable carrying this message to the policy level. However, if the changes are at a more fundamental level—changing the original policy completely and reformulating the issues of the conflict—then participants will be less willing to carry out this result at their political reality or policy level. The policy makers may also refuse such advice.

Most of these approaches are concerned with international conflicts and diplomatic negotiations. As Kelman stated, the model is helpful in a pre-negotiation setting which raises the question of the effectiveness of these models in cases that involve majority-minority conflicts and a high level of disparity between the parties. Would these models be applicable in promoting justice, as well as equality within states, where power disparities dominate the conflict course?

Another criticism of these intervention models is that most of their participants are academics, educators, journalists, and diplomats who must have a certain educational level and expertise to be able to take part in their sessions. Therefore, conflict resolution models exclude most of the populations and deal with elites, assuming that these elites will be able to identify with and represent their people's needs.

In ethnic and national conflicts, participants in these conflict resolution models are mainly middle-class, educated people who already have agreed to meet with their enemy, and they are prepared to negotiate. This assumption excludes those parties who refuse to meet or recognize the other party's right for independent representation.

## CONFLICT RESOLUTION RESPONSES TO CRITIQUES

To deal with these critiques and to establish an effective intervention model of conflict resolution, some scholars and practitioners suggest empowering the weaker party, particularly in the case of power disparity between the parties in conflict (Laue & Cormick, 1978; Susskind, 1981). This notion of empowerment is a crucial component of intervention models in dealing with the argument that an intervention in an asymmetric conflict (inequalities in power) may lead to further inequalities.

In response, some scholars even argue that a third party should not intervene in such cases unless he or she is aware of the context and can apply commitment to values of freedom, justice, and proportional empowerment (Laue & Cormick, 1978).

In response to the claim that conflict resolution functions as a social control factor, Scimecca (1987) excludes the ADR approaches and limits the definition of conflict resolution to those techniques and interventions that have the potential to engage and contribute to the processes of social change (i.e., distinguish between resolution/settlement and management). To deal with this issue, Scimecca (1987) argues that if conflict resolvers commit themselves to the values of empowerment, justice, and freedom, then the dangers and negative implications of institutionalization and becoming a social control instrument will be prevented.

Another response to the long list of critiques is made by Burton (1990a) and Rubenstein (1990) in their attempt to present the idea that basic human needs theory and its application in conflict resolution should be developed as a political system. They both argue that conflict resolution as a political system and as a movement can be effective in promoting structural change, though neither of them proposes ways or methods to consolidate the various conflict resolution methods into one political movement or political system. (They both claim that ignoring the power framework and adopting the analytical human needs approach will produce this change.)

Finally, in response to the critique of "lack of effectiveness," scholars in conflict resolution propose different techniques. For example, Burton (1990b) suggests an alternating power framework and establishing a valued relationship between the parties in order to reach a lasting resolution. Kelman and Cohen (1976) suggest injecting the outcome of the workshop into the political decision-making process, thus ensuring substantial changes in the formal policy. Kriesberg (Kriesberg & Thorson, 1991) point out that by selecting and including powerful parties who can influence implementation of the agreement, the intervenor can increase the possibility of achieving lasting agreement.

In conclusion, conflict resolution as a theory and practice in comparison to the contact hypothesis has the potential to address intergroup conflicts on both individual (micro) and collective (macro) levels. Conflict resolution models, if applied according to both Burton's and Kelman's models, can lead to systematic and structural changes because all conflict resolution models have either a direct or an indirect goal of reeducating the parties involved in the conflict. Based on these features that distinguish the conflict resolution model of intervention, an alternative educational approach and principles will be proposed for implementation in dealing with Arab-Jewish relations in Israel. Prior to the examination of the case studies, Arab-Jewish encounter programs, it is necessary to provide basic background information on the context of Arab-Jewish relations in Israel and the specific encounter programs that this research is concerned with.

# 3

# Arab-Jewish Conflict in Israel

## Historical, Social, and Political Background

### CONTEXT OF ARAB-JEWISH RELATIONS IN ISRAEL

With the declaration of the State of Israel in 1948, a minority of 156,000 Palestinians of an estimated 1.5 million remained under the authority of the newly established Jewish state. This resulted in a sudden shift in the status of this small Palestinian community from being members of an Arab majority to being a minority. There are 700,000 Arabs in Israel and they comprise 17 percent of the Israeli population.[1]

Since 1948, the Arab-Jewish conflict in Israel has been predicated on three main factors:

1. The establishment of the State of Israel on Arab lands, followed by Israeli military occupation of the Palestinian territories in the West Bank and Gaza in 1967, and the absence of a political framework of self-determination for Palestinians in general.[2]
2. The social, economic, and political inequalities resulting from a discriminatory policy inherent in the definition of Israel as a Jewish state.
3. The Arab traditional and nonindustrial social and cultural structure as opposed to the dominant Western-type Jewish social and cultural structure.

Much research and many studies present empirical data supporting the influence of each of these three main sets of factors on the Arab-Jewish conflict in Israel: Rosenfeld, 1980; Tessler, 1980; Al Haj, 1987; Smooha, 1984; Smooha and Peretz, 1980; Mari'i, 1978; Zuriek, 1979; Lustick, 1980; and others.

Ian Lustick's (1980) research considers the three previous categories in one of the most comprehensive studies. According to his analysis, the Jewish Zionist movement, represented by the Israeli government from 1948, managed to control the Arab community in Israel by establishing a control system that has three main components:

> (a) Segmentation compromises both isolation of Arabs from Jews and the internal fragmentation of the Arab community. (b) Dependence constitutes the conditions created to perpetuate the economic and political reliance of Arabs on the Jewish majority. (c) Cooptation is described as the use of side payments to Arab elites, or potential elites, in order to extract resources and maintain effective surveillance of the community. (Lustick, 1980:77)

Such a control system resulted in a great deal of inequality and discrimination against Arabs on all levels of legal status, economics, and policy.

Kretzmer (1991) listed overt statuary discrimination, covert discrimination, and institutional discrimination as three different types of direct and indirect discrimination toward Arabs in Israel. The main source of discrimination is reflected in the Jewishness of the state, which is expressed in the flag, anthem, celebrations, feasts and national holidays, language, and other cultural symbols. Legally, there are several laws to ensure the Jewishness of the state. The *law of return* ensures the ultimate right of any Jew on this earth to immigrate to Israel. Such a right is granted to any person with a Jewish mother and to his or her children. The *law of citizenship* grants Israeli citizenship to any Jewish immigrant and to those who were present in Israel after 1952. The *law of the land* indicates that lands in Israel belong to the Keren Kiemit of Israel (a Jewish organization). These lands cannot be transferred or sold to non-Jews.

Thus, Israel is a national property of its Jewish citizens, and it cannot reflect any national aspiration of the Arab minority. Any Israeli company that has a Jewish national goal excludes the Arabs from its services, membership, and interest. The application of such laws contradicts the democratic principles that Israel claims to follow in the independence charter, which indicates that all Israeli citizens will be treated equally without regard to race, religion, gender, and so on.

In terms of official policy, the main consideration of the Jewish government since 1948 regarding Arabs in Israel is described by Bligh (1991), who divides the government policy toward its Arab population into three phases: (a) 1948 to 1966, (b) 1967 to 1977, and (c) 1978 to 1987.[3]

Until 1987, the policy was one of segregation and separation in order to prevent the integration of Arabs into Israeli high governmental offices and, ostensibly, to protect the security of Israel. Such policy guided the military administration of Arabs from 1948 to 1987. However, since 1987, Bligh argues, there has been a decrease in the security-oriented policy because there has been a decrease in the perception that the Arabs in Israel represent a potential security threat. There is now coexistence and integration of Arabs into the political system.

There is no empirical evidence or proof to support such an argument of integrating Arabs into governmental offices. On the contrary, the recommendation of Bligh's office has been to deal with Arabs as being divided into Moslems, Druze, and Christians, and to provide economic benefits for those Bedouins, Christians, and Druze who serve in the Israeli Army. The security system continues to perceive the Arab community as a potential security threat (this is in essence the cooptation and "divide and rule" policy described by Lustick, 1980).[4]

Since 1948, the Arab sector has been economically excluded from any development plans by the government (except for two development plans that were never implemented). This discriminatory policy based on the governmental priority of developing the Jewish areas has resulted in a lack of any substantial economic initiatives in the Arab sector. Therefore, only 10 percent of the Arab workforce are employed in their villages. This policy is the main core of the economic dependence created by the government in order to control the Arabs in Israel.

According to *Davar*, May 30, 1989, 51.8 percent of Arabs in Israel live below the poverty level, and 59.2 percent of all children. The Arab poor in Israel is 55 percent although they make up only 17 percent of the Arab population. Of the 121 poverty housing areas in Israel, 111 are Arab communities.[5]

The Arab sector receives 10 percent of Israel's social services. In the entire Arab sector there are fewer than 10 community centers. There is a shortage of 564 social workers. Of the 5,000 social workers in Israel, only 150 are in the Arab sector.

According to Al-Haj (1989), the situation is no better at the institutional or governmental level. Of the 200 major governmental companies (more than 4,000 directors), there is only one Arab. Most hospitals do not employ an Arab as a section manager. In universities, of the approximately 5,200 professors, only 12 faculty members and appointed faculty are Arabs.

On the municipality level, local Arab municipalities serve 12 percent of the population and they receive 3.3 percent of the Interior Ministry budget. The Arab to Jewish ratio in terms of local and municipal budget allocation is 1:4, and the ratio is higher in the development budget allocation.

The main employment for Arabs is in construction, at 24 percent, and with public and community services at 12 percent. Water and electricity employ only 0.6 percent; industry, 20.3 percent; commerce, restaurants, and hotels, 20 percent; and agriculture, 10 percent (Haidar, 1991).

Since this research is concerned with the educational encounters between Arab and Jewish students and teachers, the following section compares the educational context and setting in which Arab and Jewish teachers operate.

## ARAB-JEWISH RELATIONS ON THE MICRO LEVEL: IMAGES AND PERCEPTIONS

Considering the previously described relationship and situation on a macro level, the relationship on the micro level between Arabs and Jews is limited to employee–employer, and appears to be characterized by suspicion, mistrust, hostility, and misperception.

One of the main gaps in Arab and Jewish attitudes is reflected in a survey conducted by the Israel Institute for Applied Social Research in 1988, which indicates that 65 percent of Jews think that Arabs will move to the Palestinian state. However, only 7 percent of Arabs think they will move to the Palestinian state.

In terms of individual identity and self-definition, Arabs and Jews also differ significantly. Rouhana (1987) indicates that 57 percent of the Arabs in Israel choose the term "Palestinian Arab," "Palestinian," or "Arab" to define their identity, while only 24 percent choose "Israeli Arab" or "Israeli Palestinian" to define their identity. In addition, he states that the meaning of "Israeli" is perceived differently by an Arab than by a Jew in Israel.

On the level of images, perceptions, and stereotypes of each other, the Arab-Jewish relations were reflected in several attitudinal surveys of Arab and Jewish youth. In a survey in 1984, Mena Tzimah found that among Jewish youth between fifteen to eighteen years of age, 25 percent expressed consistent antidemocratic attitudes. This percentage increased to 50 percent when related to non-Jews or Arabs.

In a 1984 survey, Tzimah indicated that 47 percent of the Jewish youth agreed to limit and restrict Arabs' rights in Israel; 42 percent supported the restriction of democratic procedures to limit the Arabs' rights; and 60 percent thought that Arabs do not deserve full equal civic rights. In a fourth survey by Van Leer (1986), 58 percent were opposed to equal rights for Arabs in Israel.

In regard to trust between Arabs and Jews, a survey by the Van Leer Institute in 1986 showed 80 percent of the Jewish youth interviewed (599) thought that one-half to three-quarters of the Arabs in Israel are not loyal to the state. Among adults, Tzimah, in a 1981 survey, indicates that 57 percent of the Jews think that all Arabs, or a majority of them, are not loyal to the state. Ironically, a report by Hareven, based on information from the Israeli Secret Services, indicates that only one percent of the Arab population was involved in any hostile action against the state.

In terms of Jewish attitudes and perception of Arabs, research conducted by Benjamini (1980) concluded that the Arab image among Jewish interviewees was completely negative. In other studies that examined social and intellectual characteristics, Jewish respondents related negatively to the intellectual ability of Arabs and positively to social features (Mahameed & Gootman, 1983; Tzimah, 1980; Bizman, 1978).

As in other areas, the attitudes of Arabs toward Jews are less reported in research findings and studies. In one of the few early studies, Hofman (1977) reported on an Arab youth who perceived the Jews in a positive manner ("progressive" and "smart") even more than they perceived themselves in those terms. Bizman and Amir, in 1984 research, supported the previous findings by Hofman.

In terms of readiness for social contact, Hofman (1972, 1977, 1982) reported that the Arabs' willingness and readiness for social contact is consistently higher than that of Jews. Support for such findings was reported by Smooha (1989) and Peres et al. (1970).

## SPECIAL CHARACTERISTICS OF THE ARAB EDUCATIONAL SYSTEM IN ISRAEL

The role of education in general and the school system in particular can be crucial to the individual's personality and relationship to others. An examination of the Arab educational system clearly shows that the role of education is to maintain control over the Arabs in Israel and to nationalize the Jewish students and population, by any means, against the threat of Arabs. Such an argument is reflected when comparing the educational goals of Arab and Jewish school. The Arab schools prepare students to be peace lovers while the Jewish schools prepare students to be good soldiers of Israel (Shammas, 1981: Saad Sarsour, 1981).

Despite structural constraints the Arab community increased its educational level significantly. The illiteracy rate has decreased from 50 percent in 1960 to 16 percent in 1983, particularly among women—76 percent in 1960 to 22.8 percent in 1984. The high school and higher education rate increased from 1.5 percent in 1960 to 8.2 percent in 1983. In addition, since the 1950s the number of Arab students in the schools has increased significantly (Al-Haj, 1989).

Although progress has been made in the educational system, the results are not bright when comparing the Arab and the Jewish school systems. Actually, the figures speak for themselves (based on the report of the Ministry of Education, Executive Director's Committee, 1985): 50 percent of Arab high school students drop out. Of the ten thousand Arab academicians, 30 percent are unemployed, and 70 percent of the Arab academicians do not work in their area of specialization.

Furthermore, great gaps between the Jewish and Arab educational systems exist in physical facilities, teachers' qualifications, level of special services (i.e., special education, curricula, allocation of resources, counseling and psychological services, extracurricular activities, vocational technological tracks, and overcrowding). In addition, Arab students are required to learn the Hebrew language beginning in the third grade, while Jewish students only recently have been obligated to learn Arabic as a third language, beginning at the seventh-grade level (Al-Haj, 1995).[6]

Arab students learn the Zionist Movement history, biblical studies, and general Jewish history instead of their own religious and national history. However, for Jewish students, in both secular and nonsecular systems, biblical studies are overemphasized. Simon (1985) warns that this could result in a lack of tolerance, exaggerated ethnocentricity, and reinforcement of stereotypes. In describing the situation of the Arab education in Israel, Mari'i states:

> Arab education in Israel was administered by a special department within the Ministry of Education and Culture until the late 1980s. Since the creation of the state, this department was headed by a Jewish official, thus depriving Arabs of the opportunity to run their own affairs in an area of most relevance to them. Further, curricula and subject matter in all areas of learning are decided upon by the authorities. (Mari'i, 1988:13

In addition to the lack in physical facilities and other resources in the Arab educational system in Israel, there are certain problems that the Arab teachers and students face that influence their participation in any dialogue or encounter. These features reflect the special needs and the unique backgrounds of the Arabs in such encounter groups. The following are some of these dilemmas and problems:

a. Student–teacher relationships are still based on an authoritarian model and on obedience—the teacher is always correct. Such a relationship also exists between the principal and the teachers. In fact, it can be illustrated in a hierarchical order headed by the Ministry officials:

Ministry → Inspectors → Principals → Teachers → Students

b. Most of the teaching is conducted by frontal techniques and in overcrowded classes. There are no substantial informal or extracurricular activities.

c. Principals are primarily occupied with their administrative duties instead of pedagogical duties and, in many cases, lack pedagogical authority.

d. Since the principal is threatened by the Department of Arab Education in the Ministry, there is little trust between the teacher and the principal. Therefore, the teachers do not develop sympathy or involvement in their roles as educators.

e. Based on these conditions, the education for democracy or coexistence is conducted by teachers in order to please their principals, and by principals to please their inspectors.

f. In spite of changes in the goals of education in the Arab school system, these goals remain unappropriated in the political and social context of Arabs in Israel. For example, the general goal of education in Israel is to reinforce the values and culture of Israel in the children (i.e., as perceived by Jewish people) and to establish a strong bond between the Jewish people in their land, state, and diaspora. Such a goal avoids and neglects the national and cultural uniqueness of Arabs in Israel.

Although Jewish education focuses on and stresses the development of a national identity for Jewish students, Arab students have no comparable focus in developing an Arab national identity. Arabs are raised to "be peace lovers" and share the country with all Israeli citizens. There is no indication of such a goal in the Jewish educational standards.

Finally, the essential balance in developing Israeli civic identity among Arab students while preventing the development of national identity among them remains the main motivation and underlying assumption of those who design curriculums and manage the Arab educational system.

g. As a result of the conflict between development of an Arab nationality and an Israeli identity (i.e., with Jewish components), Arab teachers are torn in their loyalty to their employer (the State of Israel) and to their community and students.

h. There is a tight security inspection of Arab teachers (an Arab teacher is appointed only after he or she passes a security examination performed by a special official in the Ministry of Education).

i. Such conditions have resulted in "paralyzed" Arab teachers who cannot assume a leadership role or function as a role model to their students. Students generally expect their teachers to take a political stand on the conflict between Arabs and Jews. However, even when the Ministry of Education issued new instructions encouraging the Arab teachers to introduce the discussion of current issues into the schools, teachers hesitated and expressed mistrust and suspicion, fearing this might be a trap by the Ministry of Education to examine their political views more closely.[7]

In conclusion, in addition to the physical gap in resources and facilities between Arab and Jewish schools, there are problems that are unique to Arab schools and students. Such features stem not only from the discrimination policy against Arabs in Israel, but also from the traditional social structure of the Arab community in Israel. The existence of these conditions requires special consideration for the needs of Arab students when designing any symmetric educational intervention in both Arab and Jewish schools.

# 4

# The Arab-Jewish Coexistence Programs

## DEVELOPMENT OF THE COEXISTENCE PROGRAMS

In the main communique (*Hozer Mankal*) that instructs schools on educational policy regarding political and social issues, the Arab-Jewish relation issue was mentioned only twice between 1961 and 1976 (Mahameed & Gootman, 1983). This indicates the importance of this issue to the Israeli governmental offices until the rise of Khana's antidemocratic movement, which threatened the dominance of the liberal Western (Eurpean and American) Jewish Eshkinazi society. (It became evident when Jewish youth expressed great sympathy with Khana's movement ideology prior to the 1984 elections.)

Thus, education for democracy and coexistence was introduced officially by the Ministry of Education during the 1984–86 period, in which the Ministry published two reports (*Hozer Mankal*) that encouraged students, teachers, and schools in general to deal with these issues in their classes and school activities. In the first report (1984), the program of Arab-Jewish education for coexistence was "intercultural interaction with respect and equality," which was to be achieved through: (a) knowledge; (b) attitudes and approaches of openness, understanding, respect, and tolerance to other cultures; (c) new skills and training (Ministry of Education, 1984).

The Ministry also created a special office, the Unit for Democracy, in 1985 to centralize and coordinate the new programs on democracy and coexistence produced by the different Ministry of Education departments.[1] Although this seemed to be a comprehensive plan to deal with Arab-Jewish relations in schools designed by the Ministry of Education, it unfortunately had neither authority nor ability to apply such a plan. So it was partially implemented, but with mixed messages from other government offices and from the political development.[2]

## ARAB-JEWISH COEXISTENCE PROGRAMS

In general, Arab-Jewish organizations and programs have existed since the 1950s, but they were related to or associated with the local Jewish municipalities, such as Haifa and Jerusalem, with the Hestadrut (Jewish Labor Union), and with the Mapai Party (ruling party between 1948 and 1976). They did not focus on the educational system of both communities.

In fact, such activities of coexistence were part of the Israeli governmental policy toward Arabs. Jewish officials from the ruling party used to attend religious, cultural, and social celebrations in the Arab community as part of their efforts and plans to mobilize political support, mainly voters, to the specific party among Arabs. Coexistence activity was also a vehicle for the Arab-educated and elites to gain the trust of the officials. It was an indication and tool for cooptation with the Israeli authority.

After the 1967 (the occupation of the West Bank and Gaza Strip) and the 1973 wars, however, the Jewish majority rediscovered the existence of Arabs in Israel. Both Arabs and Jews in Israel began to realize that they ought to live together in one state, and that their dreams and expectations that the other side would disappear could not be achieved in the new political context. At this time Jewish political activists began establishing different organizations with the aim of exploring the relationship between Arabs and Jews in Israel. The new organizations' targets were students, teachers, and grassroots citizens in both communities. Some of these organizations still exist today: Neve Shalom/Wahat el Salam (Oasis of Peace), Givaat Haviva, Netzani Shalom (Interns for Peace), Oaz Le Shalom (Power for Peace), Netevot Shalom (Paths for Peace), Shutfoot (Partnership), the Interreligious Committee, and the Truman Institute Project. Some other organizations have ended their activities, such as the Society for Friendship and Understanding and the Center for Arab-Jewish Education and Coexistence .

A third stage in this field took place after 1983, with the rise of the radical and extreme racist attitudes among Jewish youth, who through the surveys expressed antidemocratic attitudes and low tolerance of Arabs in Israel. Such results revealed the threat to the Ministry of Education and to government officials. In response, in 1983, the Ministry of Education launched for the first time a plan to incorporate education for coexistence and democracy in the Jewish and Arab schools. After this decision by the Ministry of Education, Arab-Jewish relations, or the coexistence field, received more recognition among the Jewish public and the schools. It was introduced into the curriculum through geography, history, and civic studies. Following these developments, a third wave of organizations became operational (in many cases, an organization will be launched after a strong or violent confrontation between Arabs and Jews)[3] Some of these organizations are: Youth Sing Different Song, the Institute for Education for Coexistence between Arabs and Jews, the Van Leer Project in Arab-Jewish Relations, Medrashat Adam (Adam seminar), Medrashat Alon (Alon seminar), Re'oot (Friendship), and others. These new programs focused on various activities: encounters, curriculum-building, teacher training, and the like.

In this third stage, at least two of the programs started addressing the conflict between Arabs and Jews while the other programs still acted and intervened on the basis of human relations and prejudice reduction models of contact. Also in this phase, there was an explicit resistance among the Jewish community to engage in such programs. This resistance was very strong among the religious Jews. One of the famous and powerful rabbis in Israel stated in *Hamodee'a* October 18, 1985:[4]

> We should relate to the issue of Arab-Jewish youth encounters as one of the most dangerous threats that we face in the state today, a threat that who knows where it can lead. One soul of Israel people for us is the whole world. In the Arab-Jewish encounter programs we are threatening thousands of souls. This is a threat to our existence and uniqueness in our country.

This reflects the religious resistance to take part in such encounters when they were encouraged by the Ministry of Education reports in the mid-1980s. During this stage, resistance from the religious parties attracted more secular people to such activities. This increased the recognition of the importance of this issue among Jews.

The Islamic official religious leaders were supporting such encounters as part of their Islamic ideology interpretations.[5] As a result of the increasing official recognition of the importance of dealing with democracy and coexistence, Arab-Jewish encounters received wider coverage in the Israeli newspapers and academics, especially after specific violent incidents during the Intifada (the Palestinian uprising between 1987 and 1992).

In Hall-Cathala's (1990) book about the Peace Movement in Israel, he classified the Arab-Jewish Intervention programs (AJIP) or Intervention programs in Jewish-Arab contacts (IPJAC) as part of the Israeli Peace Movement. Their members have ad hoc links that represent dual membership (in the Peace Movement and in the APJAC). To contextualize the work of these organizations, Hall-Cathala presents them as related to the Jewish peace movement organizations (represented by Peace Now). It is an ad hoc and ambiguous relationship that is reflected mainly through dual membership (activist in the Peace Movement work in these encounter programs). The encounter organizations do not have a direct, clear organizational link

with Peace Now or any other peace organizations in Israel. (see figure 4.1).[6]
The IPJACs include three categories:

    a. A few organizations that are usually managed by professionals
       who work on a full-time basis. They are up to date on group
       encounter techniques and at the forefront of international
       experimentation and research in the field of group encounter
       and conflict resolution.
    b. Movement Organizations (MOs) include organizations that
       carry out their IPJAC activities within the broader context of
       their activities, such as Ulpan Akiva, in which pairs of Jews and
       Arabs live together, spending twenty-one days together, learning
       Hebrew and Arabic from each other and from the institute's
       language teachers.
    c. A third category includes organizations and institutions that
       conduct Arab-Jewish encounters and programs on an ad hoc
       basis. Hall-Cathala associates them with disastrous results
       because they have been poorly organized and mismanaged.

Since 1992, the field (this includes those organizations described by
Hall-Cathala in the first category) has a professional course for facilitators;
it has been introduced to several higher academic institutes, which offer
special courses on Arab-Jewish relations, including Arab-Jewish encounter.[7]
More reports evaluating the work of these programs are being published,
while in the past (especially in the second phase), no evaluation reports
were produced. After 1985, with Ford Foundation funding, some of these
programs managed to design and conduct an evaluation of their work.

One of the recent reports on coexistence and democracy in the Arab
and Jewish schools was published in 1991 by the Ministry of Education's
Unit for Democracy, which is responsible for these activities in the schools.[8]
The report indicates that 28 percent of the schools conducted some sort of
activity during 1991. Only 245 of the Jewish schools participated in such
activities while 50 percent of the Arab schools did. Only in 14 percent of
the schools did the teachers take part in the activity. The main leading
organizations conducting these activities were the Unit for Democracy, Van
Leer, Giva'at Haviva, Adam, and Beit Hagefen.[9]

The activities in the schools included fifty different types of programs,
including curriculums, encounters, seminars, conferences, lectures, and so
on.

The eleventh and sixth grades are the most popular targets of such
interventions. More Jewish teachers and principals think that this activity is
unessential to the school and students (50 percent), especially in the
religious schools. Jewish principals listed other issues such as immigrants,

# Figure 4.1. Context of Arab-Jewish Intervention Programs

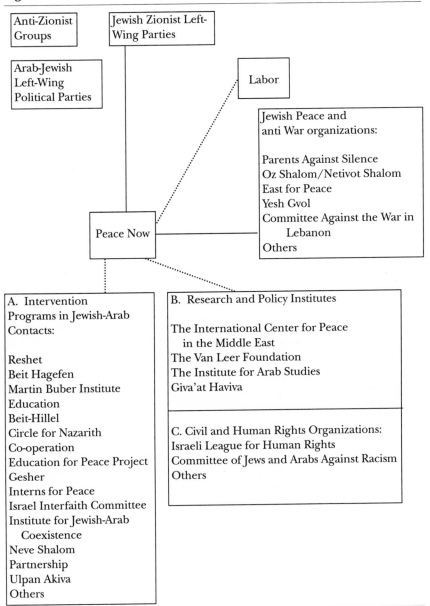

*Note:* Clear organizational links between spheres are indicated with an unbroken line (—); more ambiguous ad hoc links—often representing dual membership—are indicated with a broken line ($\cdots\cdots$).

violence and society, and alcohol and drugs to be more important than Arab-Jewish coexistence. The Arab schools focused on violence and society, coexistence, and alcohol and drugs.

Based on the Ministry of Education report, the following factors would be obstacles to such activity in the schools: (a) lack of appropriate staff, (b) lack of time, and (c) the sensitivity of the issue. On the Arab side the obstacles are mainly insufficient budgets, inadequate time and staff, and the frustration of the program. In the Jewish religious schools the obstacles are moral and political. Arab inspectors discussed this issue more often with their principals than did the Jewish inspectors. Eighty-two percent of the Arab schools have a special individual who is in charge of these programs, while only 37 percent of the Jewish schools do. Twenty-five percent of the general activities were encounters; 25 percent are curriculum-based activities; and 23 percent are a variety of other activities. Of these activities, only 5 percent include intensive encounters; 75 percent during class hours and 22 percent outside the class. Forty-four percent of the 675 activities did not have encounters; 65 percent of the activities dealt directly with Arab-Jewish coexistence while others dealt with related issues; 90 percent of the activities in the Arab schools focused on coexistence while Jewish schools had a variety of issues.

The length of the activities varied. More than 50 percent did not last more than a month; 42 percent of the activities took place during a year; and 56 percent conducted one to four units of activities. Arab schools tended to conduct the activities in both sides while most of Jewish schools conduct the activities in their schools.

In terms of content, the 300 surveyed activites in schools were focused on; 16 percent theoretical concepts in Arab-Jewish relations; 16 percent interpersonal and intergroup Jewish-Arab activites; 11 percent sport activities; 5 percent working on joint projects; 12 percent pleasure and social activities; 11 percent activities on creativity; 10 percent culture (music, art, theater); 14 percent history, geography, or civic education; and 5 percent other. In regards to the degree of satisfaction of the program, 24 percent of the principals were satisfied with the activities when they included encounter, while 11 percent were satisfied when it did not have encounter. Beit Hagefen and school-based initiatives were the leading organizations that provided satisfying activities to principals. Twenty-four percent of the principals were satisfied with the activities when they included encounter, while 11 percent were satisfied when it did not include encounter. Beit Hagefen and school-based initiatives were the leading organizations that provided satisfying activities to principals.

In terms of goals and interest, Arab principals expressed interest in developing willingness for relationship and involvement in Arab-Jewish issues through these programs, while Jewish principals indicated their interest in raising awareness to democracy in general. But principals expressed higher satisfaction with programs that included encounters and contact than those programs that were conducted without contact. In addition, the Arab principals were more interested in programs that facilitate "knowing the other side" than were the Jewish principals, who were interested in programs that reduce negative feelings.

In conclusion, the report suggests that if more Jewish principals believe that their school system has a supporting or accepting environment for Arab-Jewish relations programs, they will be more willing to conduct such programs. On the Arab side there are technical problems (resources and time), while in the religious schools there is a political dilemma.

The authors of the report recommend introducing democracy and co-existence issues to kindergarten children because this is the most neglected area for introducing Arab-Jewish relations.

In addition to the methodological problems that the authors list in this report, the major problem is that the Arab sector schools are divided into three categories of Bedouins, Druze, and Arabs. Such division is derived from the governmental policy of segregation and segmentation of Arabs in Israel. Such policy also guided the Ministry in applying its Arab-Jewish programs in the schools. Based on the report, there were no substantial differences among these three segments.

Another report, produced by the Hebrew University Education Department and Ministry of Education Curriculum Department (1990), indicates that since the 1985 announcement of "Democracy Year," 148 different curriculums were developed for this purpose by the Ministry and other outside organizations. The term "Education for Democracy" also included education for Arab-Jewish coexistence; therefore the curriculums are a mix of coexistence issues and education for democracy in general. Of these curriculums, forty-five were designed by the Ministry of Education while the others were designed by outside organizations. Both types of curriculum, however, focus more on cognitive and less on emotional and psychological aspects. The curriculums are implemented on a cognitive basis without relation to personal attitudes and behaviors because teachers still lack the appropriate training to deal with the emotional aspects of the issue.

In short, the report indicates that the curriculums were applied in classes in a sporadic fashion, without any follow-up or evaluation of their impact, and without determining the number of curriculums used by the schools. The curriculums themselves lacked direct relation between the theoretical concept of democracy and its practical application in tIsraeli culture. In many curriculums there was no relation between the goals and the titles of democracy and the content.

It is important to mention that all these curriculums were designed initially for the Jewish schools, and that there is a lack of such programs in the Arab schools. In fact, many of the curriculums used in the Arab schools are adopted or translated literally from the Jewish programs, which are based on and motivated by Jewish Zionist national interest, idealogy, and values.

In conclusion, we have described the social, political, economic, and educational background in which the coexistence and dialogue programs have been operating, as well as the three phases in the Arab-Jewish relations field development. It is clear that the Arab-Jewish programs operate in a highly complicated, asymmetric, and complex context. Therefore, one of the main questions of this research is whether these programs consider such complexity in their design and implementation.

## RESEARCH ON ARAB-JEWISH PROGRAMS

This research is not concerned with the natural contact between Arabs and Jews in Israel, but with organized encounters between students and teachers from both sides. Therefore, this review will focus on research that dealt with the encounters between Arabs and Jews in Israel.

During the first phase of the coexistence field historical development all of the documentation was written by Israeli Jews affiliated with the major political parties or Histadrut. They wrote reports to illustrate the Arab minority acceptance of the Jewish state and to describe a manufactured reality of peaceful Arab-Jewish relations. Only during the second and third phases of the field's development were more serious research or reports produced.

### Research on Arab-Jewish Encounter, 1970–80

Although Arab-Jewish encounters and contacts (without regard to their function, goals, and degree of planning) were being conducted as early as the 1950s, there are very few research or planned interventions that examine the appropriateness, effectiveness, and applicability of these "contact encounters" to the Arab-Jewish conflict in Israel. Until 1981, the main studies were Lakin et al. (1969); Greenbaum and Abdul Razak (1972); Levi and Benjamin (1976); Cohen et al. (1977); Bizman (1978); Levi and Benjamin (1977); Gordon (1980); Smith (1981); and Cohen and Azar (1981).

The first serious conceptualization of research on Arab-Jewish encounters during this period was conducted by Peled and Bargal in 1983. They examined ten studies that focused on Arab-Jewish encounters specifically, and divided them into two categories.

*(1) Problem-solving encounters:* Lakin et al. (1969) conducted the first workshop between Arabs and Jews in Israel. Lakin and his colleagues designed a workshop with three sessions of dialogue, communication skills, and a prejudice-reduction planned project. Based on subjective evaluation methods (interviews and self-reports of participants), the participants in Lakin's workshop indicated the success of the encounter in gaining more insight into Arab-Jewish relations. Emotionalism, as described by Bargal and Peled, remained until the end of the workshop and prevented further success.

Another conflict resolution-oriented workshop was conducted by Levi and Benjamin (1975, 1976, 1977). In their workshop, participants (high school students and university students) engaged in five steps of problem solving (defining the conflict issues, gathering information, selecting options, redefining the conflict, and designing propositions of resolutions). Although it was a very rationalistic design, on several occasions the participants managed to reach a solution, and they learned problem-solving procedures. In general, however, Levi and Benjamin reported difficulties in balancing the content with the process (emotional and cultural differences). They also recommended that the leading team of such a workshop, which did not have an Arab facilitator, should include an Arab facilitator who might better relate to the interaction between the two groups.

*(2) Intercultural sensitivity training and communication:* Workshops in this category were designed to improve communication, reduce stereotypes, and train for intercultural sensitivities. Greenbaum and Abdul Razak (1972) conducted a workshop which was co-led by an Arab and a Jew. Participants reported general positive changes but no relative improvement at the outgroup or intergroup level.

Bizman (1978) conducted a three-hour structure meeting to reduce prejudice without any consideration or relation to the political content. In his report of the workshop's outcomes, he indicates that Jews viewed Arabs more positively when the Arab group was in a similar or higher status. The Jewish participants also perceived the Arabs more favorably on the interpersonal level than on the intellectual level. Such an outcome confirms Amir's (1976), and Amir and et al's (1980) findings on outcomes of natural interaction between Arabs and Jews in Israel.

Smith (1981) conducted a comprehensive evaluation of two models of encounter that were implemented by the Shutfoot Partnership.[10] Their model consisted of human relations' training of voluntary participants. It included discussions, lectures, and interpersonal dynamics. The second model, implemented by Beit Hagefen,[11] included home visits and other structural activities focused on stereotype reduction. The students were brought by their teachers and principals. According to Smith, there was a

limited change in attitudes among Jewish participants, and Arab participants expressed their disappointment regarding the meeting and the way
they had been treated by the Jews. The program did not have a strong
impact on Arab participants. Furthermore, the change (if it occurred)
among the Jewish participants was negative on the group level (they viewed
the Arabs as a group in a negative, prejudicial manner), but was positive on
the interpersonal level.

The outcomes in the Shutfoot model were more successful. Jews
viewed Arab participants more positively, but in comparison with Arabs,
they perceived themselves significantly lower after the encounter. One
explanation for this result may be that the Palestinian identity of Arab
participants was diffused, while both Arabs and Jews strengthened their
Israeli identity. Such an outcome results from the absence of a uninational
framework that would assist and prepare Arab participants in clarifying and
crystallizing their national identity, and would aid Jewish students in coping
with their fears and insecurity prior to the encounter. In explaining the
differences in outcomes, Smith refers back to the different assumptions in
the two models, arguing that the Beit Hagefen program was predicated on
the assumption that once personal relations had been established between
the groups, political concerns might be addressed via lectures and discussion. But as with any contact hypothesis model that focus on similarities
only, the degree of intimate contact constitutes an insufficient condition
for collaborative behavior in a hostile environment. On the other hand, the
focus of Shutfoot program was on creating conditions for nondefensive,
inquiry-oriented dialogue. As participants identified specific areas of
possible conflict and gained a more accurate and emphatic understanding
of the position of the other side, the degree to which interest appeared to
conflict was lessened (Peled & Bargal, 1983:212).

In another qualitative paper, Smith (1981) reports on a two-step
approach (based on five years' experience working with the Partnership
Association) to ensure dealing with prejudice, fears, and power struggles in
the encounter: first work on trust, empathy, and self-disclosure, then
conduct a structured discussion on political concerns. Support for such a
rationale was provided earlier by Robert Blake and Jane Mouton (1964),
two social psychologists in the field of industrial relations, who argued that
only after the basic problems of relationship have been eliminated is
effective interaction possible.

If this is an effective role for settling disputes in industrial conflict,
then it could certainly be effective in ethnic conflicts that involve a long
history of violence and grievance among both ethnic groups.

Another attempt to conduct Arab-Jewish encounter was launched after
Sadat's visit to Israel and after the signing of the Camp David Peace Treaty

between Egypt and Israel. This attempt was led by Gordon (1980:20), whose intervention is based on Buberian learning groups. This approach consists of five stages: "the impression-making person, the conscious person, the person who educates himself to relate dialogically, the dialogical person, and the dialogical educator."

Participants in the encounter course experienced an intensive two-year course of biweekly meetings, in which they had text readings, subgroup interaction, a trip to Cairo, and other activities. Only twenty-four of the forty participants reached the third stage of development. Five Arab participants were unable to comprehend the Buberian conceptual framework. Six Arab and four Jewish participants left the course.

In short, there were no precise measurements developed for the changes in the encounters' participants' behavioral patterns during this period, but there were some indications of a possible change in their perceptions and attitudes if the encounter was conducted appropriately. However, the main importance of the research at this period is that it set the stage and reflected the need for a more serious and longitudinal research designs to evaluate the encounter programs. Such development took place in the second phase.

### Research on Arab-Jewish Encounter, 1983–present

Since the 1980s, there has been considerably more interest in Arab-Jewish relations and encounters, reflected in the Ministry of Education announcement of the Arab-Jewish year in 1986 (which resulted from the concern of the general public with the popularity of Khana's movement among Jewish youth). Therefore, other research has been conducted on Arab-Jewish encounters: Hofman (1986); Bar and Bargal (1985, 1987); Bar and Asaqla (1988a, b); Bar, Bargal, and Asaqla (1988, 1989); Bargal and Bar (1990a, b); Bargal (1990); Bargal and Peled, 1986; Hertz-Lazarovich (1989); Smith (1987); and Abu-Nimer (1993).

When comparing the two periods, this recent period includes research that examines more aspects and factors that influence the encounters between Arabs and Jews in Israel. For example, researchers began to stress the impact of context and the role of facilitators in determining outcomes of Arab-Jewish encounters. To determine these effects, researchers combined the use of longitudinal and control group research design.

Bar, Bargal, and Asaqla conducted the most systematic study of Arab-Jewish encounters in Israel during the years 1985–89, based on Peled and Bargal's (1983) first comprehensive study of conceptual, theoretical, and practical frameworks. They published eight reports based on their evaluations of two projects (Neve Shalom/Wahat Al Salam and Giva'at Haviva).

They were the only researchers to examine the work of the Arab-Jewish staff systematically and on an "action research" basis.

Peled, Bargal, and Bar were the first to introduce the notion of "living with the conflict." In addition to the typical goals of unfreezing stereotypes and promoting contact and acquaintance, their encounter designs and evaluation research were aimed toward achieving: (a) awareness of the complexity; (b) acquisition of nondiscriminatory attitudes; and (c) skills and ways for living with the conflict: trust of the other group, political attitudes, and identity and belonging.

There were several common findings stressed in both action research projects. In their first-year report (1985),[12] Arab and Jewish participants come from different social, political, and educational backgrounds and realities; therefore, they are very different in their motivations, expectations, anxieties, and language. These differences created an asymmetric situation that prevented the participants, especially the Palestinians, from gaining full and equal benefits from the encounter.

In their second-year report (1986), they found that the differences between the two encountering groups conditioned the direction and intensity of the change. Participants in the experiment group (as opposed to the control one) were selected carefully to include those with a high popularity level, a potential for leadership, and an ability to acquire skills that would enable them to live with the conflict. As a result of the encounter, changes occurred in both Arab and Jewish groups in terms of their deep understanding of living with the conflict topic. But, generally, the Jewish intervention group was found to be the main beneficiary of the short, one-time encounters.

In the third year (1987), due to a relatively calm year politically, the readiness for contact with the other nation increased in both Arab and Jewish groups, but notably among Jewish youth. More changes in the desired direction were registered in the attitudes and skills for "living with the conflict." Also, further support for the importance of emphasizing the strategy of knowing one's self as a basis for knowing others is an effective technique of intervention. Knowing one's self includes a more emotional and experiential than cognitive emphasis, especially on personal, socio-cultural, and political issues, as well as the reality of living with another nation.

In the fourth year (1988b), in a politically tense year (Intifada threatened Israeli youth and empowered Arab youth), the "action research" staff developed two different models of intervention. Model A includes long uninational activities in the group's own community, followed by a one binational encounter in a neutral location in a supporting atmosphere. Model B includes two binational encounters in a neutral location. In addition, the staff is continuing for the third year with intensive training and professional development.

The combination of the differential uninational intervention with the encounter workshop in model A, under a new political reality, contributed strongly toward more symmetry, so that both Jewish and Palestinian Arab groups benefited more. Among the Jewish youth who took part in only the two binational encounters of model B, there were fewer changes in the desired direction. The researchers also provided clear proof for the advantage of applying a uninational framework to the encounter. They indicated that the changes in any model were greater in the Arab groups than in the Jewish groups.

Bar and Asaqla (1988b), in their evaluation research of the staff of Giva'at Haviva, identify, for the first time in this field, several criteria with which to evaluate and approach the degree of professionalism among Arab-Jewish trainers. Such criteria were essential in conducting our research because they are concerned with the perception of conflict, goals, and assumptions of the third party in Arab-Jewish intervention models:

1. Strict consideration of the asymmetry in all life areas between the participating youth from both nations.
2. Egalitarian consideration of the needs of both nations. Their needs are different, which means that a single response (i.e., model) might not always contribute to equality.
3. Neither one of the groups will be manipulated to change the other.
4. The task of handling Jewish-Arab-Palestinian encounter groups requires skill, knowledge, and experience; hence, a need for meaningful and long training is a continuous investment, and accumulation of knowledge regarding self as well as formal knowledge is essential.
5. The closeness of the trainers to the participants of their own nationality is a basic necessity and is desirable. However, a combined team is assigned to these encounters, taking into account the necessity of attaining common goals, which are considered on an egalitarian basis.
6. In order to ensure a desirable change, emphasis should be placed on realistic expectations (what is possible to attain from the encounter workshop).
7. To improve professional skills in the encounters, there are certain conditions to be provided: less difficulties and worries for trainers; institutional and personal investment in developing professional skills; a feeling that the trainer can

influence; a feeling that the investment is fruitful; and a minimal feeling of alienation both from members of one's own nationality as well as of the other's; social and political closeness to primary reference groups; and optimism regarding the future.

Most of the reports and research were focused on students' encounter. However, in a unique study that focused on Arab-Jewish teacher training, Smith (1987) identifies important factors for an effective encounter. First, teachers should experience the curriculum before applying it, and they should clarify their feelings, attitudes, and positions before they begin dealing with Arab-Jewish relations in their schools. Otherwise, they will become overzealous advocates of certain viewpoints.

Second, the nonauthoritarian intervention style is more effective because it enhances the learning process or the experience, which is more important than the content that the participants are discussing. Therefore, establishing a process of feedback between the trainer and trainees is essential for the internalization of the process.

Third, the creation of a cohesive group of participants supports them in applying and discussing their experiences in classes, especially if the group involves more than one teacher from each school (Smith, 1987).

In additional research that supports the differential impact that Arab-Jewish encounter can have on Arab and Jewish participants, Hofman (1986) examines Beit Hagefen's encounters and reports several outcomes.[13] (a) There is an increase in readiness for contact among both Jews and Arabs, especially Arab girls. (b) There is a higher readiness for proper social relations among Arab students than among Jewish students (as reported by Amir, 1976; and Ben-Ari and Amir, 1988a). (c) Since Arab students' starting point is higher than that of the Jewish participants, it is harder to achieve further changes in their readiness. (A similar outcome was reported in Bar et al., 1989.) (d) Readiness is higher among Jewish secular nonreligious than religious, and Jews of European origin are more tolerant than those whose parents were born in Arab countries. (e) Readiness for proper social relations is reportedly higher among Druze, Christians, Moslems, and Jews, respectively.

Most of the reviewed research was based on quantitative surveys of attitudes. However, Katz and Khanov (1990) describe, in a qualitative study, their experience in leading Arab-Jewish teachers' encounters. They identify the main motivations and goals of participants in attending these encounters: (a) willingness to know the other group members and learn about them (especially those Jews who are less acquainted with the Arab minority culture); (b) an interest in encountering moderate participants, in order to prove that they exist; a wish to produce more moderate people on both sides. They also distinguish some basic features of these encounters:

a. There are two types of encounters: those that were conducted in a cultural island (Lewin, 1948) to separate or isolate the group from outside reality, and those that take place consecutively in both sides. Both were generally conducted in small groups (15–20) of participants for two to four days. Such encounter is an opportunity to conduct face-to-face contact with the other group. This type of encounter is limited to Palestinians and Jews in Israel.

b. The encounter is usually conducted with some association or relation with the Ministry of Education, which has supported, at least formally, these types of encounters since 1984. By giving the Ministry of Education the responsibility to deal with phenomena such as racism, or anti-coexistence movements, this fact or policy enables officials to avoid structural and social changes to prevent the causes of this conflict. Others argue that the legitimacy that an encounter achieves (with the support of the Ministry of Education) is the main gain.

c. All of these encounters and their organizations are conducted through Jewish initiative and sponsorship. Therefore, some argue that these encounters mainly serve the Jewish cause and interests. This fact, as some argue, limits a free and full expression of some participants of their identity or interests (mainly Palestinians). Participants who attend have a positive attitude, or at least, have accepted the coexistence ideology, or their organizations have such an attitude.

d. Most of the groups have an explicit goal of educational learning and experience; some aim to construct a curriculum, some aim to learn about the others' culture. But, at the same time, these encounters function as a stage on which to express emotional and political attitudes of both sides and to serve the different needs of the two encountering groups.

Katz and Khanov categorize two perceptions in these encounters: (a) the instrumental approach of the Arab participants to achieve certain interests and needs through the encounter; (b) the expressive approach of the Jewish participants, who wish to encounter in order to know other individuals and their culture better, and to produce a positive experience.

The differences between these two perceptions are reflected in the expectations, goals, process, and measures of success (both approaches were reported in this research too; see chapter 6 on intervention models).

In terms of the third-party/facilitator work, Katz and Khanov point out that the group facilitators are Arabs and Jews who are more committed to the group and to the issue than to their roles as facilitators. During the 1970s, these encounters were conducted mainly by Jews who specialized in group dynamics or other psychological aspects of group interaction, but they realized the need for an Arab co-facilitator (Benjamin & Levi, 1979). Both Arab and Jewish facilitators bring their backgrounds with them to the group process, which influences their roles separately (Bar & Asaqla, 1988a). Arabs are more positive about the encounter than Jews. Jews who belong to right-wing political ideology are not attracted to these encounters.

Katz and Khanov identify two separate approaches to the processes in the encounters, which were reflected in the findings of this research as well: *the conflict between the political person and the psychological person.* This is one of the three dilemmas in Arab-Jewish encounters. Arabs prefer the intergroup-political approach. Jewish intervenors prefer the interpersonal and psychological approach, which equalizes the members as individuals. The apolitical approach frustrates Arab members because it reflects their inability to influence outside reality or the structure.

Although scholars and practitioners (see review of the contact hypothesis: Hewstone & Brown, 1986; Reicher, 1986; Lemish, et al., 1989) overcome this by providing "action" and practical application in follow-up, of the program's participants might still feel the structural victimization (Azar, 1979).

In general, Katz and Khanov list three main dilemmas which they argue exist in the process and content of Arab-Jewish encounters:

| Intergroup-political | Interpersonal-psychological |
|---|---|
| Harmony (similarities) | Conflict (differences) |
| Focus on the group members | Focus on the outside reality |

Finally, influenced by Kelman's approach, and in contrast to Amir and Ben-Ari (1987) (who suggest the interpersonal approach), Katz and Khanov suggest a third approach instead of the intergroup or the interpersonal: an interpersonal-political approach that deals with political issues on an individual basis. Participants examine their personal attitudes and perceptions toward the conflict and toward the other group, asking themselves what skills they will need to deal with the conflict. Although they suggest the incorporation of political issues, the general framework that they propose remains on the interpersonal (micro) level of interaction and intergroup interaction and conflict. Dealing with the interpersonal approach can individualize the conflict issues and neglect the members' need for group identification.

In conclusion, since the 1980s, evaluation research on Arab-Jewish encounters has increased considerably. The quality of the research designs has improved. Researchers conducted action research and longitudinal studies for the first time. In fact, in 1995, Bar and Bargal published, in Hebrew, the first book in the field that deals with a specific model of intervention based on their action research in Neve Shalom/Wahat Al Salam. In addition, such action research (designed mainly by Bar and

Asaqla, and Bargal) introduced initial criteria with which to evaluate the effectiveness of Arab-Jewish encounters. It also assisted in sharpening the focus and designs of encounter models.

## RESEARCH ON ARAB-JEWISH ENCOUNTERS:
## LIMITATIONS AND NEEDS

Having indicated these changes, it is clear that there are basic limitations that still characterize the existing research and evaluation reports on Arab-Jewish encounters. First, in spite of the fact that Bargal's and Bar's research methodology and techniques were systematic and longitudinal, they remain vague in terms of the influence of the context on the effectiveness of encounters in changing the attitudes of the participants. However, they did confirm the assumption by Amir, Cook, and others that "contact is not enough," and that there are certain necessary conditions that should be systematically considered in order to prepare the ground for attitudinal change. Nevertheless, they found that even if these appropriate conditions exist, there is no guarantee that a change in attitudes will occur, or, if it does, that behavioral change will follow.

Second, a considerable amount of the research on the subject has been written and designed by scholars who make several obvious assumptions about the State of Israel and the status of the Arab minority in Israel. Their perception and definition of positive and negative attitudinal change are derived from the definition of Israel as a Jewish state that has an Arab minority. Researchers and evaluators rely on the assumption that Arabs and Jews in Israel can and will continue to live together in the same current political ideological framework, without any challenge to the definition of Israel as a Jewish Zionist state, which is based on the notion of excluding non-Jews from certain fundamental rights, such as the law of return (preventing a non-Jew from acquiring citizenship by immigrating to Israel). This assumption is clear in Ben-Ari and Amir's paper (1986), in which they state that in addition to the general goals that any Arab-Jewish encounter aims to achieve, Arab participants can gain the benefit of learning skills and adjustment to the fact that they are minority members who will have to accept living in a Jewish state.

Another example is the use of the term "Israeli Arabs" to describe Arab participants in the workshops and the research, instead of the term "Palestinian Arabs," which Arabs in Israel generally select as their primary identity (Rouhana, 1988, Hofman, 1988). This political attitude of the researchers is supported by Israeli governmental policy toward Arabs in Israel. In fact, the use of this term only supports the critique that these encounters assist in diffusing the Palestinian identity of Arab participants.[14]

Such assumptions influence the researchers' definitions of an effective or successful encounter. The researchers' reality influences their perception of the needs and power relation among the trainees and trainers too.

Third, most of the research relies on social-psychological approaches, which are mainly concerned with perceptional and attitudinal changes, rather than structural or political changes. They measure stereotype reduction and changes in readiness for contact rather than dealing with behavioral aspects or actions taken by participants following the encounter experience. Most reports do not relate to the output produced by the encounter on the macro level. In general, they only measure impacts on the interpersonal level of attitude change. They neglect the impact on schools, parents, or peer levels. None of the research conducted followed up or measured the impact of the encounter (or the contact) after the end of a specific intervention program.

Fourth, in their research designs, evaluation methodology, and theories, most of the scholars (except Bargal & Bar, 1985, 1987, 1990a, 1990b, 1995; and Bar & Asaqla, 1988a, 1988b) did not consider the structural context and constraints in determining the quality of relations between Arabs and Jews in Israel. Some of the researchers, mainly during the early 1970s, adopted the assumption that improving communication skills, reducing stereotypes and prejudice, and promoting understanding are means and ends by themselves to resolving the conflict between Arabs and Jews in Israel (Stock, 1968). These researchers argued that structural change is beyond the scope of the encounter and that there are limitations of the school system over these issues. However, the responsibility and the involvement in actions to produce political changes are threatening to the existence of these educational programs because, as in any other educational framework, these programs have their own common interests with the institutions (Lemish et al., 1991).

Fifth, in the past two decades, all the reports and research were conducted either on one or two Arab-Jewish organizations or programs or reviewed the coexistence field in general. There was no single comparative research that examined in depth several Arab-Jewish encounter programs.

In conclusion, these limitations and critiques that characterize the research on Arab-Jewish encounters signify the need for conflict resolution as an alternative perspective and approach in researching these encounters.

# 5

# Methodological Considerations and the Arab-Jewish Programs

There is a pressing need to examine more than one or two case studies that focus on the relationship and process of interaction rather than on quantifying changes at the individual level only, which causes the loss of impact of the context as well as important insights and nuances. Therefore, this research is designed to explore the meaning and influence of context on both macro and micro implications of intervention.

This qualitative study combines the three goals of explanation, exploration, and description. Hence it refers to meaning, concepts, symbols, characters, definitions, metaphors, and descriptions of Arab-Jewish encounter experience. For example, measuring the change in the attitudes of Arab and Jewish participants in a workshop is possible, but missing the meaning and the context of these attitudes is likely, as they are described by the participants in their communities. For instance, many scholars describe the change in identity among Arab participants, but none of them asked about the meaning and content of such identity according to Arabs.

In the research, I relied on the nonscheduled (nonstructured) interview and direct observation (participant-as-observer) as the two main methods of gathering data. In all the interviews the method of semi-standardized interview was used; the interviews were tape-recorded in both Hebrew and Arabic and the data were transcribed verbatim.

During a year of intensive fieldwork and several visits to these intervention programs, seventy-five interviews and eight observations were completed. Also full transcripts of previous workshops were attained.[1]

The purposeful selection of the six case studies in this research ensures that different types of programs and organizations, teachers, students, intervenors, directors, and facilitators are included. It covers at least 50 percent of the community of Arab-Jewish encounters' facilitators that constantly operate in this field.

The selection of each specific organization was made according to the following criteria:

 a. The model of intervention has to include at least one encounter of Arab and Jewish participants.
 b. The staff includes at least 4 Arab and 4 Jewish facilitators.
 c. The organization has been functioning for at least the last five years.
 d. Conduct encounters only between Arabs and Jews in Israel, and not Arabs from the West Bank and Gaza (territories under Israeli military control).

All the directors of the organizations are Jews, except in one organization, in which an Arab director is temporarily fulfilling the duties of a previous Jewish director. In general, the directors of these organizations are more involved in the financial and organizational aspects of the activities. None of these directors personally facilitates any of their organization's models of intervention.

From each organization, an Arab and a Jewish facilitator were selected. They were the most experienced facilitators and they all had at least three years of experience in facilitating Arab-Jewish encounters. All the Arab facilitators who were interviewed were males. Of the Jewish facilitators, 60 percent were females.

Four of the organizations' activities are directed toward high school and secondary school students, while the two other organizations focus on high school and secondary school teachers. All participants were selected randomly before the actual observation took place, or they were selected by their teachers. When there was no opportunity for actual observation, subjects were interviewed about their previous encounters.

A total of eight observations were conducted during the three phases of the fieldwork. They were basically detailed descriptions of the participants' and facilitators' verbal expressions. An additional set of interviewees includes nine facilitators (four Arabs and five Jews) with at least five years of experience in leading Arab-Jewish groups. These informants were asked about: (a) the ideal and most effective model of intervention in Arab-Jewish relations according to their experience; (b) limitations and advantages of the existing models of intervention in Arab-Jewish relations; (c) impact of the political context on intervention models.

Informants also included five Arab community leaders, three Arab Parliament members, a religious leader, a lawyer, and four Jewish Parliament members. Each informant was asked to evaluate the impact of intervention models on Arab-Jewish relations. Among the Jewish Parliament leaders there is representation of the Labor Party, the Mapam Party, and the Hat'hia Party. Several Likud members were approached for interviews, but none of these members agreed to be interviewed on the subject.

In data analysis, both latent and manifest content analysis techniques were applied, but with special focus on manifest content. Latent content analysis was applied only on particular occasions when special and different meaning was given to the same term or expression used by the Arab and Jewish interviewees. In general, we tried to avoid semantic content analysis; therefore, I applied thematic content analysis, which examines the themes in each response to every question.

Both types of content analysis, the latent and the proportional presentation of material, were blended. But the strength of this research is the focus on the overall intervention models in terms of their function in a specific conflictual context. In order to identify and examine the level or degree of the intervenors' professional integrity, several criteria were applied to the four research concepts. Some of these criteria are :

1. Does the subject relate to the political context in presenting the model?
2. Does the subject differentiate between theoretical and practical models?
3. Is the model presented clearly and in sequence?
4. Are intervenors aware of their: (a) goals, (b) assumptions, (c) rationale behind the intervention stages, (d) placement of the intervention in a political or a reality context, (f) clear perception of the success they are achieving in their intervention?

## THE SIX CASE STUDY ORGANIZATIONS: BASIC FEATURES

Before reviewing the findings, it is necessary to present and describe briefly the organizations that sponsor and apply these encounters. The following section briefly describes the six organizations and their case study programs used for this research. The description is mainly based on the Abraham Foundation Directory of Institutions and Organizations Fostering Coexistence Between Arabs and Jews in Israel (Weiner, et al., 1992) and the data gathered in this research.

### Students' Encounter Programs

*(1) Program A (Neve Shalom/Wahat Al Salam):* This program is part of the School for Peace educational activities. The School for Peace is a part of

Neve Shalom/Wahat Al Salam village (NS/WAS). The village was established in 1972 on a hundred acres of barren land leased from the Latrun Monastery, settled in 1978. It is a cooperative village of Arabs and Jews with Israeli citizenship.

The two basic principles of coexistence and equality are reflected in the village activities and programs:

    a. Village educational system. This school is the only Arab-Jewish bilingual school system in Israel. Arab and Jewish children are learning in an open school plan.

    b. The School for Peace. This program brings four hundred Arab and Jewish students together each year. The school applies several different models in these encounters.

    c. Teachers' project: The teachers assist educators in dealing with issues such as democracy and current events.

    d. There is an ongoing training course for new group facilitators.

    e. NS/WAS organizes an Arab-Jewish festival of music and art, which is attended by several thousand students each year.

NS/WAS does not receive any financial support from Israeli government sources; it depends completely on foreign funds. The staff and the members on most of the committees are equally divided between Arabs and Jews. The School for Peace has always been co-directed by an Arab and a Jew.

*(2) Program Medrashat Adam (MA):* Adam means "human being" in Hebrew. The organization's basic philosophy is that Israel can and must create a society in which individual rights and worth are respected. It was founded in 1985 and is dedicated to the memory of Emil Greenzweig, a research scholar and reserve officer in the Israeli Army, who was serving in Lebanon when he was killed by a grenade thrown during a peaceful protest opposing the war in Lebanon.

The founders believe that the Israeli immigrant society has been especially susceptible to extreme and antidemocratic attitudes. Therefore, the organization's first act was to teach Jewish students about the democratic components of the Israel Independence Charter. The organizers later expanded their activities to include Arab students.[2]

Although the organization's main purpose was to teach and address democracy in Israeli society, for different reasons and motivations the organization conducted several other related projects: (a) Project Encounter was designed to overcome conflict caused by a lack of understanding. In 1990, it reached four thousand Arabs and Jews, secular and religious, urban and Kibbutz primary, secondary, and high school students (our case study is concerned with encounters with Arabs and Jews only). (b) Training of teachers (about 1,200 each year) was conducted to teach political philosophy and democratic principles in special seminars in their headquarters. (c) The Pedagogical Center for Democracy and Peace was set up to develop curriculum for teaching democracy in the schools.

The organization recruits most of its funds from foreign resources, but it receives some support from the Ministry of Education. Of the fifty-four board members of the organization, there are four Arabs. The organization is led by a Jewish director.

*(3) Program Giva'at Haviva (GH):* Giva'at Haviva Institute for Arabic Studies was founded in 1963 by the Kibbutz Artzi Federation, which is affiliated with the Mapam Party (a Jewish Zionist left-wing party). The Institute conducts several projects in order to promote coexistence and understanding between Arabs and Jews in Israel: a. The Jewish-Arab young people's encounters include the following: (1)Children teach children through pairing or working in groups of four classes, in which Arabs and Jews teach each other Arabic and Hebrew through art, drama, literature, and music. (2) A vacation-time junior high school seminar includes cultural and social activities for Arab and Jewish high school students in which they can get acquainted. Part of the program is a joint tour of Arab villages. (3) Three-day intensive live-in workshops for Arab and Jewish eleventh-graders are conducted at Giva'at Haviva facilities. The program is directed by a Jewish director with the assistance of an Arab and a Jewish facilitator from the staff. (This is one of the programs included in our case studies.) In 1990, 2,700 students participated in the last two programs. b. Arab youth leaders and social activist seminar is a training program of sixty professionals in community work. c. The Jewish-Arab Art Center, opened in 1987, offers courses in sculpture, ceramics, painting, and so on. In 1990, eight hundred Arab and Jewish students participated. d. A study group on the Middle East allows participants to meet five to six times a year to discuss historical and contemporary issues and tour the Arab villages. e. The Institute maintains an information center and library on the Middle East. f. The Institute undertakes publication and research on the Middle East. g. The Institute holds an occasional one-day symposium on its research and current Arab-Jewish issues.

About 60 percent of the Institute's funds are provided by non-Israeli sources.

*(4) Program Beit Hagefen (BH):* Beit Hagefen, Israel's largest Arab-Jewish community center, was established in 1963 in Haifa's mixed Jewish and Arab residential and commercial areas. Its activities include the following: a. Educational activities: In Arab-Jewish encounters high school students meet together five times a year for an entire day to promote better understanding and to lessen intergroup hostilities and misperceptions.

(This program is one of the case studies for this research.) b. Cultura activities: an Arab-Jewish folk dance troupe tours Israel and participates ii at least one festival; an Arab Mobile Theater performs for adults an( children; and there is an annual Arab Culture and Book Week. c. Soci; and personal improvement activities: there are various clubs for wome and young couples, sports activities, and art studies.

Haifa Municipality and the Ministry of Education provide the func for the organization's activities. The center does not receive any suppoi from non-Israeli sources. In 1990, when the Jewish director (since 1960: resigned, his Arab assistant was appointed as acting director.

### Teachers' Intervention Programs

Only two programs were studied. There are several other programs tha include Arabs and Jews in the same framework, but few have a structura program that aims to engage the two groups in a direct encounter. Foi example, there are at least three institutions in Israel that bring Arabs anc Jews to the same building to teach them Hebrew and Arabic languages, or to arrange a seminar on psychological problems, art, journalism, and so on. In the programs studied, the participants were Arab and Jewish teachers who work in the Ministry of Education and belong to the largest organizations.

*(1) Program Van Leer (VL):* The Van Leer Institute was established in 1956 by the late Polly Van Leer, a Dutch Jewish philanthropist. It is dedicated to the reduction of tension and advancement of pluralism in Israel and the Middle East. Although the Institute is academic, intellectual, and research-oriented, intervention projects have been developed since the 1970s. The activities that are related to Arab-Jewish coexistence began in 1980. a. With the support of the Institute, the Ministry of Education in 1983 adopted a nationwide education program on Jewish-Arab relations. Since then the Institute has produced twenty textbooks on this subject, and has helped train more than three thousand teachers on the essentials of Arab-Jewish mutual coexistence and ways to introduce the textbooks into their schools. b. The teachers' encounter project, developed in 1987, has become "The Pairing Project" for Arab and Jewish schools. In this program teachers meet regularly to establish professional and personal ties and work together on the introduction of "current issues" into their schools. In 1989–90, this project was introduced into eight pairs of schools with 150 teachers. The project is led by a Jewish director and an Arab-Jewish staff. c. Four international conferences on Jewish-Arab and Israeli-Arab relations as well as on the development of a civic covenant model between Arab and Jewish citizens of Israel have been held. Non-Israeli sources provide 95 percent of the Institute's funds.

*(2) Program Unit for Democracy (UFD):* The Unit for Democracy and Coexistence of the Ministry of Education and Culture is a governmental agency founded in 1986 to help stimulate education for democracy. The Unit was established after an increase in extremism, violence, and intolerance in Israel, especially among Jewish youth. (Several surveys were conducted in that period indicated the prevalence of antidemocratic attitudes among Jewish youth. See chapter 3: Background Review.) The Unit's role is to coordinate the activities on democracy and coexistence in the school systems. One goal of the Unit is to build an interschool link that can create a climate of trust and partnership among the different ethnic schools. Another goal is to provide schools with opportunities to experience democracy in each school system. The following are activities of the Unit:

    a. Clusters is the main project of the Unit: each "cluster" incorporates different schools (religious and secular, Arabs and Jews, and urban and Kibbutz). Together these schools discuss their roles and mutual interests as citizens of Israel. They talk about current social and political issues, and develop activities for their schools. The program is designed to start with principals and then expand to teachers and students. In 1990, there were seventy schools led by twenty-five educators (facilitators). The program is led by the Jewish director of the Unit with four Jewish and one Arab regional coordinators. (This project is included in our case studies.)

    b. The Unit provides financial support to most of the Arab-Jewish organizations that conduct activities in the school system. (It supports five of our case studies.)

    c. The Unit provides publications to the schools on democracy and coexistence in Arabic and Hebrew. The Unit is totally funded by the Ministry of Education.

# 6

# The Encounter Programs' Designs

## *Components of the Intervention Models*

Arab-Jewish programs, as any other intervention models, have certain characteristics that describe the essential components of the intervention. (1) Participants are the beneficiaries of the program. (2) Assumptions underlie each program of intervention. (3) Goals of the programs are perceived by beneficiaries and intervenors. (4) The structure of the framework contains the interaction processes and the programs' contents (procedures, setting, and time frame). (5) Processes of interaction take place during the application of the program. These processes are presented and classified as they are perceived by both practitioners and beneficiaries. (6) The content of the program describes the issues and topics that are addressed during all activities. (7) The third party plays a role in the types of activities and strategies of intervention that are implemented or adopted in these programs.

In addition to the above characteristics, this chapter addresses these questions: (a) What are the differences and common features of these intervention programs? (b) Does each program have its own separate model? (c) Is there a single common intervention model that has been implemented by the different intervenors?

## PARTICIPANTS

*(A) Students' programs:* It is important to indicate that the Arab students who participate in such programs are usually selected by their educators and are well-spoken and competitive students. In four of the observed programs, the Arab students were from science classes; usually science classes include the best students of the school, who are competitive as well as socially and politically involved. On the other hand, Jewish students are not carefully selected because, as one facilitator explains,

In the Jewish side, because there is so much resistance to participate in such programs, we take any student who is willing to take a
part, regardless of his/her level of awareness, social involvement,
or school achievement.

All the Jewish participants indicated that the people who did not agree
to meet Arabs stayed at school or home on that specific day. The schools
provide individuals with the opportunity to choose whether to participate,
resulting in Jewish participants who are willing to participate and whose
resistance or fear of Arabs does not prevent them from attending such
encounters.

This result supports the criticism raised by those who oppose this type
of activity that these encounters only involve people who are already convinced of the importance of discussing Arab-Jewish relations, while the real
need is to address the students and teachers who would not agree to take
part in such encounters. In fact, this is one of the most difficult matters that
face the organizers of these programs who basically work with the same type
of participants again and again. They are not reaching out to those who
refuse to meet at all, to those whose political and emotional attitudes
prevent them from attending these programs (Hall-Cathala, 1990).

According to all organizers, many of the Jewish students reject or resist
taking part in the encounter, but the Arab schools always welcome the
encounters because they perceive it as a privilege. Some organizers claimed
that sometimes they are forced to reject Arab students because they do not
have enough Jewish students to meet with them. The intervenors explain
this difference in motivation to attend the encounter by the fact that the
Arab participants usually lack opportunities to spend time outside their
schools or to participate in extracurricular activities (Been, 1991). An
additional support for such a finding is Hofman's (1986) report, which
indicates that Jewish students are less willing to encounter Arabs and also
are more prejudiced and have antidemocratic attitudes.

*(B) Teachers' programs:* For the most part, Arab teachers are males and
Jewish teachers are females . This situation influences the process, output,
and content of the encounter. However, this issue was not addressed by
any facilitator during the observed teachers' encounters. A Jewish facilitator describes the influence of the female–male relations in teachers'
encounters:

> In fact, when we have Arab males and Jewish females who are
> young and have sexual chemistry, this eases the process of facilita-
> tion. But when there is no sexual harmony or attraction between
> several participants in the group, this mostly will increase the level
> of tension, anger, and frustration during the discussion. It will not

help us, as facilitators, in reflecting the similarities between the two sides of the conflict.

On the students' level, the male–female relationship dimension was essential on both the content and process levels. It was the issue that Arab and Jewish students discussed during every encounter: How are Arab female–male relations different from Jewish female–male relations? In some groups Arab girls accused Jewish students of being impolite, inconsiderate, and even *monhaleen* (amoral). In other encounters, male–female relations was an instrument used to learn about the cultural differences between Arabs and Jews.

Arab teachers' willingness to participate in such programs is similar that of to their students. They also tend to participate in these meetings more than the Jewish teachers because they are not offered many seminars by the Ministry of Education and do not have the opportunity to travel or participate in other seminars. However, the Jewish educational system offers teachers a variety of informal activities that they can choose to attend. A Jewish facilitator said:

> If the Jewish teacher selects Arab-Jewish relations as the subject to be discussed in two to three education classes [i.e., social class] during the whole year, this should be very appreciated and considered as a successful result of our intervention, because the Jewish teachers have many programs from which to choose. Arab-Jewish relations is one of eleven programs each year which is suggested to the Jewish schools.

In summary, Arab teachers and students tend to participate and attend this type of program more than Jewish teachers and students for the following reasons:

  a. Lack of alternative informal activities provided by the school or the Ministry of Education.
  b. Arab participants have, as minority members, a more pressing need to express their discomfort and frustration with Arab-Jewish relations than the Jewish majority members.
  c. Until recently, Arab teachers were accused of radicalism or being anti-coexistence if they refused to attend such activities. The impact of this threat is still strongly felt among certain groups of Arab teachers.

## ASSUMPTIONS

Upon examining the assumptions that were stated by facilitators and directors of the programs, four categories were identified: (a) theoretical assumptions, (b) educational assumptions, (c) professional assumptions, and (d) assumptions about the Arab-Israeli conflict.

*(a) Theoretical assumptions:* This set of assumptions is related to the philosophy and theories of social science that underlie each program or intervenor's work. There is only one interviewee who indicated such a set of assumptions. Others were not aware of these theories' existence or relation to their intervention.

*(b) Educational assumptions:* These are related to the educational perceptions and beliefs of the interviewee. In general, five of the seven directors agreed on common educational assumptions; for instance, they argued that the main assumptions of their programs are the nonviolence, compromise, and *heddabroot* or "talk" principles. At the same time, more Jewish facilitators addressed this assumption as important to their work than did Arab facilitators. Jewish subjects were more explicit in expressing this set of assumptions. Arab intervenors did not highlight these assumptions. In explaining such differences, an experienced facilitator argued that since Arab facilitators are more politicized, any explicit expression of nonviolence, dialogue, or atypical political activity will be perceived as a cooptive effort.

The Jewish facilitators and directors assume that the encounter is an educational and nonpolitical instrument; only one Arab facilitator stated this as an assumption.

Several Arab facilitators pointed out that the program should be based on equal setting and interaction between Arabs and Jews. This statement refers to conditions that Arab students have to speak in Hebrew and that the group dynamics (i.e., group discussion and informal techniques of education) are less familiar to them than to Jewish students. Both conditions cause an asymmetric setting. A Jewish facilitator claimed that "Arab participants should not be a majority in the group, even if they are a majority in the geographical region, because this will threaten the Jewish participants in the group." Such an argument is an indication of the Jewish groups' sensitivity in losing their dominance in any setting, even in an encounter.

Several Jewish directors and facilitators perceived the Arab-Jewish issue as not being the main subject to be addressed by educators, but as only one of many issues that are related to education for democracy. Their emphasis is on education for democracy and freedom of both sides. The Arab intervenors' assumptions are generally based on the principle of equality which coincides with their tendency to be more specific and explicit about their political agenda when they interact with Jews because the main political agenda for the Arab minority in Israel is obtaining equal rights (Lustick, 1980; Rouhana, 1988).

One Jewish program director stated that his program's assumption is that there is no conflict between Arabs and Jews in Israel and that the program should focus on positive images and similarities between the two sides. Such an assumption reflects the perception that conflict is negative and destructive and should be avoided to promote cooperation.

Finally, all intervenors agreed on several educational assumptions: (1) developing understanding, listening capability, and communication skills; (2) reducing mistrust, fears, anger, and knowing each other to improve relationships between Arabs and Jews in general.

*(c) Professional assumptions:* In regard to their work a as professional third party and their ideas about the intervention design, intervenors agreed on the following assumptions:

1. Continuity and follow-up are important.
2. There is a need for a uninational setting during the intervention.
3. A flexible model of intervention is necessary.
4. A facilitator has to have a democratic personality to be able to work in the field.
5. Content should not be separated from process.

Several Arab facilitators stated that they perceive the model of intervention as a political instrument, while the Jewish directors indicated that they perceive it as an educational tool.

*(d) Assumptions about the conflict:* In regard to the nature of Arab-Jewish conflict, these assumptions were predominantly stated by Jewish interviewees in at least five of the organizations:

1. Israel is a Jewish democratic state.
2. The Arabs in Israel are part of Israeli society. "Our destiny as Arabs and Jews is to live together."
3. Arab-Jewish relations should be based on dialogue and nonviolence.
4. The Arabs are a minority in a Jewish majority culture and society.
5. The issues involved in the conflict between Arabs and Jews in Israel are different from the issues involved in the conflict between Arabs from the West Bank and Gaza and the Jews in Israel.
6. There is no conflict between Arabs and Jews in Israel; it is a typical case of minority–majority relations.

The Arab facilitators disagreed explicitly with their directors' assumption that there is no conflict between Arabs and Jews in Israel, and also with the assumption about the nature of the state.

The nature of these assumptions on the conflict, which are acceptable and approved by the Israeli Ministry of Education, are the main factors that have enabled these programs and their organizations to operate during the past forty years in Israel and to survive all the political crises that have taken place (seven Arab-Israeli wars).[1]

In conclusion, neither facilitators nor directors are used to being asked to address this type of question about their intervention models. They were very confused and stated their assumptions as goals and objectives. Only two facilitators addressed both types of assumptions and drew a clear distinction between each type in their responses. Several intervenors were thankful for the opportunity to examine and explore their assumptions about the model, which they had been applying for at least two years.

Some of the intervenors explained that they did not think about this issue prior to the interview because, as practitioners, they are more concerned with the day-to-day arrangements and procedures of the process and with the results of their intervention than they are with the theoretical and educational assumptions that underlie the model. Others explained this lack of examination of their models' assumptions by stating that most of the organizations lack continuous staff meetings, professional counseling and supervision, or tight schedules.

Regardless of the explanation, most participants, both Arabs and Jews, were not aware of the professional or educational assumptions. They argued that the organizers did not provide any information on this issue and did not even explain the general field of Arab-Jewish relations. Both Arabs and Jews, both students and teachers, indicated that the only assumption of which they are aware is the importance of Arab-Jewish encounters in bringing peace and improving Arab-Jewish relationships in Israel.

Most of the programs consider neither the educational nor the professional assumptions of their work to be an important or essential component of their implemented program. Therefore, they did not introduce them to their participants. An additional explanation was provided by an Arab facilitator, who argued that if political and educational assumptions that underlie the intervention program (i.e., conflict between Arabs and Jews does not exist, or focus must be on similarities only) are presented explicitly and clearly to the Arab participants, then certainly some of them will not be encouraged to take part in such activities.

It is important to emphasize that this finding supports the hypothesis that encounters and discussions of Arab-Jewish relations that are actually based on the principle of revealing cultural and political similarities are basically additional settings in which the Arab group is being exploited by the dominant group. In such contexts the inequality and asymmetric goals and needs of the two groups are preserved as in the outside reality (Said & Hitchers, 1988).

The nature of these assumptions provokes immediate questions: (1) Can any program, based on these assumptions, promote political change in terms of equal national and civil rights for both Arabs and Jews in Israel? (2) Can a program that ignores the similarity and interdependence of the two conflicts between Arabs and Jews in the West Bank and Gaza and Israel promote freedom and equal rights to both communities?

An in-depth discussion of these questions will be raised in the section that focuses on intervention models and social and political change.

## GOALS
### *Intervenors' Goals*

Again, Arab and Jewish intervenors had different sets of goals. In response to the question "What are the three most important goals for you in the intervention model?" they listed the following:

| Arabs | Jews |
|---|---|
| • Change political attitudes personal acquaintance | • Encourage cultural and |
| • Empower participants conflict | • Teach complexity of the |
| • Develop a sense of respon-sibility toward the conflict | • Change negative perceptions |
| • Develop culturally and personally | • Encourage openness, acquaintance, and tolerance |
| | • Teach democratic values |

Most of the Arab facilitators had a goal, latent or explicit: to change the political attitudes of the Jewish participants; in particular, to make them become more in favor of a two-state solution, including the right to self-determination for the Palestinians in the West Bank and Gaza Strip, and support for the implementation of equal rights for the Arab minority in Israel. In most cases, this goal was mentioned explicitly, but in others it was described as a wish or a result that would be considered. Such a finding is echoed by Bar and Asaqla's (1988b) report on Giva'at Haviva staffwork.

The Arab facilitators also intended to help Arab participants formulate their national identity, raise their awareness of this identity, and provide them with an opportunity to express their concerns and ideas. Having such goals can be better understood when considering the fact that Arab teachers and students do not have the opportunity, as do Jewish students or teachers, to discuss political issues in their schools.

Such an opportunity is lacking for two reasons. First, the strong security measures that were placed in the Arab educational system to prevent *hasata* (instigation) prohibited Arab teachers from raising political issues. Second, although teachers in the Jewish educational system have the opportunity to address such issues without security limitations, they have not had sufficient training to obtain skills that would enable them to raise political issues in a learning context. In addition, as indicated by teachers, they were always more terrified than their students to raise the Arab-Jewish issue in their classes (Hareven, 1981).

Another important goal indicated by the Arab facilitators was to develop a sense of practical responsibility (or personal obligation to act on behalf of the minority) among participants, especially Jewish youth and teachers. Responsibility was presented as a sense of commitment toward the Arab-Jewish subject. This is also related to the pressing need among the Arab minority to obtain their civil rights in Israel, or at least to address this issue constantly. A similar statement was reported by Katz and Khanov (1990).

Although both Arab and Jewish facilitators and directors stated the importance of conducting such intervention models for the personal and cultural acquaintance cause, many Jewish intervenors stated this as being more important than the Arab intervenors did, and listed it more frequently than other goals. Other Jewish subjects listed teaching participants the complexity of the conflict in an attempt to prevent young students from adopting radical, easy, or "black-and-white" solutions. Jewish interviewees stated more often the goal of reducing violence, hostility, anger, and fear on both sides.

These findings support the hypothesis that Jewish intervenors tend to focus on psychological and communicational aspects more than Arab intervenors, who in their turn, focus on a political agenda that includes their community's persistent need to improve its political status as a minority. In one specific example, the facilitator argued that he clearly does not agree with his organization's goals or mission statement, and that he is looking for political change through his intervention.

Seven years ago I could agree with these goals, but today I am not satisfied with cultural and personal acquaintance or tolerance and openness. My goal is to change the political attitudes of the participants.

Another Arab facilitator argued that:

My goal is to change the reality, but the sponsors of this program adopt the goal of "talk" or *heddabroot* and cultural sensitivity. This applies more to conflict in the USA. . . . It also ignores our national conflict.

The explanation for such a difference in goals is that the organizations' directors (mostly Jewish) are responsible for the organization's public ima-ge and for raising funds, which are raised mainly from Jewish foundations and sponsors. Therefore, these directors claim they are apolitical, and they tend to focus on positive content as well as goals.

### *Participants' Goals*

**Students' goals.** The following list reflects the participants' responses to the question: What were your goals when you attended the program? Arab and Jewish participants have almost the same goals, but the priority of these goals was different among the two groups.

| **Arabs** | **Jews** |
|---|---|
| • Change Jewish students' attitudes | • Get to know Arabs culturally and personally |
| • Get know the Jewish youth and culture | • Have fun |
| • Get out of school | • Explore the Arab students' political attitudes |

The Arab students' goals are similar to the Arab facilitators' stated goals, particularly in the notion of changing the political attitudes of their Jewish opponents. An Arab student declared during the interview his goal in the encounter:

We have to tell the Jewish students what our life looks like, because they are the majority and they can go back and tell their leaders that we, the Arabs, should have our rights and that the Palestinians have the right for a state.

This motivation also explains the typical dynamic of interaction during the encounter, in which Arab participants ask, and sometimes demand, that Jewish participants return to their community and become involved in political activities that aim to assist the Arabs in obtaining equal political and national rights as a minority in Israel. Such a position was reported also by Katz and Khanov (1990) and Hertz-Lazarovitz (1989).

Only a few Jewish participants expressed their goal as being to explore and know the Arab students' political attitudes, while the Arab participants were persuasive, clear, and explicit in their goal to change the Jewish students' discriminatory attitudes, as they perceived them to be.

The Jewish students constantly stated that their goal was to have "fun," which means spending quality time with their peers. The Arab students, on the other hand, used the phrase "just to get out of the school," which again indicates their lack of opportunity to leave the school or to take part in extracurricular activities. There were many students, especially Arabs, who described the encounter as a "field trip." These descriptions indicate a lack of sufficient preparation for the program, in which educators and facilitators aim to present the encounter as a learning experience and certainly not as a pure "trip" or "to have fun or pleasure." The students' overall misperception of the program as a "trip" lessens their ability to relate to the encounter as a learning experience.

**Teachers' goals.** All teachers were interested in acquiring skills and tools to enable them to cope with the Arab-Jewish conflict in their schools for the following reasons:

a. There is a growing number of radical and fanatic students, especially in the Jewish schools (Tzimah, 1984).
b. The subject of Arab-Jewish relations was not recognized and introduced formally by the Ministry of Education until the mid-1980s. Therefore, there are not enough courses on how to deal with the issue.
c. Arab teachers were not allowed to discuss political issues openly.
d. Many Israeli teachers lack the educational skills that enable them to introduce current events in their class.

The teachers' goals were as the follows:

| Arabs | Jews |
|---|---|
| • Acquire skills to deal with Arab-Jewish relations (AJR) in class | • Acquire skills to deal with AJR in class |
| • Explore the Jewish teachers' political attitudes | • Know Arab teachers personally and culturally |
| • Present the problems of the Arab minority in Israel | |

The goal of cultural and personal acquaintance was not introduced by Arab teachers as being the important or the essential issue because almost all Arab teachers obtain their academic degrees in Jewish academic institutions. As minority members, they are often in daily contact with the Jewish majority culture. On the Jewish side, however, a Jewish teacher does not need to interact with Arab minority members on a continual or constant basis. As one Jewish teacher from Ramat Gan announced in one of the workshops: "This is the first time throughout my fifteen years in Israel that I have met Arabs and discussed with them any issue besides cleaning my building."

Jewish teachers' main goal is to know the Arab culture better, since they do not have to interact with Arabs in their daily life. For Arab teachers, it was important to explore the Jewish teachers' political attitudes and sometimes to present the Arab minority problems to the majority members, who are perceived as being responsible for the status of the minority.

In short, Arab participants and facilitators share a similar set of goals (promoting political discussion and awareness). Jewish participants and facilitators, and even directors, shared a different set of goals (from their Arab partners), which is basically to promote cultural and personal acquaintance.

Such a result supports the claim that several encounter programs, at least those whose directors and facilitators consider cultural and personal goals more important than political goals, are based on an asymmetric evaluation of the participants' needs. In examining the activities of such intervention programs, it is clear that cultural and personal aspects are the focus of most programs.

## STRUCTURE

The structure of an encounter program relates to the type of preparation, number of encounters (meetings), the use of a uninational meeting format, and the implementation of follow-up activities (table 6.1).

There is no single program that has any *follow-up activity* after the participants return to their normal environment. In one program, facilitators explain that they do not know what to do in the follow-up activity that will be satisfactory to their participants, especially those who are interested in a continuing relationship between Arab and Jewish students. As an illustration of this problem, one facilitator claimed that one year the concluding session was conducted by a researcher who used the session to hand out a questionnaire for his master's thesis! Such an act indicates confusion and lack of professional commitment to participants.

The students' programs (NS, MA, GH, BH) concluded the intervention with a single session of one to two hours in which most of them asked questions such as: What has happened to you since the last encounter? How do you feel today about the experience that you had? There are some facilitators who claim that they sometimes go back to the schools after the encounter and distribute a questionnaire or an evaluation form for research purposes.

In the teachers' programs the case is slightly different because some, for instance, program VL, continue for almost a full year, and each group has at least two sessions after the encounter. Generally, the encounter is not so central in this program; it is perceived and presented by the facilitators as a method and tool for completing the training of their teachers. At the students' level, the encounter is the goal and aim of the intervention program. In spite of this fact, however, the criticism of program VL is still valid, because there were no follow-up activities after the teachers ended the one-year participation. In program UFD there is continuity because the group is meeting for the third year. But there are no follow-up activities that will provide support to the teachers at their schools.

Regarding the *uninational setting*, it appears that what was once an illegitimate and unrecognized framework has now become part of the program's intervention design. However, facilitators in program MA indicated that they are using this method only when there is a problem or when the group is "stuck." The purpose of this uninational framework during the encounter is to examine the problems of each group in the interaction. In program GH the workshop that was observed was the first encounter to include a uninational setting during the encounter. Several comments were expressed in the facilitators' meeting that indicated their satisfaction with the uninational meeting, although they were still unclear about its function or importance. In fact, a facilitator used the uninational meeting to continue a political discussion that had started in the mixed group and to instruct the national group on how to respond to the other side's political arguments.

The preparation stage is very brief. Most programs have two to four hours to prepare each group for the encounter, except program NS, which has a two-day intensive uninational workshop that functions as a preparation period. Although program VL only assigned two sessions for preparation prior to the encounter, the amount of uninational work that is invested in both Arab and Jewish groups was considered adequate time to work on the weaknesses of the two groups and to address their needs prior to the workshop.

In program GH the preparation of five sessions was also part of a new intervention design since 1992. The director and the facilitators were praising their decision to invest more in the uninational preparation stage, and they even called it a uninational work. Both facilitators and directors cited the Gulf War as a reason for this change in the program (see the Gulf War's impact in the political context section). All Arab and some Jewish facilitators indicated the need for the framework of uninational preparation and the necessity for a separate uninational activity to be incorporated into the program itself.

This finding is supported by the critique of the contact hypothesis, "contact is not enough" (Bargal, 1990) and by Bar and Asaqla's (1988b) conclusion, which indicates the need for differential investment in the groups before the encounter.

**Table 6.1. Programs and Frameworks**

| Program | Preparation | Uninational Setting | Encounter | Uninational Setting during Encounter | Post Encounter | Follow-Up |
|---------|-------------|---------------------|-----------|--------------------------------------|----------------|-----------|
| NS | 2 Sessions | 2 days | 2–3 days | Yes | 1 Session | No |
| MA | 2–3 Sessions | No | 3–4 days | Yes | 1 Session | No |
| GH | 5 Sessions | No | 3 days | Yes | 1 Session | No |
| BH | 2 Sessions | No | 3 days | No | 1 Session | No |
| VL | 2 Sessions | 7-8 days | 2 days & 2–3 Hours | No | 2–3 Sessions | No |
| UFD | 1 Session | No | 9–10 x 5 Hours | No | 1 Sessions | No |

In programs MA and BH there were mutual visits to each other's houses. All students, Arabs and Jews, expressed their satisfaction and pleasure in being received in each other's homes. Even teachers in the UFD program were conducting their meetings in a different location each time in order to learn about the places and locations where members of the group were living.

*The quest for uninational structure:* A major disagreement among the intervenors was reflected in their attitude toward the use of uninational sessions, in which participants meet separately based on national affiliation. All the Arab intervenors and some Jewish facilitators agreed on the necessity and pressing need for uninational meetings. Facilitators and directors who reject the incorporation of a uninational framework in Arab-Jewish encounters argue that its activities: (a) highlight the differences between the two groups; (b) function as a tool to unify each national group's attitudes; (c) prevent the two groups from focusing on similarities; (d). add the uninational activities on account of the binational framework because of the limited resources available for the organizers; (e) Increase the mistrust between the two national groups, since they will be divided during the encounter, which is supposed to result in greater trust.

On the other hand, those who support the incorporation of uninational activities argue as follows: (a) These activities help narrow the gap between Arab and Jewish participants and make the encounter less asymmetric. It is an empowerment to the Arab students; it closes the gap between Arab and Jewish participants in terms of the Jewish group's ability to express themselves, in experiencing an informal setting, and in examining their internal social and political differences; (b) Uninational frameworks threaten the directors and facilitators, especially Jewish intervenors who are not comfortable in being outsiders in such activities; (c) Uninational activity improves the interaction between the two groups during the encounter because it helps them focus on the essential issues, rather than on marginal issues determined by a dominant group or by individuals; (d) Uninational sessions can function as a valve for participants' emotions, such as disappointment, anger, and so on, which are produced by intensive joint interaction sessions.

In general, it is important to mention that during recent years there has been an increasing number of programs that have incorporated uninational activities in their intervention frameworks. Such change has been taking place especially since the Gulf War, because Arabs and Jews could not meet and these programs were forced to work only in uninational frameworks (see more details in chapter 9: political context).

*Language as a structural barrier:* All facilitators, except in program BH, describe the encounter's language as a limitation that must be addressed. This is especially true for Arab facilitators, who stated their discomfort with having to translate both languages in addition to being facilitators. This issue also bothers Arab students, who complained on several occasions that they were unable to express their ideas properly because they were not fluent in Hebrew. For instance, in the opening session of one workshop, an Arab female student announced that she would not speak in Hebrew during the encounter. She also demanded that her peers follow her lead:

> We should have the right to speak in our language in this encounter, because we cannot express ourselves clearly in Hebrew, while the Jews can fluently say what they want during the discussion. Why can't they learn to speak our language?

This student spent the first day speaking in Arabic, while the Arab facilitator was her translator. But, on the second day, when the facilitator stopped translating (per instruction by the staff counselor), the Arab student was forced to speak in Hebrew.

Many other Arab participants, during the observation of students' encounters, described their struggle to express themselves in Hebrew during the encounter to be an obstacle that prevented them from saying everything they wanted. An Arab student said:

> I felt like I knew every answer to the Jewish students' arguments, but I could not respond because I did not know how to say it, because our Arab facilitator did not like to translate, and my friends will think that I cannot speak Hebrew well and they will laugh at me.

Some Jewish participants argued that even they had a problem understanding the Hebrew of the Arab students; others indicated their mistrust of the facilitators, who might not be translating objectively, or as a Jewish student argued, "this Arab facilitator was changing what the Arab students said, and we discovered it because one Jewish student understood Arabic well."

The encounter programs have techniques, such as group discussion, simulation, and role play, which are used by most programs. There is a new type of exercise in which Arabs and Jews in the same group have a joint mission, a task to perform, or a substantive issue to explore, such as Middle East negotiation setting or building and designing an Arab-Jewish mixed school. This type of framework has been adopted by several programs since 1992 with the idea that participants do not have to focus on the conflict or on the differences directly, but can learn about each other by focusing on a mission or task-oriented activities instead of directly focusing on conflict issues.

## CONTENT

Four categories emerged from the classification of the issues listed by every intervenor in response to the question: What are the main issues discussed or presented in your program's intervention model?

*(a) Personal issues:* All programs include in their intervention a section on personal acquaintance. In students' programs the personal level includes hobbies, information about the family, and things they like or dislike about themselves. In teachers' programs the personal information shared is basically for the participants to introduce themselves to the other group members, but there is no continuing activity on this level. The personal information is used in an attempt to "break the ice" among the unacquainted participants and to enable the facilitators to pursue their agenda. In the students' program, personal acquaintance is an essential instrument to develop a sense of closeness among participants (see table 6.2).

*(b) Cultural issues:* In discussing the cultural aspects, Arabs and Jews in the group address and exchange basic information on issues such as Islamic, Christian, and Jewish feasts and religious traditions, family habits, leisure time, home visits, male–female relations, and teacher–student relationships. A separate aim that programs NS, GH, and BH have during the discussion of cultural and social components is to reveal the stereotypes that each side has of the other group. A list of such stereotypes is made by each group during one session and the students are requested to listen without an immediate reaction or evaluation to the opinions and beliefs of each side on the other. Some of these stereotypes listed by Arab and Jewish participants are:

**Table 6.2. Content of Intervention Programs**

| | Content | | | |
| --- | --- | --- | --- | --- |
| Program | Social and Cultural | Personal | Political | Task or Professional |
| Students' | | | | |
| NS | X | X | X | No |
| MA | X | X | No | X |
| GH | X | X | No | No |
| BH | X | X | No | No |
| Teachers' | | | | |
| VL | No | X | X | X |
| UFD | X | X | No | X |

*On Arabs:* "killers," "rapists," "dirty," "can't trust them," "fanatics," "religious," and "all Arab families have many children."

*On Jews:* "can't trust them," "don't practice religion *khafer*," "stronger than Arabs," "do not respect the older people," "have no respect for women," "have no control on their desires (*monhaleen*)," "stubborn," and "oppressors."

The discussion of such cultural issues in the students' programs is an essential part of the programs, and it was stated as a goal that both intervenors and participants were interested in pursuing. Cultural issues, such as traditions, norms, and values of Arab and Jewish societies, are the focus of programs GH and BH. Programs NS and MA relate to the social and cultural issues as secondary or as supplementary factors that assist them in pursuing their main content.

In the teachers' programs, at least in program VL, the cultural aspects were not important and were not discussed or addressed throughout the different stages of the intervention.

*(c) Political issues:* The political content is predominantly divided into two sets of issues:

1. One set is related to the Palestinian-Israeli conflict, such as: (a) the legal status of the Palestinians in the West Bank and Gaza; (b) the PLO's role in representing Palestinians in the West Bank and Gaza and in Israel; (c) terrorism, Intifada, Hamas, the peace process, the Gulf War, and so on; (d) the Palestinian state, autonomy, or transfer.
2. The second set of issues is related to Palestinians in Israel having the status of equal citizens. Some of these issues are as

follows: (a) Arabs serving in the Israeli Army, or in a sort of National Service system; (b) equal civil rights for Arabs in Israel (equal distribution of budgets to local municipalities), and equal employment opportunities, in a Jewish state that provides preference to its majority, and Israel as a democratic state; (c) national claims of Arabs in Israel: land confiscation, recognition of Arabs as a national minority in Israel, and national identity of participants.

In their descriptions of their programs' content issues, only two programs (NS and VL) included, clearly and explicitly, clarification of participants' political attitudes as part of their agenda. In programs NS and VL, the political issues are introduced by the facilitators. In program NS, political attitude clarification is part of the overall design that the intervenors intend to implement in order to achieve their goals. In program VL, as stated by the facilitators, the clarification of political issues is an instrument and strategy that they follow in order to help teachers gain the skills necessary to address the subject of Arab-Jewish relations in their classes. It is important to indicate that the director of this program argued that there is no need to focus on the political content, especially the conflictual issues. Instead, he suggested addressing the issues that Arabs and Jews agreed on, or in which they share common attitudes—issues such as joint initiatives or "tasks" conducted by Arabs and Jews that would reflect positive relations between the two groups.

The four other programs share the same notion about avoiding political content. In the students' programs MA, GH, and BH, the political issues came up during the discussion but were not suggested, provided, or stimulated by the facilitators.

In program MA, the facilitators explained that they do not conduct the traditional classic political discussion; the two national groups prepare a separate list of political questions that they ask the other side to answer. "The political conflict is not the most important conflict; it is another conflict in Israeli society."

During the observation of the encounter in program GH, the facilitator did not stimulate or direct the group to political issues in a specific group, but when the group engaged in such a discussion (e.g., as the role of PLO discrimination against Arabs in Israel, Palestinian identity of Arab participants), the facilitator attempted to facilitate the discussion in that specific session but avoided it in the following sessions. In the same program there were four discussion groups, and facilitators reported that in at least three of their groups political issues were discussed, but were not introduced by the intervenors.

It is important to indicate that the director of program GH stated that political discussion is not and should not be part of the essential content. On the contrary, the director felt the program should focus on the positive and pleasant and not on the conflictual experiences between Arabs and Jews in Israel.

Those who avoid political content suggest that participants define their social and national identity, in order to deepen the personal and cultural acquaintance, and not to clarify the participants' political attitudes. However, during the observations and through interviews, it was indicated that students engaged in political discussions and arguments during these sessions on the national identity of both sides.

(d) *Professional and task-oriented issues:* This type of issue was a part of three programs, MA, VL, and UFD. The students' program focused on teaching Arab and Jewish participants democratic values and principles, such as equal rights and freedom for individuals and groups, tolerance of those who are different, and freedom of choice. The director and the facilitators indicated that they discuss political issues only as an instrument to teach democratic values to the students. They also argued that they teach these values to the participants through gender and peer relations, and it does not have to be through the subject of Arab-Jewish relations.

In the teachers' program VL, the professional issues that were discussed are related to how Arab and Jewish teachers are coping with current events in their classes. In this program participants were focusing on their profession as teachers who face common problems with their varied students. Since the main substantive issue was current events, the participants had the opportunity to address many political issues related to current events in Arab-Jewish relations. But their main content focused on developing educational and facilitation skills to deal with current issues in schools.

In the teachers' program UFD, the professional content is also at the center of the participants' activity, but the overall program, as it was described by its designer and by the director and facilitators, did not have a specific professional issue to be discussed. They explained that any issue which concerns Arabs and Jews, and secular, religious, private, or government teachers is a legitimate subject for discussion. All the interviewees in this program stated that the main content of the discussion certainly was not intended to be on Arab-Jewish relations, but because the main participants ended up being Jews and Arabs (religious Jewish schools reject or refuse to take a part in such programs), most of the discussions concerned Arab-Jewish relations and teachers' concerns on both sides.

In conclusion, the discussion of political issues in the encounter in general is an indicator of how much the specific program or encounter is *conflict-oriented.* Therefore, it appears that there are only two programs, NS and VL, which are in practice and theory related to the conflict between Arabs and Jews as an important content to be explored and addressed. The other programs can be considered *multicultural sensitivity learning* models or *professional task-oriented training.* These programs' designs attempt to ignore, neglect, or avoid the political issues that differentiate between Arabs and Jews in the encounter group. Their goal is to reveal more similarities among the participants. They basically aim to bring the two groups into a closer relationship by introducing them to each other culturally and personally.

In support of this notion, several directors claimed that their programs are interested in addressing nonpolitical and nonconflictual issues. One of them stated:

> our students have so many opportunities in their normal life to experience and learn about conflictual and political issues, but they lack any opportunity for positive experience or the focus on similarities between Arabs and Jews. Therefore, I believe this is what our program should provide them with.

*Participants' perspective on content:* In the participants' interviews (which were conducted an average of two to three weeks after the last encounter), students were able to recall some details about the person that they met during the encounter. Students were not able to recall details on the actual activities; however, they did recall issues such as female–male relations, family traditions, norms, and political attitudes expressed by the other side. In general, Arab students were able to indicate at least 50 percent of the exercises that they experienced in the last encounter, while Jewish students were not able to recall such exercises.

Moreover, it was always the Arab participants who argued and demanded that more political issues be introduced to the intervention program (especially programs MA, GH, BH, and UFD). Actually, several Arab students stated that this was their ultimate goal in taking part in the program, while Jewish participants in the same programs indicated their satisfaction with the issues and the content of the encounters.

## PROCESS

The process of intervention includes levels and types of interactions that characterize the set of activities carried out. When examining data from each program's set of activities, intervenors' and participants' perceptions, and the direct observation, several categories emerged.

*Levels of Interaction*

*(a) Interpersonal interaction* occurs when Arabs and Jews in the group relate to each other as separate individuals, and the programs' content and third-party intervention are designed to focus on differences and similarities, relationships, perceptions, and changes on the individual level only. All six programs had activities that emphasized this level of interaction.

In the students' programs the interaction on the interpersonal level is aimed to promote personal acquaintance among the group members from both national groups; it is also utilized to reduce the perceived homo-geneity and polarization within and between the two national groups, by stressing the uniqueness of each individual. In the teachers' programs (and also in program MA), as a result of the emphasis on substantive and instru-mental focus (professional discussion), the facilitators' intervention and the model in general are focused on individuals and their understanding of their professional roles or as individual citizens.

*(b) Intragroup processes* are those where interaction within the same national group is facilitated and addressed as an essential part of the inter-vention program. Only three programs (NS, GH, and VL) apply the issues relating to problems and concerns of the individuals in the same national group, and these were addressed directly and explicitly by facilitators and directors. In fact, during the observations of several encounters, the mixed group was broken down into two separate national groups in which each discussed different issues separately. In these sessions facilitators focused on the intragroup level of interaction by asking such questions as, Do you think that your Arab friends agree with you in this same attitude? Do all the Jewish group members think the same on this matter?

In these programs, an essential part of their intervention is structured as a uninational preparation activity. In some cases, as in program VL (teacher training) 75 percent of the invested work was on the intragroup level or uninational setting. In the three other programs (MA, BH and UFD) there was no substantial or direct focus on the intragroup interaction during observations and interviews of facilitators and directors. This type of interaction was not addressed as an important manner (see table 6.3).

*(c) At the intergroup level,* the interaction is mainly a set of interventions and processes that reflect two separate collective groups. All six programs have activities designed for intergroup interaction. It is important to distinguish two types of interactions on this level. *(1) Cultural and social intergroup interaction* is mainly an exchange of information or experience between Arab and Jewish students who are trying to understand each other's cultures. They examine most similarities and some differences between their two collective social and cultural identities. This type of inter-

**Table 6.3. Intervention Programs and Level of Interaction**

| | *Level of Interaction* | | |
| Program | *Interpersonal* | *Intragroup* | *Intergroup* |
| --- | --- | --- | --- |
| NS | X | X | X |
| MA | X | No | X |
| GH | X | X | X |
| BH | X | No | X |
| VL | X | X | X |
| UFD | X | No | X |

group interaction took place in all programs. But, in some of them, it was a secondary interaction, while in others, it was the main interaction during the entire program. *(2) Conflict-oriented intergroup interaction* occurs when the facilitation process and content of the program are focused on group conflicts. In this type of interaction, the members of the two national groups perceive each other as two different conflictual collective national identities. Facilitators through this process reflect the fact that there are two different groups in the encounter context. Some of the directors and facilitators (programs GH, BH, VL, and UFD) argued that this intergroup interaction should indeed recognize the fact that there are two conflictual groups, but in general it should be focused mainly on the similarities, not on the differences, between the two groups. Others argued that the intervention programs ought to recognize several assumptions in the intergroup interaction:

1. There is a conflict.
2. There are differences between Arabs and Jews.
3. There is no defined and complete Israeli identity that can unite the two groups.
4. That if "we" ignore the differences between the two national groups, it will be more difficult for the individuals to recognize the similarities between the two groups.

### Intervention Approaches

When examining the type of facilitation and activities used by each program, three sets of tools (or processes to be engaged in) were used to change the participants' attitudes. These tools could be classified as "affective," "cognitive," and "contact experience" (or social and cultural interaction).

*(a) Affective processes:* Only programs NS and VL were concerned with the immediate expressed emotional aspects of the interaction and the conflict. The facilitators were constantly asking questions about feelings of

anger, frustration, disappointment, and support or strength that the participants expressed during their interaction. This process of intergroup and interpersonal (but mostly interpersonal) interaction that focuses on emotional aspects was facilitated by a "here and now" type of intervention or questions (Table 6.4).

In program VL, the group dynamic interaction took place only during the encounter between Arabs and Jews. During the uninational sessions, the focus was on cognitive processes of learning and interaction, which means that this was the only program that combined both aspects or processes.

*(b) Cognitive interaction process:* The main assumption is that the new way of processing information and providing logical reasoning through value and attitude clarification will result in cognitive learning processes that will produce new attitudes and behaviors. Some of these processes were described by Amir and Ben-Ari (1989). Although most of the programs utilize activities based on cognitive learning processes, there are those that directly and explicitly apply certain contents or instruments assuming that promoting cognitive learning processes rather than affective processes will produce more attitudinal changes among the participants.

In program MA, the cognitive learning process is applied by focusing on teaching students, Arabs and Jews, principles of democracy. The teaching strategy is through mixed national group discussions. Facilitators stated that they hope that introducing issues and exercises on freedom, equal rights, and freedom of expression in an interaction group of Arabs and Jews will enable students to learn and adopt democratic principles and values.

In program VL, the cognitive learning is taking place through a specific training skills strategy in which teachers are expected to obtain educational skills and facilitation skills that enable them to discuss current events with their students.

In program UFD, the cognitive learning process is introduced through discussion of common problems by teachers who gather each month to discuss subjects of their choice. Intervenors who supported such an approach argued that they preferred the cognitive, instrumental learning processes, or socializing interactions, instead of the affective-oriented process, because the focus on questions such as: How do you feel with this attitude? Are you hurt? or Are you angry?, provokes more conflicts and can bring the participants to disagreements instead of exploring common interests or even enjoying a simple positive dialogue.

Another director claimed that

> the group dynamic techniques are enforcement of the group on the individual; therefore, it stands against our democratic principle. Group dynamic process can be an instrument for oppression.

**Table 6.4. Intervention Programs and Interaction Processes**

| | *Interaction Process* | | | | | |
| | | | | *Interaction:*[a] | | *Instrumental* |
| *Program* | *Affective* | *Cognitive* | *Value* | *Conflict* | *Experience* | *or Task* |
|---|---|---|---|---|---|---|
| NS | X | — | X | X | X | — |
| MA | — | X | X | X | — | X |
| GH | — | — | X | X | — | — |
| BH | — | — | X | X | — | — |
| VL | X | X | X | — | X | X |
| UFD | — | X | X | X | — | X |

[a] Conflict or experience interaction.

*(c) Experiential aspects (or socializing):* the main process focuses on the fact that Arabs and Jews are interacting socially and personally in one group for a certain period of time. The assumption is that by having a "good time," the interaction process serves to achieve coexistence and improve the relationship goal. Programs GH and BH focused mainly on this type of interaction, in which they do not have an instrumental or substantive issue for discussion, but they do explore the values and attitudes of students in regard to their social and cultural differences. Program NS also considers the fact that Arabs and Jews are experiencing the same encounter and sharing the same setting, which is a powerful process by itself and has its own momentum.

All the programs have several sessions in which the main focus is on values and attitudes clarification. These are prejudice and stereotype reduction exercises, which have been implemented in most of the students' programs. In some cases this is the main process that is adopted (programs GH, BH, and UFD). In others, clarification of values and attitudes is only another activity that should lead the group into a discussion of substantive/ professional or political concerns.

Figure 6.1 integrates the data derived from the observations and from the intervenors' interviews. It illustrates the processes of interaction and approaches of intervention, combined with the contents that each program applies.[2] It attempts to classify the programs according to their processes and content issues, which are observed in the encounters and described by intervenors.

It is clear that there is a continuing process of interaction on the interpersonal level in which facilitators focused on the individual's attitudes and positions. At the same time, participants are consistent in their responses on a collective or intergroup level. In fact, these two attempts of interaction by participants on the intergroup level, and by facilitators on the interpersonal level, continued throughout the entire observed activities. Facilitators explain their strategy of interpersonal interaction as a method that prevents participants from being stuck in a group confrontation situation or group-to-group interaction, which delegitimizes differences separate group members have. This situation also causes participants to stand behind the group's attitude. On the other hand, the focus on the interpersonal level of interaction does not recognize the conflict as being between two national groups, but as being about misperception, miscommunication, or conflict between individuals.

In programs GH, BH, and UFD, when the participants engaged in sporadic political discussion, the facilitators were persistent in pointing out that each person in the group should express his or her ideas and not the collective opinion.

The main difference between Arab and Jewish intervenors on this level was the tendency of Arab facilitators to focus on intergroup political discussion, particularly on the Arab-Jewish conflict, while the Jewish subjects (especially directors) argued that it is more effective and successful to focus on interpersonal and intergroup interactions that address cultural and personal issues. A Jewish facilitator explains the disadvantages of focusing on intergroup interactions during the discussion of political issues:

> The political discussion could start at any time. There was no fixed timing, or structured unit. It can start at the end or middle of the workshop. But, until then, everything was good and satisfying, when the (argument) fight started, the environment was to say as much as you can before the political discussion ends. This blocked the joint learning process, because it was group representative arguments. Only a few groups succeeded in achieving some learning after the political interaction. Mostly we feel the tendency to separate, because they become two paralyzed groups.

In conclusion, there is neither one single set of processes that was adopted by a single program nor a complete, single, and common set of processes applied by all the programs. There are several levels and types of interactions that take place during one program. The timing of these processes depends on:

a. The topics for discussion.
b. The participants' cultural, political, and social awareness of the conflict.
c. The facilitators' perceptions of their roles.

**Figure 6.1. Programs and Interaction Processes in AJR**

| | Conflict & | | Value & | | Interpersonal |
|---|---|---|---|---|---|
| NS---- | Socialization--- | Affective ----- | Attitude --------------------- | | Intragroup |
| | Interaction & | Cognitive | Clarification | | Intergroup |
| | | | Value & | | Interpersonal |
| MA--- | Socialization--- | Cognitive --- | Attitude ------- | Instrument --- | Intergroup |
| | Interaction | | Clarification | | |
| | | | Value & | Interpersonal | |
| GH --- | Socialization--- | Cognitive --- | Attitude ------- | Intergroup | |
| | Interaction | | Clarification | Intragroup | |
| | | | Value and | Interpersonal | |
| BH --- | Socialization--- | Cognitive --- | Attitude ------- | Intergroup | |
| | Interaction | | Clarification | | |
| | Conflict & | Affective | Value & | | Interpersonal |
| VL---- | Socialization--- | and -------- | Attitude ------- | Instrument --- | Intragroup |
| | Interaction | Cognitive | Clarification | | Intergroup |
| | | | Value & | | Interpersonal |
| UFD-- | Socialization--- | Cognitive --- | Attitude ------- | Instrument --- | Intergroup |
| | Interaction | | Clarification | | |

   d. The overall strategy, goals, and focus of the entire intervention
program (see table 6.5 on programs, content, and processes).

For instance, the interaction, on affective or cognitive level, depends
on facilitators and intervention models in general. Whether the interaction
is on an interpersonal, intergroup, or intragroup level depends on a
combination of the interactive facilitation strategy and the level of strength
of collective identity among participants. If the Arabs and Jews are united
and unified in their attitudes, and the facilitators focus on an intergroup
level, then the encounter will be concentrated on the intergroup interaction. But if the facilitators' strategy is mainly on interpersonal interaction,
then during the encounter or the program, there will be continuing
struggle and tension between the intervenors and the participants over
setting rules for the interaction.

But, in general, through the Arab-Jewish groups that were observed,
both Arabs and Jews have the tendency in this context to express themselves on the intergroup level, especially when there is a confrontational

**Table 6.5. Programs, Contents, and Interaction Processes**

| Content & Program | | Interaction Level | | | Intervention Process | | | |
|---|---|---|---|---|---|---|---|---|
| | | Interpersonal | Intergroup | Intragroup | Affective | Cognitive | Social | Conflict |
| Cultural | NS | — | X | X | X | — | X | X |
| | MA | — | X | — | — | — | X | — |
| | GH | — | X | X | — | X | X | — |
| | BH | — | X | — | — | X | X | — |
| | VL | — | — | — | — | — | — | — |
| | UFD | — | X | — | — | — | X | — |
| Personal | NS | X | — | X | X | — | X | — |
| | MA | X | — | — | — | X | X | — |
| | GH | X | — | X | — | — | X | — |
| | BH | X | — | — | — | — | X | — |
| | VL | X | — | X | — | — | X | — |
| | UFD | X | — | — | — | — | X | — |
| Political | NS | X | X | X | X | — | — | X |
| | MA | X | — | — | — | X | — | — |
| | GH | — | — | — | — | — | — | — |
| | BH | — | — | — | — | — | — | — |
| | VL | X | X | X | X | X | — | X |
| | UFD | X | — | — | — | X | — | — |
| Task | NS | — | — | — | — | — | — | — |
| | MA | X | — | — | — | X | — | — |
| | GH | — | — | — | — | — | — | — |
| | BH | — | — | — | — | — | — | — |
| | VL | X | X | X | — | X | — | — |
| | UFD | X | — | — | — | X | — | — |

context. Such behavior can be explained as a defense mechanism that the participants adopt to protect their prior attitudes.[3]

It must be noted, however, that the main assumption, which is common to all of the intervention programs, is that the interpersonal level of interaction has to be implemented during most of the issues in discussion, except in two programs (NS and VL), where the strategy also focuses on the intergroup conflict. They assume that the encounters are between two conflicting groups of Arabs and Jews.

A strategy of a group dynamic of "here and now" questions was followed and applied by facilitators in program NS and during the encounter in program VL. This strategy is not completely followed by facilitators in other programs.

Facilitators in program MA indicated that they do not deal with group dynamic techniques or with emotional tension, and aspects that are usually presented when Arabs and Jews are sharing the same discussion group. One of these facilitators claimed:

> We deal with fears and suspicion in rational strategies or modes: Our process is based on rational understanding, *Tovanah.* Our process that we used should be in harmony with the content. It should be a democratic process of discussion and learning.

But facilitators in program UFD, for example, indicated that they lack the appropriate training and the specialization to conduct such a strategy of intervention in their sessions. Both facilitators in these programs stated that they are content facilitators and not "group dynamic" facilitators; they prefer to work on specific content and clarify the attitude toward it, rather than to work on interaction among group members.

On the participants' level, the examination of the teachers' and students responses to the type of process used by their facilitators indicates that:

a. Participants in general did not recall questions about their feelings in a consistent manner, except in programs NS and UFD.

b. In all the programs, participants declared that they expressed their attitudes and beliefs on social and personal matters. In addition, in programs VL and NS participants argued that they also had the opportunity to discuss many political and conflictual issues concerning Arabs and Jews in Israel as well as the West Bank and Gaza.

c. In most programs, especially at the beginning of the encounter, participants were directed by the facilitators to talk about themselves as individuals. In some cases, such as programs MA, GH, BH, and UFD, intervenors constantly requested participants to use the term "I" instead of "we," even in sessions when the group discussed or explored cultural traditions and norms in which participants had to speak in a collective manner.

d. Participants in all the students' programs indicated that the social interaction and the experience of contact with the other national group had the most powerful impact on them.

## THIRD-PARTY ROLE

In every Arab-Jewish program there is a co-facilitation team that consists of an Arab and a Jewish facilitator (in most cases an Arab male and a Jewish female). This team, or third party, has several roles that are implemented throughout each program. Some of these roles are as follows:

*(a) "Activator" or "content intervention":* This role provides activities and instructions to help participants socialize and experience activities, which will facilitate cultural and personal acquaintance. This is the most common role that the third party plays in students' programs. This type of role has the lowest average of substantive process interventions that aim to reflect on conflictual issues, contradictory opinions and beliefs, and insights into the intergroup dynamic.

*(b) Pedagogical instructor:* This third-party role exists in the teachers' programs, which have substantial professional issues to be discussed. The third party provides pedagogical instructions aimed to train teachers in how to deal with Arab-Jewish relations in classes. In this case, the third party is an intervenor who focuses on the participants' joint "tasks" (such as learning techniques and strategies of dealing with Arab-Jewish relations in class).

*(c) Process facilitator:* He or she clarifies conflicts and differences; monitors the discussion by giving participants permission to express their ideas; summarizes what each participant or group said in each session; provides insights into "here and now" interaction, especially those that apply the group dynamic techniques (programs NS and VL); reflects and confronts the participants with their attitudes and beliefs.

An important feature of the third-party intervention in these programs is that in any binational setting there should be two facilitators. All the programs have a co-facilitation strategy, in which Arab and Jewish facilitators jointly lead the group. In all interviews, facilitators and directors stressed the need for such co-facilitation, except program GH, where directors and facilitators indicated their intention to change this strategy in 1992.[4] Indeed, in the observed activity of program GH, a single facilitator led the group.

It is interesting to point out that sixteen of the nineteen participants expressed agreement on the need for two facilitators and the advantages of having a facilitator from their own national group. But, in program GH, during the observed encounter, two of the four groups in discussion expressed their acceptance and agreement to having only one facilitator. The two other groups, especially those Arab participants who had a Jewish facilitator leading their group, stated their dissatisfaction and discomfort with the fact that they had no Arab facilitator who could translate for them or explain what they needed to say.

In short, by having a single facilitator in students' groups, which are asymmetric in terms of the language and the social and educational background, the organizers are adding another obstacle that can prevent students from interacting genuinely or directly. This can also function as an additional factor to the asymmetric context of the encounter which already has many of these factors (see discussion on asymmetric encounters).

*Roles of Arab and Jewish facilitators:* The main difference in Arab-Jewish encounters is the fact that any Arab facilitator in students' programs, in addition to translating from Hebrew to Arabic and vice versa, should be able to function on two levels at the same time during all the sessions: (a) ensure that Arab and Jewish group members understand each other in terms of the language and vocabulary used; in this case, the facilitator's role is to translate back and forth; (b) provide process and content interventions. Several participants said that Arab facilitators were less active than Jewish facilitators, especially on the process level.[5]

The same notion was expressed by some facilitators that it is easier for them to intervene on a content level rather than on a process level because they are usually preoccupied with translation during the interaction. Other facilitators argued that this is not the main cause for the differences in the types of intervention provided by the Arab and Jewish facilitators. They claimed that since the Arab facilitators are more politicized, they tend to focus on content issues rather than on process ones.

On one hand, as a result of these conditions, there is a potential for conflict and tension between the two facilitators. In some cases, as pointed out by an Arab facilitator, this conflict is reflected and transferred to the participants' interaction level, who also are divided in a similar manner. An additional source of tension between the two facilitators is the fact that the Arab facilitators in these programs have an advantage in terms of knowledge of both Arab and Jewish cultures and languages, while most Jewish facilitators lack these capabilities.

Finally, it is important to indicate that most Arab facilitators are males, whereas most Jewish facilitators and directors are females. Several informants presented this condition as an additional factor that can either increase or decrease the professional harmony between the two facilitators.

## ARAB-JEWISH ENCOUNTERS: IS THERE A GENERIC MODEL?

Having presented the various components of the intervention programs, we move to the discussions of two questions: (1) Is there a distinctive model of intervention that has a clear and separate set of goals, assumptions, process, content, structure, and third-party role? (2) What are the intervention models that are being applied by the six programs studied?

*(1) Is there a single distinct model of intervention?* Given the findings and analysis of the data in terms of *assumptions and general goals*, all six programs have one common set of intervention model components. But in regard to structure, there are two types: (a) One focuses on one-shot or single-attempt

intervention that has no continuity. The interaction is conducted over a two- to five-day period with a short preparation time, without a conclusion and postencounter activities: (b) The other is a type that includes a continuing set of activities for a longer period of time, six to ten months. This does not mean a constant binational interaction, but it can include uninational activities.

In terms of *content* there are certainly three types of components: (a) models that include political, cultural, and personal activities; (b) models that include cultural, personal, and professional activities; (c) models that include personal, cultural, political, and professional components (see figure 6.1).

Of course, each of these types of components influences and aims to achieve a different set of goals. An example is when the goal is to achieve cultural and personal acquaintance, and there is no time capability or intention to intervene for a longer period. In this case, it is better to adopt the cultural and personal model rather than the conflict approach or model. However, if the goal is to work with conflicts to identify differences and learn the complexity of conflict, then the model should involve political components and also address affective and cognitive approaches, as was recommended by Hewstone and Brown (1986), Amir (1989), and Bar and Asaqla (1988a, b). This conflict model also incorporates the intervention on all levels of interaction: personal, intergroup, and intragroup. Only programs NS and VL came close to such a model.

Some informants (five directors and facilitators) claimed that they teach complexity of conflict by focusing on cultural and personal issues. It is obvious that one cannot teach the complexity of Arab-Jewish relations if the program ignores the conflict issues and the affective aspects of the conflict.

In addition, it is clear that there are intervenors who ignore the political aspects and conflict issues. They focus on the interpersonal level and neglect the fact that there are two different groups in the encounter. Through this design, intervenors are making a political statement, which reflects and expresses the notion that there is no conflict between Arabs and Jews in Israel, or that the main cause of the conflict is cultural misunderstanding. This design has another facet: the cultural and personal aspects are the most important components in the identity of each side.

This statement is inaccurate according to the polls and research, which indicate that 85 percent of Arab students indicate that their identity is Palestinian. In addition, 69 percent of the Jewish youth support a law limiting democratic rules to the Jewish majority only.[6] Thus, directing the selection to focus only on a cultural and personal issue does not address the core problems of the conflict in Israel.

In spite of these indicators, there are some programs that do not relate to the conflict at all. They are concerned with improving positive images of the two groups and revealing the humanitarian aspects that exist on both sides. These programs start usually with the personal acquaintance process and end with the cultural acquaintance process. Their aim is that each participant will leave the encounter or end the program with a positive and nonthreatening feeling. Program MA is the closest to this type of intervention.

There are some differences and gaps between the programs' description in the organizations' documents and their implementation in the encounters or in the field.

Based on the fact that most of the programs were developed during the 1980s, the recent minority–majority dynamic in Israel, and evaluation reports by several scholars (Bar, Bargal, & Asaqla, 1989; Hofman, 1986; Hertz-Lazarovitch, 1989), there are several features and outputs that can be identified as common to all the Arab-Jewish programs:[7]

a. They became more aware of the importance and function of revealing and focusing on differences between Arabs and Jews in Israel, and Arabs in the West Bank and Gaza.
b. The encounter programs helped in drawing the "Green Line" between the West Bank and Gaza and Israel.
c. They also reveal the similarities between Arabs and Jews in Israel by focusing on culture and identity.

The national identity issue became more important in such designs after it was introduced to these programs about eight years after the inauguration of Land Day.[8] Relative to theoretical approaches of intervention, the models that are applied by the different programs are influenced mainly by the contact hypothesis interaction theory (Sherif, 1958), in which the main assumption is to bring two different cultural groups into an interactive situation, where they will be stimulated to interact with each other, if only on the social level. Such interaction should be sufficient to reduce the conflict tension, hostility, and stereotyping. Intervenors in this field refer to this interaction as "the experience of encounter," while students refer to it as "having fun."

Only two programs are struggling with the attempt to incorporate an additional aspect of intervention into their work: the aspect of conflict and differences. These programs are providing legitimacy and recognition for the existence of the conflict, while other programs still adopt the notion of searching for similarities, thus avoiding conflictual issues. It is important to indicate that on the individual level there are more intervenors and facilitators who believe and express the importance of incorporating conflictual issues into the encounters and intervention programs, but as was mentioned, on an organizational level this idea has not yet been incorporated or adopted.

In fact, there are several contextual and interorganizational conditions that function as obstacles and preventive factors, delaying the incorporation of conflictual approach into Arab-Jewish intervention programs. Some of these conditions are as follows:

a. All the organizations need the Ministry of Education's permission to enter the schools to recruit their beneficiaries.
b. These organizations and programs are mainly designed to work with the school system.
c. All these programs receive their funds from foreign sponsors (mostly Jewish), whose main interest is in promoting a positive image of the State of Israel. Therefore, they would not readily approve the focus on conflictual issues.
d. Professional and academic experts who are involved in this subject of Arab-Jewish relations are lacking.
e. Jewish intervenors in these programs are either directors, whose main job is to raise funds and administer the program, or university students, who consider their work in this program as a short transitional period in their careers. On the other hand, Arab intervenors are in many cases those educators who could not find a professional job or those graduates whom the Ministry of Education did not accept as teachers or educators.

Therefore, many intervenors lack the professional examination of their intervention models, and only a few are fully committed to the development of this field.

In spite of these conditions, it is important to indicate that the process of legitimizing conflict in such programs is in progress mainly as a result of the macro-contextual conditions of the Israeli Palestinian conflict environment. Since 1987, with the outbreak of the Palestinian Intifada, Jewish society and officials increasingly recognize the fact that they do have a conflict with the Palestinians in both communities—the West Bank and Gaza, and the minority in Israel.

*(2) What types of models exist in Arab-Jewish encounters?* Table 6.6 is an attempt to address the question of what types of models exist among the six programs. Based on the data analysis, there is a typical and classical design and process of interaction in Arab-Jewish encounters, specifically those encounters that include three-day workshops.

But this typical design and process of interaction also applies to those who have a continuous program (more than one or two workshops).

**Table 6.6. Interaction in an Arab-Jewish Encounter Framework**

| Stage | Interaction Process |
|-------|---------------------|
| 1. Personal Acquaintance | Excitement of meeting the others. Tension. Surprise from the kindness of others. Explore similarities. |
| 2. Cultural Acquaintance | Tension continues, but learn differences. Explore similarities between cultures. Reveal stereotypes. Setting becomes less threatening. |
| 3. Political Discussion | Explore political attitudes. Frustration, growing mistrust. Accusations, blaming others. Discover and assure the differences. Exhausted from arguing. |
| 4. Common Interests (Task) or Separation | After being exhausted, now less tense and more trusting, less threatened by others. Look for common ground and similarities or solutions and alternatives. Also search for common activities or practical application for agreement. Also more able or capable of learning and understanding the others. |

The design starts with the *personal acquaintance stage,* in which participants are careful and hesitant, and show exaggerated politeness, which reflects tension and difficulties with the situation of direct encounter. The purpose of such statements is to indicate that they have no problem with the other side; for example, this is a typical Jewish participant's statement at this stage: "I have no problem with Arabs. In fact, I have many Arab friends, and I visit in Arab villages, or grew up with Arabs." Or an Arab participant might declare: "I have Jewish friends, and they even have visited my home."

This tension and careful expression continue throughout the *cultural interaction stage,* in which participants start to reveal some of their stereotypes and fears or mistrust of the other side. At this point, it depends on whether the facilitators are interested in directing the discussion and the interaction to reveal cultural differences and to address, with the group, the reasons and assumptions that underlie the stereotypes, fears, or tensions that are reflected in the group dynamic. It is clear that the facilitators who are interested in the cultural and personal activities or in the instrumental component of the encounter usually choose to ignore or neglect fear, mistrust, and tension, or they elect to follow safe interaction in this stage. Therefore, some of them choose to focus on the positive cultural experiences or to move toward discussing the professional aspects and components of the programs; some models even combine both aspects. In other cases, where the program is designed to reveal conflicts and differences as a way or strategy of learning about the perception of conflict on both sides, facilitators direct their intervention to reveal tension, fears, and differences in this second stage.

The third stage is *political discussion issues.* It begins when participants start to discuss or address political issues. In this stage some facilitators decide to ignore the demands to address political issues, arguing that this is not the appropriate time or correct context for such issues and that the aim of the program is to know each other culturally and personally (programs MA, GH, and BH); other intervenors might elect to explore the differences and the perceptions of each side on the political issues. In this case, the process between the Arabs and Jews in the group becomes more heated and tense. Both Arabs and Jews blame each other as being the cause for the conflict. In this stage some discussions can "explode," which means some angry participants will leave the group, start crying, or become so tense emotionally that they cannot stand the discussion or the interaction.

In some cases, when the Jewish group in general agrees with the accusation of discrimination against the Arab minority, the Arab participants' goal becomes to convince the Jewish participants to take an actual and practical stand and behavior that will help Arabs in Israel obtain their equal rights. But, the Jewish participants may still be unwilling to commit themselves to defending or translating their political agreement into political activities at the practical or operational level. In fact, none of the six case studies examined address such matters. Several facilitators expressed their fears and difficulties in handling such situations, and stated that they would prefer not to get into a political discussion because of the possibility of "explosion." Two directors stated that any political discussion in the third stage is worthless and blocks the students' ability to study or to learn anything about the other side. Other facilitators argued that if the encounter is not a simulation or laboratory that aims to provide an illusion, then participants have to experience the reality of their conflict, which is that political discussions and arguments are an essential part of this reality.

*The common interest or separation stage* is basically when participants realize that they cannot convince each other, or change each other, and that they have nothing left to say to the other side. At this point, some of the participants will be willing to look for the common or similar concerns and interests of both sides. In this stage the participants learn the importance of being aware of the other side's perceptions, and obtain or develop the ability to compromise and understand the other side's needs. As has been stated by several facilitators, many groups and encounters do not fully complete this stage, much less reach it. This is the "realization stage" (the "click," as facilitators call it) or insight. It is an indicator of the trust and confidence-building process that influences the behavior of participants during the encounter.

These four stages are not completely separate. The interaction between Arab and Jewish groups can be on both levels, the personal and cultural acquaintance and the political arguments, at the same time. There is no clearcut division among the four stages; on the contrary, in most Arab-Jewish encounters or interactions, there are processes from the four stages. There are facilitators in some models, though, who focus only on the first two stages of the interaction, the personal and cultural, in some cases adding the fourth stage. These intervenors try to jump or skip to the fourth stage without handling the third, or what some intervenors call the exploded stage. Such programs as MA, BH, GH, and UFD do not handle the political issues directly and neglect the conflictual issues and the emotions attached to these issues. They focus on soft and safe issues such as cultural and personal issues, or how to train a teacher to become a facilitator or better educator, without examining the teachers' biases, stereotypes, fears, or mistrust and insecurity that they feel toward each other.

In conclusion, the differences that were revealed in the examination of the different models that exist were most influenced by the fact that they belong to different programs and organizations. However, the fact that Jews and Arabs co-facilitated the workshops also influenced, and in some cases shaped, the perception and presentation of goals, assumptions, processes, and certainly the role of the facilitator. The role of the intervenor (director or facilitator) had the least influence in perceiving and presenting the process, content, assumptions, and structure. Its main influence was reflected in presenting each program's list of goals.

Having identified the different designs of intervention and their components (assumptions, goals, structure, content, process, and third-party role), the question raised is: Do these intervention programs reflect the intervenors' and participants' perception of the Arab-Jewish conflict? The following chapter addresses this question.

# 7

# Perceptions of the Arab-Jewish Conflict in Israel

Arab and Jewish intervenors and participants in the encounters responded differently when asked about their perceptions of the most important issues, solutions, and changes that relate to the conflict between Arabs and Jews in Israel. Although intervenors held similar roles, nevertheless they held different perceptions that stemmed from their opposing realities. These differences are explored in terms of each program's intervenors and participants.

## INTERVENORS' CONFLICT PERCEPTIONS
### *What Are the Issues?*

When asked to list the three most important issues involved in the Arab-Jewish conflict in Israel, both Arabs and Jews listed self-determination (national identity, sovereignty, etc.) for the Palestinians in the West Bank and Gaza, equal rights for Arabs in Israel, the Jewish state, and cultural differences. However, there are several differences in the content and language used to describe these issues. These differences reflect varied perceptions of the causes and the desired settlements of the conflict between the two groups.

For instance, for an Arab intervenor there is an issue of a direct and intended discrimination policy against Arabs in Israel. But, for a Jewish interviewee, the Arabs' social and economic conditions are an ultimate result of minority–majority relations or of a natural competition for resources between two communities. For an Arab there is an issue of occupation; but for a Jewish intervenor, it is the Palestinian problem, assuming that it is caused only by the Palestinians, thereby being their problem. In addition, some Jewish intervenors use the term "Israeli Arabs" or "Arab minority" when referring to Arabs in Israel. But most Arab interviewees refer to the Arab community as "Palestinians in Israel" or "Palestinians."

These distinctions reflect a perceptional difference between Arabs and Jews in Israel, in which the majority of the Arabs associate their national identity with the Palestinians in the West Bank and Gaza, while most Jews prefer to perceive the Arabs first as Israeli citizens and then as Arabs or Palestinians. Such an outcome was also supported in the research of Smooha (1992) and Rouhana (1988).

In addition to these essential and linguistic differences, there are two types of perceptions in terms of the issues. Each type includes a set of issues listed according to their importance. These types exist among both Arabs and Jews. (a) One set includes those who consider the Israeli-Palestinian conflict over land, national and civil rights to Arabs in Israel (which are influenced by definition of the Jewish state), and issues of cultural differences as the main components of the Arab-Jewish conflict in Israel. (b) The other set includes those who consider the issues to be a Jewish state definition and status of Arabs in Israel, Israeli-Palestinian conflict, and cultural differences. Basically, both sets include the same issues; however, the priorities and preferences of these issues are different.

Several interviewees, both Arabs and Jews, ignored the cultural components of the conflict, arguing that these are not important issues in this conflict. But, interviewees who considered the cultural issues to be an important issue were divided according to two categories:

1. Those who addressed the conflict in terms of Jewish cultural dominance and the lack of representation and expression of the Arab culture in official offices or in the media.
2. Those who perceived the religious, language, and social differences as the source of conflict without addressing the dominance of the Jewish culture as the issue.

On both sides, Arabs and Jews considered the *definition of Israel as a Jewish state* an issue and a cause of Arab-Jewish conflict in Israel. A Jewish interviewee explains the status of an Arab in Israel: "The problem that this is not their state nor their people, and they sympathize with our [i.e., Israel's] enemies." A similar idea was expressed by Abdol Aziz Zugbi, the first Arab to become a deputy minister: "My state is in war with my people." An Arab facilitator described this issue of discrimination and Jewish states: "A Jew in Brooklyn has more rights than me. We are discriminated against not only because we are Arabs, but because we are not Jews."

Those Jewish interviewees who rejected the notion that the Jewish definition of Israel is an issue in the conflict between Arabs and Jews argued that this is a basic assumption and axiom for any Jew in Israel. One Jewish intervenor claimed: "The Jewish Zionist definition is not a problem or conflict, this has been accepted by Arabs. Besides I want Israel to be a democratic state, but I will not give up my flag or any other symbols."

By the same token, two Jewish intervenors argued that the Jewish definition of the state should not be a problem because

> The Jewish definition is supposed to be a result of majority context and not to be forced by state laws. It should be a symbolic issue and not an instrument of control. It should have a similar function and symbol as Switzerland's chocolate or clock has.

Those Jewish interviewees who argued that *there is no Arab-Jewish conflict in Israel*, and that the conflict is between the Jews and the Palestinians in the West Bank and Gaza, explained their argument as follows: (a) Arabs in Israel have a problem with economic opportunities and not violence, like in the territories. (b) The problems between Arabs and Jews in Israel are a typical and natural result of minority–majority relations; therefore, they should not be described as conflict relations. (c) Discrimination or unequal rights is the Arabs' problem only; therefore, we cannot be sure it is a conflict issue.

On the program level, when examining the issues as presented by the intervenors from each of the six programs, only intervenors from program UFD did not indicate the Jewish state as an issue. All the other programs had the three set of issues.

When considering the issues based on the intervenors' roles, there were no specific characters or identifications that distinguished the definition of issues by directors from the facilitators' definitions of issues, except that directors stressed the cultural aspects more than the facilitators did. There were only three directors who listed the Jewishness of the state as an issue of conflict, however, two of them are Arab. Therefore, it is difficult to determine whether this difference can be attributed to the subjects' professional or national affiliation.

In short, the definition and perception of the issues involved in the conflict and their priority were influenced mainly by the intervenors' national affiliation; however, it is important to indicate that there was almost an agreement on the list of the issues themselves but not on the priorities assigned to these issues.

### Participants' Perceptions of Issues

Like the Jewish intervenors, both Jewish teachers and students identified the control of the land, equal rights, and cultural differences as the main issues of the conflict. However, the students could not explain in detail the subissues, causes, or historical events related to the conflict issues. Also, they added several other issues such as:

- They sympathize with the territories.
- Arabs are misinformed and misled by their media.
- The Arabs are "inferior to us"; they are the black workers.
- Intifada and territories.
- Arabs are isolated in their areas.
- Suicidal bombs and Hamas.

A Jewish student insisted in defining Arab students as follows: "They are not Palestinians, they are Arabs. The ancient Palestinians were destroyed centuries ago. Therefore, this is not Palestine."

Such students lack basic information about the territories, such as who lives there and what type of citizenship people have there. For these students both areas (1976 and 1948) are the same; Arabs in both areas have the same legal and political status. Many students were repeating political terms and distinctions without fully understanding their meaning. For example, they presented the issue of the minority's equal rights as a problem resulting from Arab sympathy with the Intifada, from Arabs not serving in the Israeli Army, or denied the existence of discrimination. The teachers were more informed and able to distinguish between the different issues in the conflict.

Arab students and teachers defined the conflict issues similarly to the Arab intervenors. They listed the issue of equal rights for Arabs as the most important issue. An Arab explains this notion:

They do not give us our rights because they are afraid we will be stronger. An Arab participant explains his problem with Israeli identity: I am forced to be an Israeli, because this distinguishes me from my people with whom I cannot express my sympathy.

Arab students, in terms of future political status, distinguished their community from the Palestinians in the West Bank and Gaza. Ninety-eight percent of them argued that they will not leave Israel even if a Palestinian state is created.

It is important to point out that statements such as "Jews have a negative image of Arabs," "they look down on us," or "they are inferior" were not defined as issues by any of the intervenors. However, they were listed by both Arab and Jewish students.

Finally, there were several Jewish participants who argued that there is no Arab-Jewish conflict in Israel, and the conflict is with the Palestinians in the "territories."

*Solutions*

**Intervenors' solutions:** Six sets of solutions were proposed by both Arabs and Jews. However, all Arab intervenors agreed on the first four solutions, while the two other solutions were less popular among Arab intervenors (see table 7.1). In explaining why Arabs in Israel support the creation of a Palestinian state, Arab intervenors said:

> Isn't it enough that we gave up our chance of having a state; then at least our brothers should have a state. In having a Palestinian state for us we can relax that our relatives will not be persecuted in the Arab countries or anywhere in the world.

On the Jewish side, all intervenors listed *equal rights for Arabs in Israel as a must solution*. A Jewish intervenor explained the nature of such a solution by saying: "Arabs in Israel should have full equal rights and not only equal rights in having luxury swimming pools." Among those Jewish intervenors who suggested equal rights for Arabs in Israel, most of them excluded the expression of the Arab minority's national rights that might contradict Israel as a Jewish state.

Jewish intervenors were divided on the other solutions. Some agreed on a Palestinian state, but stressed the need for tight security assurances. Others did not specify a Palestinian state as a must solution to solve the conflict between Arabs and Jews in Israel. On the other hand, many Jewish intervenors agreed on the need to provide some sort of self-determination to Palestinians in the West Bank and Gaza, a solution that the Arab intervenors named as a Palestinian state. Both Arabs and Jews considered *an early education for tolerance and separation of religion from state* as solutions to the cultural differences. There were also some intervenors of both nationalities who argued that Arab-Jewish encounters and interactions are solutions for the cultural issues. However, on the Arab side this solution was not presented as an immediate solution to be pursued, while on the Jewish side, it was stressed more.

In regard to changing the Jewish definition of the state, few interviewees were clearly in favor of this solution; the other intervenors expressed strong resistance to such a solution.

Recognizing the Arabs as members of a national minority was interpreted by Jews and Arabs as providing Arabs with a legal opportunity to express their Palestinian national identity within the State of Israel. For some Jews this was a threatening solution, which can be linked to the state's Jewishness, but for the Arabs it was a fully accepted and supported option.

**Table 7.1. Solutions to Arab-Jewish Conflict in Israel**[1]

| Arabs | Jews |
|---|---|
| 1. Palestinian state 8/8 | Equal rights for Arabs in Israel 8/11 |
| 2. Recognition of Arabs as a national minority 8/8 | Self-determination for Palestinians or state 5/11 |
| 3. Equal rights for Arabs in Israel 8/8 | Tolerance of cultural differences 5/11 |
| 4. Changing the state's definition as Jewish 7/8 | Changing the implementation of the state as Jewish 4/11 |
| 5. Tolerance of cultural differences 3/8 | Recognition of Arabs as a national minority 3/11 |
| 6. Autonomy to Arabs in Israel 2/8 | Autonomy to Arabs in Israel 2/11 |

*The autonomy principle* was graded by both Arabs and Jews as the least viable solution. Even though when some Arabs explained recognition of their community as a national minority, they used the term "cultural and educational autonomy," there were only two intervenors who directly and explicitly requested autonomy for Arabs in Israel. Such a finding is also supported by a survey of Arab political leaders' opinions (Ganim & Ausitsky, 1990).

Finally, all the intervenors, both Arabs and Jews, indicated that *the solution of the Israeli-Palestinian conflict will ease the Arab-Jewish conflict in Israel.* Even so, there were a few intervenors who argued that in solving the Palestinian-Israeli conflict, the Arab-Jewish conflict in Israel will disappear, because, they claimed, there is no essential difference between the two groups. A Jewish intervenor describes this assumption:

> We suspect the Arabs in Israel as long as the conflict with Arab countries and Palestinians continues, in spite of the fact that they prove their loyalty to Israel. Therefore, when there is a regional solution, Arabs will not be perceived as enemies, or traitors, or even a threat to Israel. Then the discrimination will disappear because they will not be perceived as fifth column.

Even an Arab intervenor also confirms this assumption:

> As long as the Palestinian case is not solved, we remain suspicious in the Jews' eyes. The solution of the Palestinian case will end our "terrorist" image and being a potential security threat. Hopefully, this will be translated into equal rights for Arabs in Israel.

On the other hand, as mentioned earlier, there are those who declared that in spite of a solution to the Israeli-Palestinian conflict, the Arab-Jewish conflict in Israel will continue and even escalate, because, as an Arab intervenor explains:

When there is a Palestinian state then we can't complain about our status in Israel because the Jewish mainstream argue: If you do not like it here, you can move to Palestine.

A Jewish intervenor expresses his suspicion of a future solution: "When Israeli-Palestinian conflict is solved then Arabs in Israel will not move, and some of them will continue to look for problems and conflict with Jews."

In short, the main argument is that a solution to the Israeli-Palestinian conflict will ease and reduce the tension between Arabs and Jews in Israel. It is a necessary first condition to solving the Arab-Jewish conflict in Israel. Several Jewish intervenors perceive it as a solution to the national aspiration of Arabs in Israel. However, Arabs argue that they will continue to demand a national recognition within Israel.

When classifying solutions proposed by the directors and facilitators, six directors asserted Israel as a Jewish state and rejected solutions that could influence or threaten that status. Only one director (an Arab co-director) who considered changing the Jewishness of the state as a solution. Only three directors mentioned the creation of a Palestinian state as a "must" solution, and two of those did so with a precondition of security assurance for Israel. Most directors mention tolerance as an element in a solution to the conflict.

To explain these results, it would seem that the director's role, requiring the person to be responsible for the public image of the organization, leads him or her to protect the organization's access to and credibility with the Ministry of Education, which provides the organizations with participants. Thus, the organizations remain in the Israeli Jewish national consensus by avoiding solutions such as a Palestinian state or challenging the Jewishness of the state.

**Participants' solutions:** Jewish students' attitudes were more radical than their teachers' attitudes. Only two students suggested the return of the West Bank and Gaza, and only two students agreed on equal rights for Arabs in Israel. Students in general proposed Arab deportation and keeping the territories as part of Israel. Such solutions reflect a superficial and noncomplex understanding of the conflict (only a few of them knew where the West Bank is, or the border of 1967, or the legal status of the Arabs in Israel). Students selected easy "black-and-white" solutions, which do not require them to understand the implications of such a solution (Haraeven, 1989). A Jewish student explains why Israel cannot give back the West Bank and Gaza: "We will returns the territories when United States return New Mexico, or when England gives up Northern Ireland." Some of the Jewish students' proposed solutions were:

- Deport all the *Mesiteem*, provocateurs.
- Establish a committee to investigate whether Arabs deserve more rights.
- Close the Palestinians up in Sinai or the West Bank.
- "Put all Arabs in one state."
- Accept the other's rights and religious beliefs.
- Keep the territories and deport all "trouble makers."
- Limit the Arabs' rights.
- Land for peace with the condition that Arabs stop the Intifada.
- Don't return territories for peace; they belong to "us."
- Arabs should receive equal rights although they don't serve in the Israeli Army.

On the teachers' level, all Jewish teachers expressed their deep and strong belief that Israel has to continue as a Jewish state. Some of them agreed to full equal rights, while others suggested that Arabs cannot get their full rights in Israel, including the expression of their national identity.

Solutions proposed by Arab teachers and students were similar in content and even in order. They both suggested two-state solutions, equal rights for Arabs in Israel, and cultural integration programs to be conducted by the Ministry of Education.

Although Arab students demanded equal rights, many of them indicated that they do not believe that Israel will provide them with such equality: "Because it [i.e., Israel] is their state and they have the power, why should they give it up? Israel can be democratic but not with security matters and Arabs." Even a teacher describes his frustration regarding the equality solution: "Jews will not let us be equal to them because they are threatened; therefore, they keep us economically controlled."

Some of the Arab students proposed solutions were:

- Palestinian state.
- Equal rights.
- Respect the other's traditions, but integrate in education.
- Jews don't insult Arabs and respect them, while Arabs look at Jews as brothers: this can happen through encounters.
- Arabs participate in controlling the government.
- Constitution to ensure democracy.
- Access to religious sites.

Teachers' responses:

- Palestinian state.
- To express national identity without threatening the state.
- Palestinian state with security assurance to Israel.

- Equal rights.
- Integration of Arabs and Jews from the kindergarten stage.

In comparing Arab students' and Jewish students' solutions, the first completely accepted Israel and the right of the Jews to a state. They had more moderate solutions. However, they were less divided in their solutions, and provided more details in explaining each solution. There are several explanations for such findings: (a) Some facilitators argued that the Arab students were prepared by either their teachers or Arab facilitators to memorize all these issues and solutions. (b) They unify their attitude because they assume that, as an oppressed minority, they have to be united in order to convince the Jewish participants of the justice in their demands. (c) A Jewish facilitator suggested that because the Arab students are more politically involved in their community life, and because they belong to a discriminated minority, they know more about their problems and demands than the Jewish majority students, whose lives do not require them to interact with Arabs on a daily basis.

Arab students proposed more peaceful methods, such as dialogue groups or encounters, as solutions. They stress more democratic values and principles. There was not a single Arab student or participant who suggested deportation for Jewish radicals or any act such as limiting the rights of Jews. Such differences can be explained by the following:

a. Arab students are raised according to curriculum goals and content designed by the Israeli Ministry of Education. The two main goals are: first, to maintain the security of Israel and to recognize it as a Jewish state, and second, to adopt democratic values and principles (Al-Haj, 1995).
b. There is a strong security inspection network among Arabs in Israel that prevents them from expressing their political and radical attitudes. Therefore, teachers and students believe that by expressing radical attitudes and extreme solutions, an Arab in Israel will eliminate his or her chances of being employed in the future.
c. The young Arab generation is being raised by parents who lived and experienced an Israeli military administration from 1948 to 1966, in which Arabs' social, political, and even religious movements were restricted. Therefore, the students are threatened by their parents' image of and historical experience with the Israeli authorities.

The findings in this section are also supported by the micro-analysis of Arab students' attitudes and perceptions conducted by Hofman (1986) and Rouhana (1988) (see review on Arab-Jewish research, chapter 4).

*Changes Required for Solutions*

Arab and Jewish intervenors identified three shared or common sets of changes required to reach the desired solutions: (1) changes related to the political level; (2) changes related to education; and (3) changes caused by external factors.

In the first type of changes, both Arab and Jewish intervenors stated the need for political changes. The Arab intervenors were more explicit on the practical and concrete changes that they wished to see. Such political changes include control of the government taken away from the Likud Party, emergence of a new political party that will favor negotiation with Palestinians, government adoption of policy of equal rights to Arabs, and a satisfactory solution to the Palestinian case. An Arab intervenor stated this notion clearly: "It is a political decision and not a work of organizations. I don't believe in the organizations' broader impact." A Jewish intervenor supporting the need for policy changes added: "As we did with placing the *alia* (immigration) in our first national agenda, we ought to do the same in regard to equal rights for Arabs in Israel."

Several Arab intervenors described the need to change the government's approach to Arabs in Israel, indicating that since 1948, there has been no official governmental policy in how to deal with the Arab minority in Israel. The second type of changes are educational changes, which Jewish intervenors cited more than Arab intervenors. Components include educational and perceptional changes in terms of recognizing the other's equal rights, more education for democracy, changing the curriculum in Jewish schools to learn more about Arabs, convincing the people not to be afraid of Arabs and to be willing to get to know them personally and culturally, and stopping the Israeli media from presenting Arabs negatively as "killers" and "rapists."

When introducing these changes, only two intervenors described the encounters as an effective method (or a change) that can be influential in solving the conflict between Arabs and Jews. A Jewish intervenor describes this notion: "Although there is no serious attention to my work in interaction between the two people, I think this is the alternative to violence."

In contrast to this view, most intervenors, especially the Arabs, were convinced that Arab-Jewish encounters and educational activities in general cannot solve their conflict: "It is an illusion to think that people can influence; it is only matter of resources. . . . Educational encounters can't solve the problems of sewage, school classes shortage, or health system and services."

The third type of changes are those related to external factors. The Jewish intervenors mainly referred to economic pressure to be activated on Israel by the United States, or the entire international community, while the

Arab intervenors considered changes within the Arab countries (changes in the leadership or the creation of mass movements). Such a difference is based on the strong perception among Arabs that the United States will not impose pressure on Israel for any political settlement that will satisfy Palestinian needs (Said & Hitchers, 1988).

In short, the intervenors' perception of the changes that are required to solve the conflict are most influenced by the Arab-Jewish level of analysis. In comparing the two groups' responses again it seems that the Jewish and Arab teachers share more similar and common attitudes than their students. They both stated the need for political and educational changes as conditions to reach solutions. But their students' opinions were very different. As one Jewish teacher describes her students: "Our students are much more extremist and radical in their solutions."

Thus, the Jewish students expressed more radical and one-sided opinions. They were more likely to accuse Arabs of being the radicals and the cause of the conflict, and to propose changes such as deportation or prison. The Arab students' main focus was on: (a) political changes, such as sharing political control; (b) educational changes, such as integration and Arab-Jewish encounters; (c) changes on both sides rather than focusing on the Jewish side only. Even when they expressed negative opinions about the other side, an Arab student said: "I believe that there is a hatred inside each, Arab and Jew. . . . We cannot throw each other to the sea."

Finally, neither Arab nor Jewish students focused on or considered the international context as a source of change that might influence the Arab-Jewish conflict in Israel. Arab students provided more specific changes and had more consideration for the Jewish side in their statements. The Jewish students were less informed on the potential changes on Jewish side; therefore, their list of required changes mainly included changes needed on the Arab side.

In short, it seems that Jewish students lack basic information about Arabs in Israel, and even about those students they were meeting in the same encounter program. Jewish students also were more radical than Arab students in suggesting solutions derived from antidemocratic perceptions or ideas.

### Can the Conflict Be Solved?

The responses to the question, Can Arabs and Jews in Israel reach a situation of no conflict? were divided into two categories: (a) No, Arab-Jewish conflict in Israel will continue to exist as long as these two communities live in the same land. (b) Yes, the two communities can reach such a situation if certain conditions are fulfilled.

**Intervenors:** Most of the Arab intervenors believe that "there is such an option of a no-conflict situation between the two communities," while most of the Jewish intervenors believe that there is no such situation. The intervenors' hopes to reach a no-conflict situation indicates their perception of wishing to eliminate conflict instead of accepting it as part of their reality.

In an attempt to explain this difference in response, apparently the reason for such an optimistic (but unrealistic) view among Arab intervenors is that most of them are more involved in political activities in their personal lives than are Jewish intervenors. In addition, as minority members, they tend to believe more in political change, which they hope will solve their conflicts. Another explanation provided by some evaluation reports (Van Leer, 1990; Bar, Bargal, & Asaqla, 1989) is that, in general, Jewish intervenors are more realistic in terms of their goals and expectations and are more professionally trained to operate in such intervention frameworks.

Such an explanation is based on the assumption that it is more professional to adopt the notion that there is no such situation of no conflict; but there is a situation of living with conflict, or obtaining skills to deal with conflict, because conflict will always exist between two mixed communities.

**Participants:** Like most Arab intervenors, all Arab participants, except two students, agreed that there is a way of solving the Arab-Jewish conflict in Israel, and that they can reach a situation of no conflict. All Arab participants argue that by solving the Palestinian-Israeli conflict, their conflict with the Jews in Israel will be easier to solve; Jews will be less threatened by Arabs; and their national problem will be solved. An Arab teacher explains the relation between Arab-Jewish conflict in Israel and the Israeli-Palestinian conflict: "It is related because if I feel with Ethiopian Jews and Russian Jews, then certainly I feel and sympathize with Palestinians."

Most of the Jewish participants have no hope of reaching a state of no conflict with Arabs. Several justifications were provided by student participants: "Arabs will continue to hate us. Even if we solve the territory problem, then they will come up with another issue, they then will ask for Jerusalem." The Jewish teachers were divided on this issue. A Jewish teacher, who has been participating in an Arab-Jewish encounter program since 1989, explains her hope for a no-conflict situation: "If I don't believe that we will solve all our conflicts, then I have nothing to look for in this messy life."

## INTERVENTION MODELS AND PERCEPTIONS OF ARAB-JEWISH CONFLICT

It is clear that most Arabs and Jews, participants and intervenors in the six programs, especially the Arabs, agreed that the most important conflict issues are political. They identified self-determination for the Palestinians in the West Bank and Gaza Strip, the recognition of Arabs in Israel as a national minority, and equal rights for Arabs in Israel.

The Jewish intervenors, especially the directors, tend to add the cultural aspect as an additional important issue in the conflict. In examining the issues discussed and presented in several models of intervention, there were only two organizations that deliberately planned and designed their intervention model to include conflict issues defined as political. The other designs excluded these issues and focused mainly on cultural components that are defined by most intervenors and many participants as being less important than the issues related to political matters.

Furthermore, although Arab and Jewish intervenors, especially facilitators, perceived the definition of Israel as a Jewish state as a focal issue in this conflict, it was not addressed in four of the intervention programs. Only intervenors, particularly facilitators, in programs NS and VL provided some direct indications and statements on the importance and necessity of addressing this issue in Arab-Jewish encounters.

Although preserving the nature of the state as Jewish is one of the most sacred ideological components of the Israeli Jewish consensus (Hurwitz, 1992), there were some Jewish intervenors who considered changing Israel from a Jewish state to "a state of its citizens" as a must solution to the conflict between Arabs and Jews. An Arab facilitator argued in this regard:

> Those Jewish facilitators who truly understand the conflict and observe what is happening between Arabs and Jews not only in encounter context but in general, will reach the conclusion that a Jewish state definition is the source of the conflict between Arabs and Jews.

Another Arab intervenor indicated: "For me the workshop is effective when Arabs and Jews are engaged in a discussion about the definition of the state, because this is the core issue."

In terms of solutions, it appears that the Arabs and Jews believe their conflict can be eased by a solution to the Israeli-Palestinian conflict in the West Bank and Gaza. Even some interviewees, especially participants, believed that their conflict can be totally resolved when the Palestinian-Israeli conflict is settled.

Contrary to this assumption, there are other Arabs and Jews who claim that this could be a factor that will increase the tension between the two communities because then the Jewish population will generally believe and feel (after a settlement of the Israeli-Palestinian conflict) that they made their substantial concession by giving up the control over the West Bank and Gaza. Any indicators of discomfort or resistance among Arabs in Israel to the official government policy will be perceived as beyond the Jewish majority tolerance limits. Any Arab minority claims in Israel can provoke an extreme official and public response, such as calling for forced or voluntary population transfer, or a persecution of any Arab political movement in Israel.

In comparing the intervenors' conflict perceptions and their intervention model designs and implementation (see the previous chapter), it is clear that there is a contradiction, particularly concerning those intervenors who, on the one hand aim to achieve political change and to promote a solution to the Arab-Jewish conflict in Israel. On the other side, they perceive and describe the output and changes produced by Arab-Jewish encounters as insufficient, nonconditional, and unnecessary for solving the conflict issues between Arabs and Jews in Israel. This contradiction is very clear, especially with those Arab facilitators who present political change as an important goal of their intervention efforts. But, at the same time, they are aware that their intervention cannot be a substantial contribution to the political change for which they strive.

This contradiction raises the question: Why do these intervenors continue to work in such programs in spite of their perceptions that these programs do not produce substantial changes, and do not address the main issues of the conflict?

An explanation of these questions emerges from the argument that many Arab intervenors expressed their willingness to leave such a profession if they have gain an appropriate opportunity to work in their original profession or on academic degrees. In addition, as illustrated by a Jewish director:

> The fact is that many of the Jewish facilitators [not directors] are
> university students who consider this work as a transitional station
> in their professional career; therefore, professional and personal
> contradictions or deep commitment are not their main concern.

It is clear that deep and sufficient answers to such question will require us to look at the intervenors' motivations and the organizational arrangements and the structure of the organizations operating these programs, which are beyond the limits of this discussion and the research.

Another potential explanation lies in the differences between facilitators and directors. There is a gap between directors and facilitators (at least with Arab facilitators as well as some Jewish facilitators). This gap indicates that the intervention models' designs and goals, which are presented for publication and described by directors, are somehow different from the goals, assumptions, and perception of conflict presented by the facilitators. In addition, according to data derived from participants and observation recorders, there were several indications that facilitators do not follow or apply the program's intervention model guidelines precisely. For instance, in one incident, two facilitators stimulated and directed students to discuss the Intifada and other political issues, while their directors' program described such intervention as unacceptable or not required content.

Another result indicates this gap between directors and facilitators is because all directors listed culture as a conflict issue and tolerance and education for democracy as solutions and changes required to solve the conflict. It is clear that the directors determine the theoretical and practical aspects of the programs' designs and goals more than facilitators (because the focuses of the three students' programs are very similar to the directors conflict perceptions and assumptions on conflict assumptions).

In terms of participants, there are two extremely important findings:

(a) Most Jewish students who were interviewed or observed lack basic information about the Arab community in Israel or about the conflict in general. This finding was true not only prior to their participation, but even after they had participated in at least one intensive Arab-Jewish encounter.

(b) Many Arab participants perceived the framework of the specific encounter in which they were participating as an effective and promising strategy and even a solution to the Arab-Jewish conflict in Israel and in general. In addition to the fact that this is an unrealistic expectation, it is also misperception of the goals and assumptions of all the intervention models examined.

This outcome questions the argument that they are conducting sufficient preparations to conduct an encounter. Some argue that if a Jewish participant does not recognize his or her counterpart during the encounter, then certainly he or she will tend to rely on stereotypes, previous experience or attitudes, and impulsive reactions during the interaction instead of relying on information and ideas that should have been learned during the preparation stage.

Having identified the main conflict perceptions among intervenors and participants and having discussed their relation to the design and implementation of the specific intervention models, the next chapter presents the findings related to the third concept of this study, the intervention models' outputs and perception of success according to both intervenors and participants.

# 8

# Perception of Success and
# Impacts of the Encounter Models

## WHAT IS SUCCESS?

In an attempt to examine their macro perspectives, intervenors had difficulties responding when asked: What is success? Some began by listing ways
in which they felt the encounter had been successful; others admitted that
they had not thought about this issue before. Such confusion was not
correlated with the interviewee's program affiliation, nationality, or professional role.

In each program, at least one intervenor defines success as the fact
that the program continues to exist despite the tough political climate in
the region. One intervenor explained such a notion by arguing that
intervenors focused on the immediate needs and concerns rather than
outcomes. In that sense, surviving the political reality and bringing the
participants together becomes an accomplishment by itself.

Nevertheless, at least one intervenor from each program defined
success as producing "changes on an individual and not on the collective
group or mass level," that is, changes in attitudes of participants toward
each other on a personal level. These changes included:

(a) Raising self-awareness.
(b) Strengthening democratic perceptions and behaviors.
(c) Increasing interest in Arab-Jewish relations.
(d) Improving Arab-Jewish relations.
(e) Raising awareness of the conflict situation and its complexity.
(f) Changing attitudes of participants toward each other.
(g) Suggesting practical implications (i.e., behavioral changes)
based on the perceptional changes.
(h) Reducing tension, fear, and alienation.

(i)  Learning through a meaningful experience of conflict.
(j)  Being convinced of the value of living together.
(k)  Learning to live together in conflict.
(l)  Knowing more about the other culture.
(m) Increasing communication and dialogue.

These individual changes were usually viewed in one of the two approaches. *Conflict-oriented intervenors* defined success as teaching participants to "live with conflict" and to "understand conflict complexity" (such intervenors were associated with programs NS and VL). In the *cultural and personal acquaintance approach*, intervenors more emphasized improving Arab-Jewish relations; reducing fears; and educating for dialogue, communication, and living together (such intervenors were associated with programs GH, UFD, MA, and BH).

In all programs, success is a perceptional change with the hope that this success in changing perceptions can be translated into practical individual behaviors.

Some intervenors stressed their belief that participants should apply what they had learned through the encounter or the program to their profession (especially teachers). Those intervenors described their frustration with the fact that their programs do not produce this effect on the participants. They even do not expect the participants (teachers) to implement what they learn in their classes.

There were no substantial differences in terms of the intervenors' affiliation as Arabs and Jews in their macro perception of success, except the fact that two Arab intervenors stated the need for changes in participants' actual behavior after taking part in an encounter or a program. These intervenors expected a change in participants' political behavior: "I expect success to be reflected through acts such as a letter to the defense minister about the occupation in the West Bank and Gaza."

The reason for the lack of differences between Arabs and Jews in their definition of success stems from the Arab intervenors' awareness, when defining success, of the limited effect that any of these programs can produce. However, this contradicts the fact that in their goals, Arab intervenors stated their intention to produce political changes in the participants' attitudes. When they described the potential success and impacts of their program, however, these intervenors returned to the realistic approach and presented a minimalist definition. Thus, in this part, both Arab and Jewish intervenors are aware of the limitation of the effects of their programs on the general conflict situation. A Jewish facilitator concludes the effect and role of such activity by saying: "This will make the general solution easier, but it is not a part of the needed political solution."

## MEASURES AND CRITERIA OF SUCCESS

There were no major differences between Arab and Jewish intervenors in the responses to the question of how to measure success of the encounter. Thus, the measures indicated by the intervenors in all the programs can be classified into four major categories:

*(1) Criteria related to interaction and experience:* The fact that Arab and Jewish students are interacting and having a "good time" is, by itself, perceived and presented as a criterion of success. Establishing personal relationships and friendship between participants is certainly considered a popular criterion of success among intervenors. This type of criterion was listed by intervenors from all programs as positive encounter experience.

*(2) Criteria related to perceptional changes:* This type includes those criteria that relate to changes in participants' perceptions of themselves or the other side as a result of the deep acquaintance process with the conflict situation. These criteria mainly refer to changes in the participants' self-awareness of the existence of the other side and their equal rights. This develops a positive image, reduces stereotypes, and fosters openness to learning. In this category are only those intervenors from programs NS and VL who stated the understanding of conflict complexity as one of their criteria for success of the intervention model. In this regard, a Jewish facilitator describes a minimal success: "He [i.e., the participant] cannot simply say 'kick Arabs out of the country' without closing his eyes even for seconds and thinking that they are equal."

Most of the criteria in this category are general and not specifically defined. According to most intervenors, criteria in this category are very difficult to measure or identify, either during or after the program. A facilitator describes his difficulties: "I have no criteria for perceptional and attitudinal change. I can work years and years with the same school and I cannot say if there are attitudinal changes."

Another facilitator expressed his frustration in this regard: "It is hard to say if students hate each other more or less after the encounter. I cannot measure if it has positive or negative effect." Intervenors identified criteria such as:

- Participants perceive the conflict in more complexity and not with misperceptions, fantasy or ignorance.
- Look at the other side as equal and cope with it.
- To change their expectation from changing only the other side to realize that it is not that easy to do.
- More openness and sensitivity to both sides.
- Acknowledge contradictions in attitudes and behavior.

- Obtain positive way of thinking about the other side.
- Fewer stereotypes.
- Know the other's culture and personal identity.

*(3) Criteria relate to practical behavior:* this category included examples such as:

- Establish a professional relationship between encountered teachers.
- Deal with Arab-Jewish conflict in class.
- Participants call and visit each other in a crisis (war).
- Recommend this activity to others.
- Take responsibility on the Arab-Jewish issue.
- Act according to democratic principles.
- Initiate joint activities such as trips.
- To have an active and practical role: letters and demonstrations.
- Students react to what they have learned on political level.
- Provide help to other side (to Arab villages).

Although this set of criteria was listed by intervenors from different programs, intervenors stated in the interviews that their organizations or programs do not necessarily require them to measure it. For instance, intervenors from programs VL and UFD state that it is not necessary for their program success to have teachers (participants) who established professional relationships with the teachers from the other national group. Actually, in program UFD establishing a professional relationship between Arab and Jewish teachers was not listed as a goal or objective of either the director or the facilitator.

Thus, this criteria remains a wish and a hypothetical assumption. Therefore, intervenors would not consider their program a failure if they do not achieve these criteria of practical behavior.

Since intervenors had great difficulties in defining their criteria of success and separating them from the definition of broader success (what is success?), the result was that most of the criteria listed in this category are general rather than specific or well-defined. For instance, in defining openness or awareness to conflict complexity, intervenors couldn't elaborate and specify what the indicators are for a person who became more open after participation in their model or for a participant who became more aware of the complexity of the conflict.

Finally, it is important to mention that the last three criteria in this category, which indicated practical political involvement, were stated by Arab intervenors. The importance of a practical application of the workshop output was described by an Arab facilitator: "The participant cannot go out and conclude that I understand the conflict but I cannot do anything about it." Another Arab facilitator stated that "If a student demonstrates, then so be it, but it is not a sub-goal. . . . But, it is my fantasy to see participants active for the creation of a Palestinian state."

These Arab intervenors claimed that even if they fail to achieve such criteria (which they do), they still consider their program a successful intervention.

None of the Jewish intervenors suggested this practical political behavior was an indicator of success. For most Jewish intervenors, the practical implementation of the programs' output is not a necessary condition of success or criterion for success.

Even those Jewish intervenors who stated the importance of such practical implementation argued that these implementations can be any action taken by the participant; it does not have to be on an Arab-Jewish relation. Just the fact that the participant did take an action after the program is a sufficient criterion for success. A Jewish facilitator stated this notion clearly: "Success is when a participant takes responsibility for his ideas; for example, I had a participant that decided to contribute to Jewish immigrants' absorption after the program. I think this is also success."

It is clear that this specific output of the intervention was not considered by the Arab facilitators as a success. Such a difference also existed between Arab and Jewish intervenors in stating their intervention models' goals and assumptions, but it was more explicit and stronger.

This congruency in Arab intervenors' statements can be explained by the hypothesis that, in stating their goals, Arab intervenors explained their motivation and wishes. In describing the success and criteria of success, however, they were more aware of the limitations of these programs in achieving a change in participants' political and practical behaviors.

In order to bridge the gap between the stated goals and the criteria of success or actual or potential success, it seems that intervenors minimalize and generalize their expectations and become more aware of the intervention models' limitations.

*(4) Criteria related to program implementation:* This category includes:

- Managing to conduct an encounter as planned.
- Program continues to exist.
- Managed to conduct encounters in this reality and safely.
- How many participants took part.
- Willingness to continue in a follow-up activity.
- The school continues sending students to the program.
- Teachers express positive responses to the program.

The most important finding was the belief that the continuing existence of the program is a success in itself—"managing to conduct the program and the continuing existence of the program." Some proposed explanations of why intervenors perceive their program existence as an important criterion of their success are as follows: (a) There is a continuing high level of tension between Arabs and Jews as a result of the Palestinian-Israeli conflict, especially since the outbreak of the Palestinian Intifada in 1987; (b) The program relies on unstable foreign financial support, which can be easily redirected, bringing an end to the programs' activities; (c) The organizations face obstacles in recruiting participants, especially in Jewish schools.

Therefore, conducting an encounter safely and positively becomes a continuing test for the programs' credibility and reputation in the Jewish sector.

*Measures of success:* Most of the intervenors did not think about the question, "What are the measures that you use in your intervention to identify criteria of success and success in general?" at all; others replied that the research and evaluation project should address this; therefore, it is not their responsibility to identify the measure of success. However, programs such as: NS, VL, BH, and GH had at least one evaluation research between 1988 and 1992.

In general, there were several types of intervenors' responses to the question:[1]

- Research evaluation (8).
- No measures whatsoever (7).
- Personal and facilitator's impression (7).
- Questionnaires, but for immediate reaction (4).
- Feedback of participants during the program (3).
- Follow-up: by contacting teachers and meeting in school (3).
- School and counselor feedback.
- Request for more activities (2).

There were no differences between intervenors in terms of their proposed measures of success on neither nationality nor program level.

As concluded in the previous section, the practical and behavioral criteria of success were listed by many intervenors, but the intervenors in general did not apply these criteria in evaluating their success. Basically, the intervenors relied on the three remaining categories of criteria (perceptional changes criteria, interaction criteria, and program implementation) to evaluate their intervention or efforts.

In short, there is no clear perception, definition, or even awareness among intervenors in regard to the measures that can be applied to examine the criteria of success.

## ACTUAL SUCCESS

When intervenors were asked to indicate the successful aspects of their program, they provided specific examples (see appendix 1). These and other examples of actual success were classified into different categories.

There are no special aspects in which any program succeeds, but it is important to mention that in the teachers' programs, the successful aspect was bringing teachers together and raising their awareness of Arab-Jewish relations. In the students' program, the main successful aspect was raising the participants' awareness of Arab-Jewish relations and experiencing an Arab-Jewish interaction.

In general, the actual success of these programs is basically reflected in the four following categories:

a. Changes in individuals' perceptions of each other and the conflict:
   • Participants' awareness of democracy
   • Students' awareness of the conflict
   • Understanding of the complexity and experience of conflict
   • New insights, students acting differently
   • Students' awareness of the problem
   • Arab students' increased awareness of conflict
b. Know each other culturally and personally. A Jewish intervenor noted that: "70 to 80 percent of the program's goal of cultural acquaintance is achieved."
c. Succeed in raising awareness of Arab-Jewish relations in Israel.
d. Having a good personal experience of Arab-Jewish interaction. (Each of these programs can achieve one or more of these categories.)

There are some differences between Arab and Jewish intervenors in relation to the actual aspects of success. (1) Arab intervenors stated that raising Arab students' awareness and empowering Arab students was part of their success in these programs. (2) More Arab intervenors expressed frustration and disappointment with the actual results of the programs. An Arab intervenor stated this notion and clearly described the output of the encounter: "Yes, they [programs] achieve acquaintance, but so what? . . . Our model did not create strong confrontations because we did not speak about conflict."

Such frustration can be explained: (a) It is assumed that the Arab intervenors evaluate the actual impact of these programs in terms of their personal goals and needs for political and structural changes in the Israeli political system. Such high and unrealistic measures and criteria of evaluation, if applied on these limited impact programs, will certainly cause constant frustration and disappointment, not only among intervenors but also among participants, especially Arab teachers who attend these programs. (b) According to an Arab facilitator, there are several types of Arab facilitators in this field: those who could not get jobs in the Israeli Ministry of Education or in other offices; those who decided not to be teachers; and those who were searching for an alternative or substitute to the typical political framework for change. These types of facilitators lack the strong educational or professional obligation to their programs and to their profession as third-party intervenors. Thus, for them, it is an alternative political framework. Therefore, they continue to perceive it as a political framework and as an opportunity to promote social and political changes in Israeli society. In comparison with the Arab intervenors' responses, the Jewish intervenors' actual aspects of success were defined in more realistic terms as in the following statement: "Anything that we do in a context that is so antagonistic to coexistence and democracy is an important act for the achievement of our goals." Or, as a Jewish director said, "We produce changes in individuals' perceptions only, but even this we don't know for sure."

In general, according to most Arab intervenors and all Jewish intervenors, the programs succeeded in their intervention. However, those who declared that their programs were completely successful were mainly the Jewish directors.

## EXAMPLES OF SUCCESS

There are two differences in the nature of the examples provided by Arabs and Jews:

a. Arab intervenors' examples are focused on changes in the Jewish participants' political attitudes, and neither of their examples was related to achieving changes in the Arab participants' attitudes or perceptions. The Jewish examples are focused on a combination of changes in both Jewish and Arab participants.

b. While the Arab intervenors' examples were more specific concerning Jewish participants' practical and behavioral changes, the Jewish intervenors' examples were more general and relate to perceptional and approach changes rather than practical.

These differences between Arabs and Jews are explained by the assumption that each national group of intervenors provided examples that reflect what each of them considers successful intervention. For Arabs the important success is political and practical changes; for Jews it is mainly perceptional. This difference confirms previous differences between Arab and Jewish intervenors regarding to the intervention models' goals and assumptions.

Finally, in general, the list of examples presented by both Arab and Jewish intervenors focuses on the actual changes on the individual level rather than on the community or national level of Arab-Jewish interaction.

## PARTICIPANTS' PERCEPTIONS OF OUTPUTS AND IMPACTS
### *Criteria of Success*

Similar to the intervenors, the participants had difficulties providing a specific definition for the broader success of the intervention model in which they participated. These participants also could not respond to the question of how to measure the intervention model's success.

The participants' responses were based on their experience and not on hypothetical assumptions or perceptions of success, as most intervenors' responses were.

The main difference between Arab and Jewish participants is the fact that Arab teachers and students looked for change in Jewish participants' attitudes and political perception and context of the conflict, and they searched for agreement on conflict issues (see table 8.1). An Arab student explains the success in his program: "They changed their ideas about us. A person who said that we have twenty-two Arab countries to which we can move was convinced that this land also belong to us as much as to him." A frustrated Arab teacher stated: "I am not satisfied with the products, because we should have something to influence the policy planning and decision making in regard to Arab interests."

The Jewish participants, especially the students, are looking for a "fun" experience and a pleasant interaction with a group of Arab students whom they perceived as being violent, "terrorist," and even physically threatening. Therefore, it was very important to them to indicate the encounter's non-violent aspects.

For Arab students, to establish a friendship is an important indication of acceptance by the Jewish majority group. A friendship is also an indication of agreement, which was an important component of success. These differences between Arab and Jewish students illustrate the importance of considering the different and unique needs that each group expected to fulfill in these encounters.

All intervenors agreed that the Arab students would consider the program successful and satisfactory, if only because of the fact that it provided them with an opportunity to leave the school and participate in an

**Table 8.1. Arab-Jewish Criteria of Success[2]**

*Arabs*
*Students*

- Reach an agreement on conflict issue (3).
- Convince them of our ideas (2).
- Friendship: phone calls and visits (6).
- Treated us well and with respect.
- Changed their perceptions about us (2).
- Didn't have violence.

*Arab Teachers*

- Agree on the problems and other matters.
- To know the other people's attitudes.
- Participants attend the entire program (2).

*Jewish*
*Students*

- Friendship: call each other, visit (2).
- Had fun (4).
- Was not violent (5).
- Know the Arabs better.

*Jewish Teachers*

- Experience an encounter.
- Change in approach to the subject: more sensitive.
- Completed the program.
- A good atmosphere during the program.
- Introduce curric lums related to the issue in the schools

informal activity, which they lack in their s chool systems. Jewish students, on the other hand, attend these programs with the expectation of gaining information and acquainting themselves with the "exotic and mystical" Arab culture.

There are several variations in the Arab and Jewish students' motivations, expectations, and background that help explain such differences:

a. For Arab students, attending the encounter involves a national mission of representing their minority and their national problem in Israel.

b. Arab students maintain a certain degree of respect and seriousness in their relationship with their teachers and adults in general. This prevents them (motivated and supported by cultural politeness) from criticizing or presenting "having fun" as criteria of success because of the program's perceived seriousness. The criteria of "learning about the other side" and "learning about the complexity of conflict" were mentioned only by the intervenors. Participants did not explicitly list these components as criteria of success.

To explain such differences, again, there appears to be an element lacking in the preparation stage and the process itself, which is the fact that after participants experience the entire program, they still believe they can easily change attitudes on the other side, and that this type of interaction can be effective in changing or solving the Arab-Jewish conflict.

### Was It a Successful Experience?

In responding to this question, Arab and Jewish participants agreed that it was a successful experience, but for different reasons. For Arab students, it was successful because they convinced Jewish participants in their attitudes. An Arab participant stated this notion: "It was successful because there were good Jews who were even more left than us, and they supported Arabs' demands. We, the Arabs, did not change our ideas since there were also radical right Jews." A disappointed Arab student said: "It was successful because first they did not want to know us. Now they are interested but not in politics because in other encounter classes after one year the encounter was broken down as result of politics."

On the Jewish side, the responses were focused on the perceptional changes or changes in approach to Arabs in Israel. A Jewish participant stresses the importance of continuing in Arab-Jewish relation programs: "Before, I was a very right-wing extreme Jew. If I had an Arab I was ready to stab him with a knife, of course if the law did not prevent me. But, when I was there, I learned about Arabs with whom I can live, even in the same room." Several Jewish participants described the change in attitude that occurred after the program: "Now, I know that not all the Arabs are killers, but I am still afraid of them. This Arab group was nice but this does not mean anything about other groups." Another Jewish student expressed her enjoyment in the encounter: "They did not look like Arabs, they were like my friends. When we returned to school, I thought, what fun we had."

The new approach that Jewish participants obtain as a result of these encounter experiences was described elegantly by a Jewish teacher who became more committed to Arab-Jewish relations:

> My approach changed, not my opinion or political attitude, but I read the newspaper and listened to news with more awareness,

sympathy, and understanding. Although I did not obtain new information in the course, I guess it is the experience.

There were several disappointed Jewish participants. One of them explains his frustration: "I finished the encounter with no satisfaction, without fun, because they [Arabs] have only one opinion—Palestinian state and equal rights, and others wanted to throw Jews in the sea."

In short, the different motivations and expectations for attending the encounter influenced the participants' evaluation of success. The Arab students focus on the changes in attitudes and perceptions, while the Jewish students express their surprise and excitement that they "made it through safely," meaning they managed to talk to Arabs safely. Such a response indicates the different needs and concerns on both sides. The Arabs were concerned with their status in Israel as a discriminated-against minority, and their national identity. Jews were more occupied with security and the threat they feel from interaction with Arabs. As Hofman (1986) and Bar and Asaqla (1988a) reported, Arabs are more oriented in their goal of convincing Jewish participants to change their political attitudes, while the Jewish participants avoid such output and are more concerned with the enjoyment of the encounter, or the "fun" of the contact, or learning about the "mystical" Arab culture.

## PERCEPTION OF SUCCESS: THE NEED FOR SYSTEMATIC MEASUREMENT

The Arab intervenors were closer to the Jewish intervenors' perceptions in their evaluation of success, criteria of success, and actual aspects of success. Arab intervenors were more aware of the fact that these programs are limited in their impact on the macro level. Such awareness (which was especially a source of frustration to Arab intervenors) was not expressed in the section where Arab intervenors describe their goals and assumptions.

The frustration is not only voiced by Arab intervenors, but is also expressed by some Jewish intervenors. Aloof Haraeven, a Jewish director who is known for his pioneer work and leadership in the field of Arab-Jewish relations, justifies his change of focus by arguing that:

> We worked in education for coexistence and cooperative Arab-Jewish relations for eight years, but I cannot say that we did achieve or we managed in creating an alternative reality for Arabs and Jews in Israel. Therefore, I think it is time to focus on the decision-making level and policy planning where there is a lack of Arab officers or any representation for Arab interests as a minority.

Another source of frustration for intervenors, which was expressed especially by Arab intervenors, is related to the fact that the most important success, particularly in the students' programs, is the experience of "contact," which also was indicated in the statement of the goals. Thus, this is an interaction that lacks the intellectual or systematic cognitive learning through new information processing. Therefore, the experience remains on a rhetorical or perceptional level (or superficial, as described by one experienced facilitator) rather than moving on to a practical level. For most participants this remained a "fun" experience that did not reach beyond spending "good" time with friends. There was no indication of applying the encounter's learning either directly or indirectly in any behavioral aspects.

On the teacher programs, there were very few teachers who implemented any of their personal and professional learning into their classes or schools. Such application or implementation was limited to just a few teachers.

There are conditions and factors that lower the possibilities and options for teachers to implement what they experience in the encounter, or even to continue being more involved or committed to the Arab-Jewish subject. Some of these factors are as follows:

(a) In general, the encounter's outputs are not followed up in any of these programs. None of the programs has a formal or specifically designed follow-up plan to trace the impact or the changes that their programs produced in students' or teachers' attitudes, if they produced attitude change at all. There was only one case in which a facilitator described an act of follow-up conducted by him personally. This facilitator usually sends a letter to his participants asking them several questions about their adjustment process back in their environment, but this was not done in a systematic and institutionalized manner.

(b) None of the programs has any responsibility or clear commitment to participants who wish to continue working on this issue after the program's project is finished. In fact, there are very few cases in which participants took responsibility after their participation and initiated a practical project to implement their agreements.

(c) On the teachers' level, such rare initiatives could be understandable, especially if we consider the fact that only a small portion of the teachers will ever take part in such activities. Therefore, the teacher who returns to his or her school environment is basically returning to a hostile and typically uncommitted environment that will resist any initiative for change.

According to intervenors' evaluation and perception of broad success (input at the macro level), the most important impact or success is their hope for the creation of a public atmosphere that pays more attention and creates obligation to Arab-Jewish relations in Israel.

The gap between Jewish and Arab participants' expectations remained even after the participants completed the program, especially those programs that dealt only with cultural aspects (see programs such as BH and UFD). Even after they graduated from these programs, many Arab participants continued to believe that political and attitudinal changes can be accomplished through these interactions. They were less concerned or occupied with what they learned about themselves or the other side than they were with causing a change in Jewish political attitudes. The Jewish participants, on average, were occupied with the fact that they made it safely through the encounter with Arabs and that the threat was not so great.

For the Jewish student, the fact that there are Arabs who are willing to talk and interact with Jews in a nonthreatening context was a meaningful learning experience. For the Arab student, the outputs that resulted from the experience of interaction were not sufficient outputs.

Since the Jewish participants' expectations were not as high and unrealistic as the Arab students' their frustration was less. They attended the workshop to know the Arabs better and to examine their fears. The interaction provided an opportunity for them to do so. Therefore, they were less disappointed or frustrated. Actually, they were able to learn more about themselves than the Arab students did. The Arab students were occupied with convincing the Jewish students of the "justice of their demands." As minority members, they were less willing to reveal or allow differences among their group. The Jewish groups are more open to revealing differences, because revealing internal differences is not a source of weakness or threat for them as a group. On the contrary, this functions as a learning opportunity by revealing differences among the group; one learns to become more tolerant.

There were several facilitators, Arabs and Jews, who stressed the centrality of the interaction experience in their work. They argued that the content of the program does not really matter. The fact that Jewish and Arab adolescents are spending informal time together is the main source of failure and success of the program or the encounter. As long as the program provides these youth with activities and enables them to enjoy spending time out of class, even among their own national group, the encounter will be successful for them.

On one hand, this argument has some truth in it, especially if we examine the fact that in the students' programs the participants are adolescents who experience unique teenage processes and have certain needs and questions, which are not addressed directly or explicitly by these programs at all. However, for them to spend time with their peers is a major need.

On the other hand, as reported by Amir (1976) Ben-Ari and Amir, (1988a, b), Rouhana (1988), and Bar et al. (1989), "contact is not enough" to change attitudes. On the contrary, contact alone might produce damaging or negative changes. Based on such a conclusion, at least those programs and intervenors who stated in this research that they perceive their ultimate goal and success is to perform the contact itself might have negative impacts on Arab and Jewish students' attitudes.

Thus, the main output of the encounter programs (except those that focus on conflict issues in their content and process) is in increasing the awareness of the Arab-Jewish relations in Israel (to relations, not to a conflict). This output is mainly produced by providing a special interactional experience on an interpersonal level between Arabs and Jews throughout the program or during only a part of it. Therefore, any attempt by the third party to present his or her goal to influence the immediate political situation directly or effectively would be a misperception and false presentation of the program, as well as an indicator of a lack of awareness of the program's assumptions and professional integrity.

Figure 8.1 illustrates the programs' range of impacts in circles. The direct and explicit impact of such programs does not reach beyond the immediate circle of the individual, in this case, students. In the teachers' case, the impact might directly be transferred into the teachers immediate circle of school and professional domain.

The Arab participants and, in some cases, the Arab intervenors, wish and hope for an impact on the far external circle, but during the interaction they become aware, at least in their statements, that the maximum they can expect is an impact on the second circle. Even this sort of impact may be too difficult to accomplish because their Jewish counterparts are not easily convinced to accept the idea of changing the situation, or becoming active, or being obliged to the Arab-Jewish subject. Such discovery or awareness produces frustration and disappointment with the program among participants and facilitators, especially Arabs. Even if there are changes in perceptions, which appear to be the main output of these programs, this does not mean that these changes are transferred into the reality of the person or even to the immediate school environment. As a Jewish facilitator explains:

> We cause a change in perceptions and not always in the same direction I want. But, for sure, teachers will not leave as they entered. I am not sure that all participants can move from changes in personal perception to a reality of perceptional changes.

**Figure 8.1. Intervention Programs' Range of Impact**

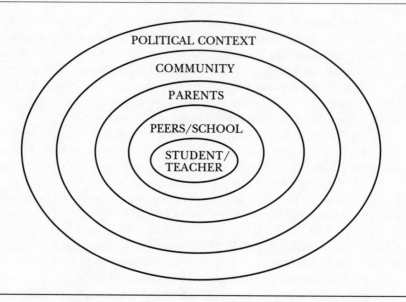

In conclusion, if friendship and positive experience of interaction or contact between Arabs and Jews in these programs are the main definitions of broader success or criteria of success, this brings about questions such as: (a) Are there other methods by which a program can produce such outputs and in greater scales? (b) Are these programs not misleading students, especially Arabs, who, after the program is over, believe that by participating in such programs they are active in political change processes? (c) By perusing only cultural acquaintance and personal friendship do not these designs serve only one side (i.e., or the Jewish participants)? (d) Should not students be prepared to be more aware of the fact that these programs do not aim, or even intend, to produce political change or input into the political change processes? These questions will be addressed in the concluding chapter.

Having completed the findings related to the design, perception of conflict, and outputs of the intervention models, we turn to the impacts of the political context on these aspects of the programs.

# 9

# Impacts of the Political Context on the Encounter Models

The lack of consideration of the impacts of context, particularly the political, on the intervention model has been one major shortcoming of the contact hypothesis model (Hewstone & Brown, 1986). Therefore, the primary objective of this chapter is to examine impacts of the political context on Arab-Jewish intervention models. Of the rapid changing Middle Eastern reality, the Intifada, the Gulf War, the immigration of Soviet Jews, and the recent peace process are the major political developments that shifted many of the regional and local politics. Thus, to explore the impact of the political context, it is essential to discuss these events and their relations to the encounter programs.

## MAJOR CHANGES IN THE ENCOUNTER PROGRAMS SINCE THE MID-1980s

Most of the changes have occurred during the past decade, and they were identified through the description of the organizations' development and specific questions on certain political events.

The timing, size, and intensity of the major changes that took place in all the programs vary by program. Some of these changes are listed below:

a. Increase the preparation for their encounter.
b. Add a uinational section to the encounter.
c. Work with smaller groups and focus on in-depth work rather than greater participant number.
d. Introduce task-oriented encounter rather than discuss political issues or groups' dynamic interaction.

131

   e. Increase teachers' involvement in order to reduce their fears
      and frustration during the student encounter.

In addition to these changes, each organization has its own unique and
specific development and pace of change. For instance, by 1991 the NS
encounter program had added two binational encounters for continuity; it
also had an integrated uninational framework by the mid-1980s. Programs
MA started as a program of education for democracy. It worked separately in
Arab and Jewish schools. Later, the encounters between Arabs and Jews were
included as part of the larger and initial design of education for democracy.
The main reason for such change, as stated by intervenors, was an imposed
precondition by the organization's foreign sponsoring foundation. They
also reduced the minimal number of required meetings because the schools
were not willing to commit their students for a long program.

The GH encounter program only introduced a uninational framework
at the beginning of the 1990s. It also restructured its facilitation staff in
1989, a change that influenced its encounter model. Program BH only
introduced uninational framework after 1991, and it began introducing
Palestinian identity questions as late as 1990.

Although a Arab-Jewish encounter program has ceased to exist in its
host organization, Van Leer's development is similar to that of other organizations in this field.[1]

   a. Started with developing curriculum for Jewish, then Arab
      schools.
   b. Initiated encounters for teachers, training them to apply new
      curriculum. There were two types of encounters: group dynamic
      encounters and training courses on specific curricula.
   c. Initiated another wave of encounters between Arab and Jewish
      teachers. This focused on value and attitude clarification.
   d. Initiated the program or model of "current events," which was
      described by the director: "This was a failure because we didn't
      create the model for teachers to deal with current events, and
      we didn't have impact on teachers."
   e. In 1991–92, initiated "Educational Task Pairs." This indicates
      the program's change from a group dynamic and value and
      attitude clarification into "task-oriented encounter."[2]

Finally, according to the program UFD directors, there were no
substantial changes in the model, which is applied by the intervenor in
different regions. The model was created in 1987 and it has been continued in fourteen different locations on the organization level. However,
this director added that today the encounter program has to compete with

other projects that are offered to all schools. Program UFD intervenors explained the impact of this change:

> As a project that involves Arab and Jews and education for democracy, we cannot compete with other projects which only address Jewish schools' needs and are less threatening to teachers, such as immigration, or other issues.

Intervenors agreed that the model stayed the same as it was created by its first director. They stressed that this is a very open and flexible model, which enables different facilitators to apply it according to their preferences and focuses.

## IMPACTS OF THE PEACE PROCESS

Since the signing of the Palestinian Israeli Declaration of Principles (DOP) in Oslo 1993 and the Cairo agreement in 1995, many changes have taken place in the Middle East political context. These major changes influenced and reshaped Palestinian-Israeli relations. For the first time, the Israeli government has recognized the PLO as a representative of the Palestinian people. Arafat is received as a diplomat rather than a terrorist by Israeli government officials, and has returned to Gaza, where he was welcomed by Palestinians in a heroic reception.[3]

Israeli troops have completed their redeployment out of the major Palestinian cities. Israel has established a strong and comprehensive peace treaty with Jordan. Israeli officials are regularly visiting the various Arab countries, initiating economic and political ties.

Meritz (represented by leaders of the Israeli Peace Movement, particularly Peace Now) joined the Israeli government coalition and its leaders are taking an active part in the peace negotiations. A sense of accomplishment and success overwhelmed the Israeli Peace Movement, which the Arab-Jewish encounter program has been in direct connection with (Hall-Cathala, 1990).

However, not all Palestinians and Israelis eagerly welcomed these historical developments. Both Israeli and Palestinian opposition groups have successfully blocked the peace process. On the Israeli side, the right wing and religious fundamentalists' campaign against the peace process resulted in further religious, political, and ethnic polarization in Israeli society. Tension and calls for violent and nonviolent resistance to the government's policy broke the Israeli national consensus. In November 1995, the prime minister was assassinated by a fanatic religious Jew.

On the Palestinian side, the Islamic movement (Hamas and the Islamic Jihad) has launched fierce suicidal bomb attacks on Israeli cities (several major explosions that killed and injured hundreds of Israeli citizens). In addition, the lack of infrastructural development (the donor countries are delaying their funds for the Palestinian authority, and the economic deterioration as a result of the siege imposed by the Israeli authority in response to the suicidal bombs, have caused a sharp decrease in popular support for the peace process among Palestinians in Israel and the West Bank and Gaza.

The developments on both sides brought Benjamin Netanyaho, the Likud leader who defeated Shimon Peres (the Labor leader) in the first direct prime minster election in Israel. The victory of the Likud in mid-1996 provoked many speculations on the continuation of the deadlock between Israeli and Palestinian negotiators and on the possibility of bringing the entire process to a total collapse.

Regardless of the future direction of Israeli-Palestinian negotiations, the peace process had influenced Arab-Jewish encounters in Israel on several levels. In general, Arab and Jewish intervenors emphasize more the need and urgency for conducting encounters between Arabs and Jews as a result of the peace process initiation.

Jewish intervenors argue that the encounter can now focus on the relationship between Arabs and Jews in Israel rather than being occupied (i.e., the encounter) by the Palestinian-Israeli conflict, which often caused tension and arguments among the participants. The Arab intervenors perceived the encounter after the peace process as a chance to further the discussion on the core issue of Arab-Jewish relations in Israel: to deal with the Jewishness of the State of Israel.

On the content level, the Palestinian-Israeli conflict has ceased to be the main topic of political discussions. Arab participants seem to focus more on the issue of equal rights and their future as Israeli citizens. The Jewishness of the state is another topic that has been stressed in several encounter programs, as reported by intervenors. Also, Arab and Jewish participants mostly agree on the rejection and condemnation of the suicidal bombs attacks—an important element of agreement that reduces the gap between the two in regards to the Israeli-Palestinian conflict.[4] On the process level, intervenors reported a lower degree of tension and fear in the course of the encounter. Intervenors are less worried about a political explosion.

In regard to willingness to meet, directors of encounter programs had indicated that in the aftermath of Oslo I (1993), Jewish schools are more willing to meet with Arab schools. In fact, in the first year after the agreement, the director of program GH complained that for the first time so many Jewish schools had interest in the encounter that they could be selective in whom to invite to the encounter. No change was identified in the Arab schools or participants' willingness to meet the other side. Intervenors did not associate any changes in the goals or assumptions of their programs with the peace process.

## IMPACTS OF THE INTIFADA ON INTERVENTION MODELS

The impacts of the Intifada were described by many intervenors as positive and negative at the same time. There are several general changes that took place as a result of the Palestinian Intifada. These can be divided into three categories: (1) impacts on Arab participants, (2) impacts on Jewish participants; (3) impacts on the encounter program.

*1. Impacts on Arab participants:* The Intifada had a positive impact on Arab participants who were empowered by the Intifada; they became more confident and more nationally aware. They were empowered by their Palestinian identity. Such empowerment was a balancing factor in the typically asymmetric setting of the encounter. A Jewish facilitator stated this notion:

> Arab students were not under the typical accusation or questioning of Jewish students to explain (i.e., justify) the brutality of the Palestinians against Jews, but it was an opposite situation: Jewish students felt the need to defend and explain the Israeli military actions in dealing with the Intifada.

This impact was very strong during the first year of the Intifada but eased as time passed, as described by several intervenors.

At the same time, the Israeli components in their identity were reflected. The Intifada caused both Arabs and Jews in Israel to see themselves as citizens of Israel because the Arabs were not involved directly with the Intifada.

The Intifada confirms the perception that "our" reality is a conflict relationship that "we" cannot continue to ignore. Jewish participants were examining and testing the Arabs in Israel to a certain degree whether they were like those in the West Bank and Gaza.

Arab participants became stronger during the encounter, as indicated by an intervenor of the GH program: "Arabs are more honest and direct in their interaction with Jews; they will not say what you wish to hear them saying." Therefore, the encounter became more equal, direct, and sharp in its focus. The Arab teachers asked for encounters or any activities that might help reduce the tension in their classes. A facilitator from program MA described such a call for help: "They were in crisis; and they did not know what to do with their students. They told 'us' [i.e., intervenors] to come and take as much time as 'you' want."

For Arab teachers, the encounter was an opportunity to ease their stress, tension, and fears from the threat of their students exploding in an attempt to express their feelings and sympathy for the Intifada. For the Arab students, this was an opportunity to vent their national case to the Jewish students. Thus, in contrast to the Jewish schools, the Arab schools, students, and teachers were more willing to meet with Jews and address the issue in any manner. Such a finding is supported also by Hertz-Lazarovich in a 1989 study of the Intifada's impact on the BH's activities.

2. *Impacts on Jewish participants:* It was more difficult for Jews to deal with the situation because they no longer can deny the conflict. Also for Jewish students, the "Green Line" was deleted completely; for them, the Intifada was everywhere.

Jewish participants suspected that Arabs in Israel are engaged in the Intifada's activities. For many Jewish students, who lack information and are ignorant of the status and conditions of the Arabs in Israel, there are no differences whatsoever between Palestinians in Israel and Palestinians from the West Bank and Gaza.

On the Jewish teachers' level, since they witness the polarization in their students' political attitudes, they were more resistant to the Arab-Jewish encounter because of fear and expectation that the encounter might explode in violence or produce damage to the school–community or school–parents relationship.[5] Therefore, they were more extreme in their perceptions of Arabs. This increased the fear, tension, and pain in the encounter atmosphere. They were terrified of the encounter, especially after the "Dome of the Rock" and "Reshion Le Tzion" incident.[6]

The number of Jewish participants dropped. The teacher encounter program stressed the difficulties in the recruitment of schools to the program. However, Jewish educators in general were more interested in the model, because they understood that they must deal with the Intifada.

During the encounter Arabs declared their Palestinian identity very clearly. This terrified the Jewish participants, who were thinking they were meeting with the PLO. They were shocked and confused. As one Jewish student said: "As human beings you are nice, but if you are Palestinians you almost violate the law."

3. *Impacts on the encounter program:* The Intifada made it difficult to hold and arrange the encounter. Teachers and schools were less willing to participate; on the other hand, it became more important to conduct such activity.

On the content level, the Intifada specified and defined the issues of the conflict. However, it increased emotional tensions that accompany typical discussions, such as control of land, equal rights to Arabs, and other issues. Thus, the Intifada imposed itself as a constant issue in the encounters, even though the intervenors did not intend to introduce it as an issue of discussion (particularly in programs such as BH, MA, or UFD). But students, especially in an informal setting, addressed the Intifada as an important issue of Arab-Jewish relations in Israel. As one Arab intervenor in program BH describes the influence of the Intifada on his organization:

> It was only after 1989, that the board or the council changed their attitude toward the PLO's. legitimacy and the Intifada. Just after that we started talking about political issues and Palestinian identity; before we only discussed cultural aspects; besides this is what the students expect us to discuss. We cannot stop this process among students.

On the process level, the main impact was to increase the level of fear among Jewish students, frustration among Arab students, and mistrust and anger on both sides.

More focus on the political issues in the encounter became a more important criterion of success than before. Programs like BH became more politicized and asked more political questions (this was done indirectly because the organization is defined as being apolitical). But because students are not satisfied with the cultural and social components of the program, they requested more political discussion.

Thus, the encounter became more dangerous to conduct; it might "explode" or the possibility of "causing damage" became stronger, especially when schools canceled at the last minute. A facilitator from program NS illustrates such a notion: "In one incident, the students were more motivated to attend the encounter than their principal, who insisted in canceling the encounter because of the killing in the 'Dome of the Rock' in Jerusalem in 1990."

This impact also influenced program MA, whose intervenors stressed that because of fear and tension, it became more difficult to control emotional aspects and remain focused on cognitive and rational learning. It became more difficult to reach the second level of the model (acknowledging the implications of double-standard behavior) because the process evoked more tension than before. Intervenors realized the need for dealing with emotional aspects and the need for integrating process and content facilitation; however, the process continues to be overshadowed by the content on democracy. Threatened by such an environment, encounter programs such as BH started working in small groups because they could not manage one large group.

Both Arabs and Jews found methods to cope with its impacts. However, the encounter's process of interaction and content was easily and constantly influenced by sudden "violent incidents" conducted by Arabs or

Jews. Intervenors in all the programs testified that their most difficult problem was coping with the Intifada's sudden violent incidents, such as the "Dome of the Rock," "Reashon L' Tzion," and the "knives stabbing waves."

The structure of the programs did not change immediately, except program BH. They all continued with the same model structure as before the Intifada. Through the last three years of the Intifada, however, at least two programs changed their focus and structure of activities: GH and BH. At this point, it is difficult to determine whether the Intifada was the major cause of such changes or whether financial factors and changes in directors of the programs were the cause. However, during the Intifada, program BH began using small group discussion and introduced more political issues into the discussion, at least in the third encounter of the model. In addition, during the three years of the Intifada at least three programs introduced or intensified their uninational activities.

> On the staff level, at least in three programs, the Intifada's activities caused arguments and revealed differences between Arab and Jewish facilitators. As an intervenor in one of these programs stated: Because of the Intifada we, the facilitators, could not stand each other anymore. It was very difficult to continue and to ignore the outside reality. We had to talk about it and then everything exploded. Arab facilitators started asking themselves, "What am I doing here? Is this my contribution to the political uprising in the West Bank and Gaza Strip?"

In terms of goals and assumptions, most of the intervenors indicated that their goals and assumptions have remained the same since the outbreak of the Intifada. But some of them indicated that their goals and expectations were reduced to a minimalist notion: they were expected to conduct the encounter and complete the program, which became their criteria of success and their definition of broad success.

In conclusion, although it appears that some programs attempted to avoid the impacts of the Intifada, it penetrated their models very easily throughout the different levels and stages. Even the director of program UFD, who argued that the Intifada did not impact the model of his program, was challenged by his facilitators, who pointed out several changes that the Intifada forced them to make.

In addition, there were several facilitators who initially stated that there were no impacts of the Intifada on their intervention model. These facilitators, when they proceeded in their explanation, reached the conclusion that there had been changes in their intervention model's process and sometimes in the content of their program. This change occurred as a result of a specific period during the Intifada. It is clear that some facilitators did not consider impacts of the Intifada in their work or relate to them. Such lack of consideration is again an indicator of the lack of professional perspective among these intervenors.

Finally, most of the facilitators indicated that their evaluation of the Intifada's impacts are not based on any research or study that they conducted but on their personal and professional impressions. The fact that studies or research were not conducted to examine the impact of a crucial political resistance movement such as the Intifada on the organizations' work aptly illustrates the lack of research and the neglect of this field among the Israeli and Palestinian scholars or academics.

## IMPACTS OF THE GULF WAR ON THE ENCOUNTER PROGRAMS

The major impact of the Gulf War on the intervention model is reflected in the fact that from the beginning of the war on January 15, 1991, the Israeli Ministry of Education issued an order to close all the schools and suspend all informal and formal activities until the middle of February 1991. Since all intervention programs operate through the school system, during the war period all intervention programs were suspended. A Jewish intervenor explains the problem during the war: "You cannot conduct a seminar on coexistence and understanding while both Arab and Jewish participants are equipped with gas masks and terrified of a Scud missile attack." Even prior to the outbreak of the war, there were some programs that were paralyzed during the crisis, and could recruit participants, especially on the Jewish side. However, the main impacts can be identified through examination of the Gulf crisis's three phases:

*Pre–Gulf War impacts:* These were noted during the crisis and period of threats of launching Scud attacks on Israel. The impacts of tension, fear, and mistrust became highlighted in the interaction between Arabs and Jews. For those who continued conducting encounters (such as programs BH and VL) the war imposed itself as an issue for discussion, and it helped in defining and specifying the fears, suspicions, and gaps in positions. Thus, students ended the encounter very angry and tense. In program UFD the crisis caused distance between Arabs and Jews, but those who were engaged in the encounters continued their program, while those who were supposed to start could not establish the contact.

On both sides, the uninational framework became the goal instead of the encounter. In program MA, the intervenors realized that they could educate Arabs and Jews separately. They could not attend the Jewish schools and were forced to work with Arab schools only (which led to the emergence of a uninational framework in this program).

The shift to a uninational framework can be better understood knowing that the Ministry of Education instructed the organizations to work in a uninational framework rather than a binational one.

In some cases, like program GH, only Arab facilitators gained access to Arab schools, while the Jewish facilitators could not attend the Jewish schools. Some facilitators argue that this was a result of the Jewish facilitators' personal problems and confusions with the Gulf War. Other facilitators explain this result by saying the Jewish schools were more threatened by the Gulf War and it influenced them more than it did the Arab students. Therefore, Jewish schools were less willing to receive Jewish facilitators to address the conflict.

Thus, an important coping attempt was achieved when these programs operated separately in the Arab schools and Jewish schools. These programs entirely adopted the uninational framework as a method of dealing with the students on both sides. A facilitator explains this phenomenon of using a uninational framework during the Gulf War:

Because the programs could not conduct encounters prior to, during, and after the war, they had to do something with the students. They came up with the idea supported by the Ministry of Education, of uninational sessions.

On the Arab side, students were hungry for such activities, while on the Jewish side, students were terrified and less willing to talk about this issue with Arab-Jewish facilitators.

*Impacts during the Gulf War:* Encounters were prevented by the Ministry of Education; schools were closed for at least a month. As a result of this decision, most programs used the war to examine and discuss differences among the staff members. Actually these discussions among the staff were part of the programs' difficulties in coping with the war situation. A Jewish facilitator illustrates the difficulties in the staff:

Personally, I have a problem with the Gulf War. I cannot discuss it with Arabs. It is illusion that both Arabs and Jews were in the same position; attacked by Scuds and have the gas masks; we were in different situations.

Finally, the war period encouraged programs to develop curricula and exercises for postwar activities. In all the organizations such curriculums were not implemented because neither Arabs nor Jews were willing to address the Gulf War.

*Post–Gulf War impacts:* Many intervenors expressed their surprise at how quickly and easily Arabs and Jews forgot the Gulf War. Neither the groups nor the facilitators wished to discuss it further. A Jewish facilitator described this situation:

The Gulf War is not mentioned so much after only one year, because it added another level or *rovid* to the existing levels, such as the Intifada and other violent events in Arab-Jewish relations. But, today, it seems like it doesn't exist. Both Arabs and Jews in the encounter ignore it, avoid it, or forgot it.

Several programs such as NS, BH, and MA designed special curriculums and exercises to deal with the postwar situation, but they were not used or applied. For the most part, the Gulf War was mentioned as a passing accusation of Jews toward Arabs as being traitors or mistrusted partners. Arabs use it as an illustration of double-standard values and political behavior against Palestinians. Intervenors describe taking a few months after the Gulf crisis for Arabs and Jews to return to their normal path and continue responding to the Arab-Jewish programs.[7]

In general, the programs in the postwar period faced several problems. An Arab facilitator describes the situation: "An Arab active principal told me after the war in despair: 'Please, I cannot deal with the Arab-Jewish subject now.'" A Jewish teacher told the Jewish facilitators who proposed an encounter with Arab teachers: "Don't bother us with this issue now." The same facilitator claimed: "We still suffer from the war because schools are slow in responding to our invitations."

During the political discussion in the postwar encounter Arab students did not have anything to say to Jewish students. But, as a program MA intervenor speculated, in the future, the mistrust will increase because Arabs supported Sadam Hussein and Jews were against him. An intervenor in the VL program suggested that the Arab participants' position was weaker in the postwar political discussion.

In general, the war had no impact on the theoretical model of the encounter programs; however, certain interactions on the process level were identified by intervenors. For example, program MA intervenors argued that there was a basic change in the postwar encounter interaction; Arabs usually insisted on democracy, but, in this case, they supported Sadam Hussein's antidemocratic regime. This created a contradiction and confusion when they requested democracy in Israel.

On the staff level, in the NS program arguments and difficulties among the staff were reported. However, in others, such as UFD, the facilitating teams did not discuss the Gulf War.

A year after the Gulf War, in examining the activity of the programs, it was clear that the main effect of the Gulf War on models' structure is the introduction of a uninational framework into all the programs. In the Gulf War crisis intervenors understood that they could not encounter Arabs and Jews just for the sake of encounter—not only because the Ministry of

Education prevented them, but also because Arabs and Jews were not ready to meet each other (see appendix 3).

Intervenors in the NS program, who were the first to include the uninational framework in their intervention model, described this notion:

> What was once described as a waste of time, in the pre–Gulf War was being applied by all the organizations, not because they believe in it or because they feel the need for such a thing, but because the Ministry of Education instructed them to do so, as the result of the Gulf War.

The gap in terms of attitudes between the two groups is so huge, and the emotional tension and anxiety on both sides are so high, that it might be a damaging rather than constructive experience to attend an encounter. It is true that such a situation could happen during one of the Intifada's violent incidents, but programs were not ready to postpone or cancel an encounter and switch to uninational activity on both sides.

A clear example was in one of the programs when the two facilitators returned to their staff for consultation, arguing that their two teachers' groups were not ready for an encounter and that the model in this case should focus on uninational work with these two specific groups. Although this was the facilitators' evaluation, the directors and the remaining staff advised the facilitators to conduct the encounter, which they did. The same two groups did not complete the program; the Jewish group claimed that they had other projects to deal with.

This is an example of one incident in which programs rejected the idea of a uninational framework prior to the Gulf War, but adopted it as a result of the Gulf War.

Another conclusion that might be relevant to the impacts of the Gulf War on such programs is that the models that had continuing encounters and activities throughout the year continued in their activity soon after the war ended. But projects that had to establish new contacts with both Arabs and Jews had more difficulty. As a Jewish intervenor described such an argument: "This is a lesson to 'us' Arabs and Jews that the creation of a human interaction helps 'us' cope with wars."

Some programs apparently adopted an alternative role during the Gulf War—a role that helped the Ministry of Education relax and calm down the students in schools and assist the students in expressing their fears and anxiety about the war. By functioning in a such a manner, these programs were converted into being another tool of the Israeli government (specifically, the Ministry of Education) to deal with Arabs in Israel in a crisis situation (an additional discussion of this function is presented in the next chapter). One facilitator described such a role: "These organizations functioned as assistants to the Ministry of Education to overcome the crisis of the Gulf War in the schools—the same role the programs had during the Intifada's crisis."

In at least three programs (MA, GH, and BH) intervenors adjusted their activities during and prior to the Gulf War when Arabs and Jews refused to meet each other. These programs focused on uninational activities, but after the Gulf War programs MA and BH returned to their typical classical activities. Program GH planned to insert more uninational frameworks into their model, and to put more focus on the positive aspects of the Arab-Jewish relations.

In short, the impacts of the Gulf War were initially in the actual existence of the intervention program: they were forced to stop their activities during the war. In terms of content and process, the Gulf War influence was less than that of the Intifada; the war only became a part of the content for a short period of time, mainly prior to the war. The interaction was more tense and fueled with more mistrust. The Gulf War caused a temporary change in the structure of most of the programs, forcing them to adopt the uninational activity framework. The goals and assumptions as reported by intervenors were not changed or influenced by the Gulf War, except for some discussions and arguments among facilitators.

## IMPACTS OF SOVIET JEWISH IMMIGRATION ON ENCOUNTER PROGRAMS

The immigration of Soviet Jews is not a sudden incident, or an act of explicit and direct violence that involves Arabs and Jews. However, since 1989, when massive immigration waves began, this issue has been continuously on the Israeli and Palestinian list of current controversial political events. It has provoked tension on several occasions, even at the international level. It is clear that the absorption of approximately seven hundred thousand Soviet Jews has enormous implications on both Jewish society and the Arabs' status in Israel.

Surprisingly, intervenors claimed that there have been no substantial or intentional changes in any of the programs' models, even when discussed the specific components of the intervention model. The main impacts of the Soviet Jews' immigration that emerged can be classified into four main categories. First, the Jewish immigration became an issue of discussion during the encounter and uninational meetings, even in a program such as NS, which was the only program to decide not to work with immigrant participants.

Second, some Jewish schools, as described by program NS staff, claimed that the immigration is their main topic and preference; therefore, they cannot take part in Arab-Jewish programs.

Third, on the process or interaction level, Arab participants have ambivalent responses. On the one hand they are accused of anti-Semitism by opposing the immigration. On the other hand, they are aware of the damage such immigration can cause to their status in Israel. However, in most encounter programs Arab participants raised the issue as another example of governmental discriminatory policy.

The Jewish participants viewed this issue as an internal matter, which was discussed in uninational sessions without touching on its implications on Arabs.

Fourth, several programs announced their plans to deal with the issue in special curricula that they have or will design. There has been no immediate consideration of this issue in any of the programs.

Several factors explain the programs' reaction to this factor in their political context: (a) There is a consensus among the Jewish society, in that they agree on the necessity of bringing Jews to Israel and have an obligation to absorb these immigrants. Therefore, there is no conflict, and Arabs in Israel should adjust themselves to this fact; (b) When Arabs in Israel raised the issue, there were ambivalent responses. On the one hand, Arabs rejected the absorption of immigrants because they will lose jobs and other economic opportunities. They also oppose sending immigrants to the settlements in the West Bank and Gaza. On the other hand, when the PLO and other Arab countries announced their rejection of immigrant settlements only in the West Bank and Gaza, but did not object to bringing more Jewish immigrants to Israel, such a policy placed the Arabs in Israel in a dilemma of rejecting the principle of bringing Jewish immigrants to Israel (i.e., the Jewish state idea), or rejecting only the notion of losing jobs and resources (land) in the process of absorbing these immigrants; (c) As one Jewish intervenor argued, encounters were not influenced so much by the immigration issue because the Arab teachers' or students' status is not threatened directly by the absorption of immigrants. Their claims and arguments are derived only from the perceptional and attitudinal level and were not based on an immediate threat related to the absorption of immigrants; (d) In opposing the Jewish immigration on the basis of principle, Arabs in Israel will be opposing explicitly and directly the nature of Israel as a Jewish state. Generally, such opposition is avoided, at least publicly or explicitly, in their political statements.

The Arab participants' ambivalence was clearly detected by a Jewish intervenor, who described the Arab teachers' reaction to the immigration issue:

One thing amazes me about Arab teachers that they do not react to Jewish immigrants in the group. In one case, two Jewish immigrants who just arrived were talking about their rights over the land, while Arab teachers continued to talk about their rejection of Zionism, but without referring to the two participants who were sharing the same room with them.

An Arab facilitator also describes his disappointment with the Arab teachers' behavior in the discussion:

Although they said their opinion frankly, they always kept a back up line such as: What can we say, after all, this is a Jewish Zionist state. Therefore, based on its legal definition it has the right to bring Jews from everywhere. But, we do not want this to be at our expense.

Regardless of these participants' responses, it is clear that this political issue was not put on the agenda of the encounters in Israel. This finding raises the question of whether the political crisis or incident should be important only to the majority in order to be addressed in the encounter. But certainly the avoidance of this matter by Arabs and Jews in the encounter illustrates the asymmetric power relations that determine the agenda of any encounter between the two groups.

Based on the participants' reports, the Intifada, as a part of the political context, has the major impact on the content and processes of interaction between Arabs and Jews in all the intervention programs (see appendix 2). The Gulf War was discussed and addressed less in all the programs than the Intifada. But, the Gulf War was addressed more than the immigration of the Soviet Jews, which was hardly addressed by the intervention programs, and it did not influence the process of interaction in terms of increasing tension or anger among the participants, which the Intifada did. This result confirms the intervenors' evaluation of the three political context components and their impact on the intervention model.

Since the teachers' programs were continuing programs (participants met during the full year or even longer), participants were more alert to the political context and its influence on Arab-Jewish relations in Israel. Therefore, teachers addressed the political issue on a more regular basis than just in the students' encounters.

There were several participants, especially students, who mentioned that they discussed the Gulf War or the Intifada in their sessions. However, in examining their intervenors' evaluations, the intervenors claimed that these issues were not raised formally in any session. This contradiction can be explained by considering the fact that many of the political discussions during a student encounter take place in their private rooms or informally and without the facilitators' awareness.

## ENCOUNTER MODELS AND CONTEXT:
## AVOIDANCE, CONFUSION, AND SLOW ADJUSTMENT

In addition to political events, there were other elements that were identified as important factors in shaping the intervention models.

First, conducting research and evaluation reports in the case of NS, the necessity of conducting research limited the facilitators' flexibility and their ability to apply their own exercises. For research purposes, they were obliged to apply the same exercises and activities at the same time in all groups. It was a very structured program, with a strong focus on professional techniques of intervention. Therefore, since 1991, with the end of five years of research, the facilitators were more flexible in applying their model, which provides more room for facilitators to be creative and open to new techniques.

Second, when results of evaluation reports brought disappointment, directors and sponsors demanded changes. An intervenor explains:

> In evaluating the program, they [evaluators and directors] looked for substantial and concrete results such as how many teachers are participating or what practical implications the project had on the students. Therefore, their main reaction to the programs' activity was: teachers have been meeting since three years, so what?

In four cases certain changes took place after internal evaluation reports. In program VL, the director and the entire program shifted its focus from encounters into curriculum building after a 1987 report. Again, in 1989, the program introduced the geographical pairing of schools after the completion of its internal evaluation. Also, the research results of Bar and Asaqla (1988a, b) and Bar et al. (1989) changed the entire NS program.

Third, lack of funds is often a crucial element that was stressed by the encounter program (particularly directors) as determining the type of changes taking place in the intervention model and the organization in general. Program MA, for example, began conducting encounters only when specific donors requested such utilization of their donation. Also lack of funds was used to explain the lack of follow-up activities in several programs. Dependency on the Ministry of Education funds was also mentioned as one of the reasons for reluctance to introduce uninational meetings.

A planned change emerges as an interaction among several factors, such as research, professional evaluation reports, personal experience of intervenors, and clear understanding of the goals and functions of the intervention as an intervenor in the Arab-Jewish context. Unfortunately, most of the changes in the programs are not characterized or based on a well-planned approach (except in the case of program NS, which conducted the only longitudinal action research between 1985 and 1989). On the contrary, the changes are related to other factors that emerge mainly from organizational necessities or as immediate responses to political crises.

The intervention programs' reactions to each of the political situations were different according to the nature of the specific political context. There were four major events in the political contexts: the peace process, an ongoing process that reduced tension in the encounter, particularly in regards to representation issues (who represent the Palestinians). Denouncing events such as suicidal bombs functioned as a common ground for the participants; however, it was not sufficient to eliminate tension and suspicion among them. The overall encounters' environment, particularly in the initial phases of the peace process, was injected with optimism and hope that negotiation and positive changes are possible. However, since the deadlock and the outbreak of violence (initiated by Islamic militant groups and the Israeli siege of the territories and the election of Benjamin Netanyaho and the Likud), intervenors have been reporting less enthusiasm and optimism among participants.

The Intifada is a continuing, direct, and violent context that relates to Palestinians and Israeli Jews directly. The programs did adjust themselves to the Intifada by changing some of their components and processes of interactions, such as inserting more uninational frameworks and addressing political questions or issues.

The Gulf War is a discontinuing situation, indirect and less violent than the Intifada. The programs made a temporary adjustment to the Gulf War situation by separating their activities into Arab and Jewish schools. But when the war ended, most of them returned to their prewar activity because Arabs and Jews in Israel soon returned to their typical relationships.

The Soviet immigration, which is a continuing condition, has no explicit and immediate physical implications for the status of Arab and Jewish teachers or of students, and it is not directly and explicitly violent. Therefore, the program succeeded in avoiding it and neglecting its impact on the Arab-Jewish relations in Israel. Another explanation is that Arabs hesitate to raise this issue consistently since the Soviet Jewish immigration is a Jewish interest, which has the entire Jewish public consensus, and relates to the Jewishness of the state.

For those programs that dealt with the political issues prior to the occurrence of these events, the content of their models was apparently less affected. For example, the Intifada only intensified the interaction processes between Arabs and Jews in the encounter. However, those programs that did not deal with political issues were forced by the Intifada to introduce such issues as part of their content. They have a problem in integrating these political issues into their model or rationale. It would seem that they adjusted themselves only at the facilitators' level, but not in directors' formal statement of publications or in the printed material of these programs. They still focus only on positive aspects and neglect conflicts.

It is clear that the nature of the political development, incident, or even context determines the agenda and focus of the organization and program. For instance, in an interview with the Ministry of Education officer, who inspects and funds the work of most of these organizations and whose department was established to deal with Arab-Jewish relations and democracy, he argued that Arab-Jewish relations is one of the several important issues on which his department focuses. According to this official, the priority of the Israeli society has changed since 1985 when this department was established to confront Khana's movement. Now the focus is on the absorption of Soviet Jews into Israeli society.

This change in priority illustrates the impact of the context on all the programs. It is a clear indicator that the main factor that determines the encounter agenda, even the development of the models, is the national interest of the Jewish majority.

Having presented the findings and analysis (chapters 6–9), we now move to examine and discuss the general contribution of these models to changing Arab-Jewish relations in Israel, and the definition of the Arab-Jewish programs as conflict resolution programs.

# 10

# Arab-Jewish Encounter Programs

## *Political Change or Control?*

Arab-Jewish encounter programs have been developing since the mid-1950s. Therefore, a comprehensive consideration of the contribution of Arab-Jewish encounter programs to the political and social processes of change and control in Israel requires, in addition to the discussion of research findings, the examination of existing critiques of this field.

This chapter addresses these two aspects, and suggests a set of conflict resolution principles to be considered in conducting encounter programs in such ethnically divided societies in general and in Arab-Jewish encounters in particular. Thus, it will address the main question of how Arab-Jewish encounter programs in general, and the specific six program models relate to the processes of changes and control in the Israeli political and social system.

### LIMITATIONS OF THE ARAB-JEWISH ENCOUNTER FIELD

There are critiques and limitations based primarily on macro evaluations of the Arab-Jewish programs. Some of these critiques and problems are directed against the field of Arab-Jewish coexistence, and others are pointed against specific intervention models. Nevertheless, they all question the Arab-Jewish programs' function and contribution in the Israeli political context.

Some of these limitations were identified by Bar and Asaqla (1988a, b), Lemish et al. (1989), and Lemish et al. (1991).[1] Lemish et al. argue that, in fact, the "contact programs"[2] are another experience of asymmetry, because the primary reasons why Jewish participants take part in such activities are as follows: (a) They need to present Israel as a liberal state and ease their

*Jewish Israelis*
*Usl to*

consciences; make it a foreign service interest; (b) It is a test of their stereo-types, (i.e., are they primitive or capable of rational reasoning?); (c) They must prove they are tolerant; (d) They must test whether the Arabs are loyal to the Jewish state.

In reality, "external knowledge control" operates by imposing the Hebrew language on Arabs in Israeli society. In the encounter, this dominance of the Hebrew language causes Arabs to feel inferior, insecure, and alienated from the process, while Jews are very comfortable. They conclude their argument in suggesting an alternative approach to deal with the five main problems of the contact model: (a) The formal or external structure is symmetric, but in practice it is asymmetric; (b) There is a need to integrate cognitive, affective, moral, and action dimensions as opposed to only psychological or affective ones; (c) Tension is created in individual-social interrelationships, both in meetings and as a structure of social-political reality; (d) On the Jewish students' side, there is a need to confront their role as oppressors and superiors. On the Palestinian side, there is a need to encourage participants to communicate their feelings and claims as well as to become involved in the development of critical political consciousness and their national-cultural identity. (There are differential processes and summative outcomes;) (e) Another type of asymmetric relation exists on the organizational level in which Jewish directors and administrational managers control all the organizations (except program NS, which is co-directed by Arabs and Jews). Some Arab facilitators left the field because Jewish partners would not share the organizational basis.

According to facilitators, this type of intervention prompts the Ministry of Education to encourage the contact approach, with no political content and only cultural issues.[3]

Other research conducted by Bar and Asaqla (1988a:77) also commented on the effects of encounter models in program GH:

> The encounter in the Giva'a is contributing to the mutual acquaintance of both Arabs and Jews, to the knowledge and awareness of the actual relationship between the two groups and their meaning in reducing strangehood feelings. However, without these encounters these processes are taking place in reality among youth who did not take part in the encounter. But the encounter group has a stronger effect on the feelings of participants' knowledge of themselves.

Thus, the encounter did not strengthen identity and self-knowledge, although these were two goals that the intervenors had precisely expected in this specific program. If this is the situation, then for the Arab facilitators to achieve their primary goal was an illusion, while the Jewish intervenors' goals will be achieved.[4] In another concluding statement Bar and Asaqla stated that:

> Plunging right into encounter workshops without preliminary ongoing activities within a uninational framework will eventually be more beneficial for the Jewish participants. This is especially so when at times the political situation preserves and emphasizes the basic asymmetry between the two groups. (1988a:78)

Unfortunately, several of the examined case study programs in this research conducted their intervention or encounter without intensive preparation efforts. In one of the cases, Arab students were brought without any preparation at all. The group of sixteen Arab participants was selected one week prior to the encounter through personal contact of one of the Arab facilitators. This type of encounter is basically to serve the needs of the Jewish students who asked or are forced to encounter Arabs. Also Hofman (1987) and Bar and Bargal (1987) argued that even if the encounter is very professional and is systematically evaluated, it still has less effect on the Jews than on the Arabs in terms of being moderate and those who are willing to talk to the other side. The Jewish participants as majority members are initially less willing to do so.

Another accurate description of the AJP field is provided by Bandler (1991), who describes the Arab-Jewish program function as a safety valve in that it provides the framework for dialogue rather than violence.

In the first study of those organizations dealing with Arab-Jewish relations in Israel (Rosen, 1970), the same notion that is attributed to the condition of these programs in the 1990s was identified: "Arab-Jewish cooperation in Israel is alive but not well." This statement, made by Rosen in 1970, still illustrates the situation and relations between Arabs and Jews. In reference to the two sections of Jerusalem, the report in 1970 stated: "No wall must divide them again." To look for the unity of Jerusalem in 1970 (only three years after the Six Day War in which Jerusalem was captured by the Israeli Army) is a purely governmental and Jewish interest without consideration of the Arab participants' rights, interests, desires, or needs. This statement also reflects the origins and interests of the field of Arab-Jewish cooperation in Israel. The inclusion of Arabs in Israel and Arabs from East Jerusalem under the same title of coexistence is another governmental policy that is conducted by some of these organizations.

There were other statements made by Arab-Jewish organizations during the 1960s and 1970s that illustrate the function of these programs (Rosen, 1970). The Arab department, Haifa Labor Council (1969), stated its aim: "To find an Arab population which is ready to link its fate with the

fate of Israel." The Arabs' Department of the Histadut established the
Israeli Society for Understanding and Friendship and its goals were "(a) To
promote brotherhood, friendship, and understanding. (b) Educate Arabs
of Israel to full identification with the state."

These are strong verifications that conducting encounters and Arab-
Jewish dialogue during the 1950s, 1960s, and 1970s in Israel was func-
tionally a part of the "control system" created by the government to control
Arabs and to ensure the security and legitimacy of the state as Jewish.
Participation in Arab-Jewish programs became another tool for cooptation,
especially when those who took part in Arab-Jewish relations and cooperation projects received economic and material benefits.

Today, another governmental policy that is adopted by these organizations is the division among Arabs, Druze, Christians, and Bedouins. Some
organizations differentiate their programs according to these divisions; they
do not question them. For instance, many programs and activities of these
organizations are not directed or even marketed in the Druze schools.[5]

An additional, parallel critique comes from Kuttab (1988), who crit-
icizes the dialogue and encounter groups of Arabs from the West Bank and
Gaza Strip and Jews from Israel. His argument is valid when applied to
Arab-Jewish programs in Israel. He argues that

> When dialogue becomes a substitute for action, there are two
> results. First, it assuages the conscience of members of the
> oppressor group to the point where they feel they do not have to
> do anything else. The conscience is soothed and satisfied. On the
> other hand, for the members of the oppressed group it becomes a
> safety valve for venting frustrations. In both cases it becomes a
> means of reinforcing the existing oppression and therefore serves
> to perpetuate it. (1988:89)

Another pitfall indicated by Kuttab toward the Israeli-Palestinian
dialogue groups, which also applies to Arab-Jewish relation in Israels, is

> The tendency to accept the status quo and take for granted the
> generally prevailing assumption. . . . They tend to begin by
> accepting many of the assumptions of the oppressor concerning,
> for example, who is an extremist, what can be done in certain
> situations, and what is reasonable. (1988:86)

The prevailing assumptions that should be accepted and not brought
up during the discussion of Arab-Jewish relations in Israel are: (a) the
legitimacy of the Jewish state as opposed to the state of its citizens, and (b)
these Arab-Jewish groups are educational, not political activities, or that
they should not have any political activity or consequences. This is based on

the assumption that education is a neutral act or process that should not take any political stand.

In the critique of this field of AJP in 1990, Hall-Cathala presented the "radical" argument:[6]

> The coexistence programs that take place in the realm of Jewish state are simply an attempt to make Zionism more palatable for Palestinians by presenting the universal face of Israel. Instead, it is argued, they should be supporting the Palestinians' right for self-determination (in a state alongside Israel) or their right to live in a non-sectarian, secular Israel. (1990:138)

Hall-Cathala also describes adequately the differences between those in the intervention programs who argue that it doesn't matter what, how, or when the Israeli-Palestinian conflict will be settled because Arabs and Jews in Israel will continue to live together after that settlement. Therefore, eliminating hatred, stereotypes, and fears at the micro level will eventually produce positive changes (understanding, knowledge, and tolerance) that will correct the micro-level problems. In this way they contribute to peaceful coexistence.

Those who oppose this argument claim that the intervention program organizations do not confront the "root causes" of the micro-level problems on which they focus their energy. Fears, stereotypes, and hatred are a result of the macro-level problems of occupation, discrimination policy against the Palestinian minority in Israel, and definition of Jewish state:

> It is argued that any attempt to alleviate the micro-level problems is futile as long as the macro level problems exist and continue to fuel the flame of hatred. Attempts to quench these flames with mere "waters of dialogue" are considered doomed to failure. (1990:137)

But several of the intervenors who were interviewed for this research claimed that they selected this approach of AJP to influence the micro-level after they became tired of the traditional and typical protest activities against government policy.

There are certain objective limitations of the IPJAC as identified by Hall-Cathala (1990:135):

> (a) Their development has been hampered by the lack of infrastructure and resources, and hence lack of stability and professionalism in their operation. (b) They are extremely limited in reaching only a small part of the population. (c) They lack institutional support and nationwide legitimation from the authorities and the public. Although the Ministry of Education backed the

Arab-Jewish encounter in 1985, the Ministry lacks any potential to implement this policy because the religious education department, headed by Haddani, and the Chief Rabbinical Council came out against Arab-Jewish encounter on the bases that these encounters can potentially promote intermarriages between Arabs and Jews. In addition, the teachers in the Ministry of Education are not yet willing to commit themselves to the principle of education for co-existence because of fear, mistrust, lack of skills, as well as other reasons.[7]

Hall-Cathala's critique of these organizations is summarized:

The IPJAC organizations may be seen as part of the "reform" side of the peace movement. This is made evident by the fact that they most often aim to restore universal values, within the Jewish state, through their encouragement of tolerance, democracy, and co-existence; they don't aim to radically restructure Israeli society. Rather, taking existing ideals, they aim to reform apparent defects in the social order. (1990:139)

Figure 10.1 (based on Hall-Cathala, 1990) illustrates that the impact of the organizations at the macro level will be produced through changes in the participants' attitudes and approaches to each other on the personal and micro levels. The effect of these organizations or this type of intervention reaches the macro-level or the political macro-level indirectly when participants translate their attitudes or changed perceptions into behavioral acts, and succeed in maintaining their new attitudes under the pressure of peers, parents, teachers, and other agents of their environment who did not participate or do not share the same attitudes with them. According to this logic, considering the tremendous effects of the macro-level context (the Intifada, the Persian Gulf War, and discrimination policy), the impact of these intervention programs on the micro-level, if not wasted or reversed by the context, is as a "drop in the ocean," considering the limited population reached.

Finally, a very strong critique of the field is presented by Hana Bieran (1990) in her examination of the work of a newly emerging and promising Arab-Jewish project.[8] She argues that for both sides there are components of *hetnasaot*, or snobbish (elitism); Arabs looked down on the issue of Jewish views on female–male relations, issues of elder and children relations, and authoritarian figures in the child's life. The Jews looked down on Arabs in Israel because of the Jewish power image that they developed after 1967.

In addition, Jews try to be affiliated with a Western mentality and lifestyle, due to the influence of Western Jews who control Israeli institutions

**Figure 10.1. Philosophy Behind Arab-Jewish Intervention Programs**

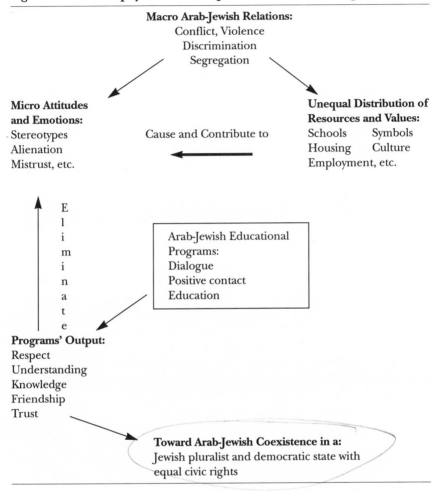

and elite, and because of their Zionist movement ideology and history. Bieran (1990) listed several components of inferiority and superiority that function as obstacles to dialogue between Arabs and Jews in Israel. She argued that: (a) the Jewish intervenors who initiated such AJP belonged to the elitist culture and they expected the Arabs to be thankful for their efforts to work in dialogue. The Jews brought Western techniques of emotional clarification through the individual exposure of himself or herself for others. This is not part of the Arab culture, which expresses attitudes through acts toward the object; (b) The Arabs have the value of interaction ritual, while the Jews adopted the direct manner of interaction; therefore, the Arabs are more polite and less direct in the encounter, which makes them more suspicious in the Jewish students' eyes; (c) The encounter is based on individualism; this expression and notion is strange to the Arab culture, which relies on the collectivism and the belonging of the individual to her or his family, *hamula* (extended family), and village; (d) Another component is the fear that Jews will become Arabs, or will be affiliated with Arabs. (e) The Jewish majority wants to preserve the image of power that they acquired after the 1967 war.

In the workshops, participants and intervenors tried to reach understanding, empathy, and even "love." They spread flowers, but they ignored the difficult problems and the asymmetric power relation. They did not talk about these issues until children exploded with hatred, violence, and rejection of each other. The above are general limitations in the various Arab-Jewish programs. The following are specific limitations that relate to the designs that were studied in this research.

## LIMITATIONS IN THE AJP DESIGNS

Every intervention model has its limitations, but when problems and limitations are identified through all the stages of the intervention (structure, process, content, goals, third-party role, and outcomes), doubts emerge whether the model achieves its objectives or whether it produces negative products. Unfortunately, this is the case in the examined Arab-Jewish intervention models in this research. The following limitations, which were recognized in most of the examined models, supports the need to reevaluate the Arab-Jewish programs' function and role in the Israeli context. These limitations include the following:

Structure:
  a. Lack of preparation; lack of uninational frameworks; high and unrealistic expectations among intervenors, as well as among participants who took part in the workshops; lack of participants' matching or uncareful selection of participants.
  b. Asymmetric access to Arabic and Hebrew languages in the encounter.
  c. Lack of follow-up activities.
  d. Lack of continuing, comprehensive intervention plans.
  e. Lack of research or evaluation of postencounter impact.

Content and process:
  a. Avoidance of political or conflict issues.
  b. Avoidance of differences and overemphasis on similarities.

c. Focus on interpersonal interaction processes.
d. Lack of "task-oriented" activities.
e. Asymmetric content; Arab students know more about the Jewish culture than Jewish participants know about the Arab culture, but the assumption and program content are designed toward equal and symmetric learning.
f. Lack of consideration of context impact and influence on the participants' attitudes and mode of interaction.
g. No consideration of practical and action output as a result of the intervention.

Third-party role (professional integrity):
a. Asymmetric roles between Arab and Jewish facilitators.
b. Facilitators less involved in the process and more focused on the content; few reflections and little feedback on the process.
c. Facilitators and directors are unaware of the philosophical, theoretical details of their models.
d. Opposed and unclarified goals and assumptions are held by directors and facilitators.
e. Lack of common goals and interest among intervenors regarding their intervention.
f. Idealistic expectation of the workshop output among facilitators, particularly the Arabs.
g. Lack of consistent professional training and support of the intervenors.
h. Confused and unclear perceptions of the Arab-Jewish conflict (issue, solutions, etc.) among intervenors.

Assumptions:
a. Asymmetric assumptions; majority-oriented assumptions such as "Jewishness of the state," a total separation of the Arabs in Israel from Arabs in West Bank and Gaza.
b. The intervention outputs and even processes are apolitical; it is an educational approach.

In addition to the above-listed problems, which are related to the design of the models of intervention, there are other factors that can influence and direct the programs' output contributing to the control or change process. Some of these factors are:

a. The lack of continuous and serious commitment and support from the general government offices.
b. The history of the organizations that operate these programs as being part of the ruling political party, which used these

programs to mobilize political support in the Arab minority.

c. The control system analysis provided by several scholars, particularly Lustick (1980). In these studies, scholars argue that the Ministry of Education (which provides support and protection in implementing Arab-Jewish programs) is an integral component of the cooptation and segmentation structure and policy that the government activates on Arabs in Israel.

## DO THE EXAMINED INTERVENTION MODELS CONTRIBUTE TO CONTROL OR CHANGES PROCESSES?

The previous two types of findings and indications support the argument that in their current structure, framework, process, content, and organizational structure, the intervention models are operating in a manner that can directly or indirectly contribute to preserving the status quo of the control system which the Israeli government imposes on Arabs in Israel. Such an outcome is seen clearly when examining the educational context of these programs.

The intervention models of AJP operate mainly in school systems, and the schools are "social agencies, created and maintained to achieve social purposes, what such purposes are, and the priorities assigned to each, are defined by majority opinion" (Stiles & Robinson, 1973:258). Thus, schools and educators are charged with maintaining the status quo rather than with producing changes that might upset the existing economic, social, and political equations. Educational professionals, by nature of their employment, are enslaved to the status quo (1973:259).

It is important to indicate that the external factors that promote changes in the educational system and in curricula are related to political pressure activated by minorities, crisis conditions, and economic and political changes. To generate change, educators and professionals should aim toward changing society and then convince their colleagues that change is both permissible and possible.

One of the main dilemmas that faces any educational system is the fact that the educational structure, the curriculum, and the educators' actions with students are social processes that can be used to maintain, intensify, confront or work to resolve the conflict. Thus, the role of education in and responsibilities for the conflict, are established by the way in which the curriculum is related to the conflict (Lemish et al., 1989).

In Israel, the main function of the educational system is no different from the above described set of characteristics. Especially when examining the Arab educational system (the policy of the Ministry of Education and the physical conditions of the schools), it is clear that the role of education is to maintain control over the Arabs in Israel and to nationalize the Jewish students and population against the threat of Arabs. The Arab minority school system, in general, and the curriculum, in particular, are designed to maintain control over Arab youth. The system is designed to educate for three main essential principles:

   a. Obeying the law and preserving the security of Israel.
   b. Accepting and acknowledging the assumption that Israel is the Jewish homeland.
   c. Strengthening the components of Arab students' Israeli identity and weakening their national Palestinian or religious identity.

Our case studies operate in this educational system and they are obligated to its principles and assumptions. They depend on the educational system to obtain their entry into the schools, and five of the six case studies receive financial support from the Ministry of Education. Thus, the operational context of these programs is part of the Ministry of Education's policy and general structure.

The Ministry of Education in Israel is divided between the religious and secular systems. The religious resistance to Arab-Jewish encounter programs is very strong and consistent. Since encounters between Arabs and Jews are affiliated with the left-wing political parties in Israel, the image of those who address this issue in their schools is "Peace Now," or people who are not right-wing oriented.[9]

Therefore, it was the Labor Party and its education minister who initiated the efforts to education for democracy and Arab-Jewish coexistence in 1983, although this fact did not guarantee that the issue would be discussed or addressed by all schools. Although the AJP intervention models are criticized in this research as being part of a control system that ensures the silence or coaptation of Arabs and Jews with the basic assumptions of the regimes, they were rejected, or avoided, among the mainstream Jewish school system, where most of the principals and inspectors expressed their concerns and fears that the Arab-Jewish relations issue might provoke the students and teachers. Therefore, they concluded that it would be better to avoid it or to focus on other issues that were more important to the Jewish community.

Such avoidance of or resistance to dealing with Arab-Jewish relations as it was presented by the Ministry of Education in the Jewish schools indicates further the fact that the Jewish schools are more conservative and less accepting of the idea of coexistence and equality between Arabs and Jews in Israel. This position is clear when we examine the report by the Unit for Democracy on the percentage of Arab schools and Jewish schools who took part in Arab-Jewish activities in the past year. (Twenty-eight percent of the schools who participated in Arab-Jewish relations programs were Arab, which is 80 percent of the Arab schools.)

The acceptance of the Ministry of Education's political and ideological assumptions is also reflected by the fact that encounter programs adopt and strengthen the separation between the political and the personal or psychological/cultural programs (interactions). The programs are defined as nonpolitical, a definition that educates young students to avoid political issues and to focus on intercultural and interpersonal relationships. Arab participants and intervenors request the discussion of political and conflict issues while Jewish participants and organization's directors and Ministry of Education officials seek to avoid such issues in the encounters. Such policy or ideology would certainly diffuse the victims' anger or resistance and alienate students of the majority from the current political issues. Thus, teaching students with noncritical, nonanalytical, and apolitical approaches, and encouraging them to avoid conflicts or politics, has strong support among those who encourage Arabs and Jews in Israel not to question the main assumptions of the state as a Jewish state. This outcome is also supported by the policy of creating and strengthening the coopted members among the Arabs in Israel.

The outcome is illustrated in figure 10.2, which contextualizes the Arab-Jewish programs in a control system analysis approach. The different Israeli Ministries apply many other policies in order to control the Arab community. In the cooptation category an important component is raising an educated, coopted Arab elite, which is implemented throughout the Israeli educational system. Arab-Jewish encounters—avoiding conflict and focusing on cultural and interpersonal relations, searching for similarities only, weakening the Arab students' national identity and strengthening their Israeli identity with Jewish components—are affiliated directly/indirectly with the cooptation policies and outcomes.

Regardless whether this role is played consciously or unconsciously, directly or indirectly, by Arab-Jewish encounter programs, it is clear that by raising the Arab and Jewish students' awareness of their Israeli civic identity only, these programs are contributing to weakening the Palestinian identity of the Arab students and strengthening the Israeli Jewish identity of the Jewish students, the Israeli identity that essentially reflects what the Jewish Zionist movement wishes to transmit to Jewish youth for generations to come.[10]

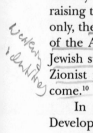

In addition, the different Israeli Ministries (Education, Economy, Development, and Interior) have discriminated against the Arab minority sector. This is particularly true of the Ministry of Education, which aims in its curricula to avoid and ignore the existence of the Palestinian identity

**Figure 10.2. Arab-Jewish Programs and the Control System Approach[12]**

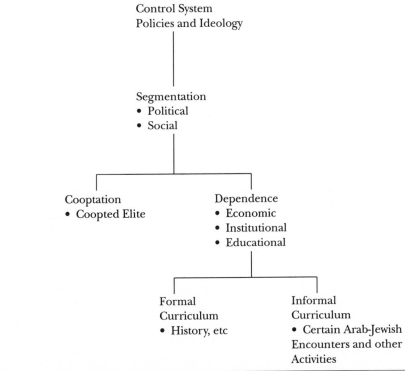

Control System
Policies and Ideology

Segmentation
• Political
• Social

Cooptation
• Coopted Elite

Dependence
• Economic
• Institutional
• Educational

Formal
Curriculum
• History, etc

Informal
Curriculum
• Certain Arab-Jewish
Encounters and other
Activities

among Arab students. The Ministry of Education with its applied policy in the Arab sector has contributed to the creation of a coopted educated elite and leadership.[11]

Thus, when these programs operate under the Ministry of Education's inspection, authority, and policy, and they are asymmetrical and implemented with low professional integrity, they contribute to the existence and production of a coopted Arab elite, educated through training to avoid political confrontation and conflict issues. This result is accomplished by following the Western models of individualization and segmentation of community. The product of these models is appropriate to the majority groups and serves the general control policy that has been implemented by the Israeli government for the past forty years.

It is important to indicate that the participants and third party in these programs are motivated by their pressing need to change the existing system (especially the Arab participants and third party); but, unfortunately, since research and professional development training are not often not available to these intervenors, they end up designing models that produce effects that satisfy primarily the interests of the Ministry of Education.

In spite of the above macro-level critique, the encounter programs achieve certain elements of success in establishing friendships on an interpersonal level between Arabs and Jews who would never meet or interact if it were not for the efforts of these programs. In addition, stereotypes and prejudice are reduced as a result of the experience; however, there is no evidence that such an impact endures beyond the immediate period of the encounter.

Also, supporters of the current work of encounter programs argue that compared with the general right extreme public opinion in Israel regarding coexistence between Arabs and Jews in Israel, these programs are offering and promoting better relationships and alternatives than those the right-wing extreme and official government offices are offering. Such an argument is true and worth considering, but based on the expected and perceived outputs of the six case studies in this research and other evaluation reports, the encounter's maximum impact remains within the general and the overall national consensus of the Jewish state. Most of the organizations do not challenge the basic assumption that the state is a Jewish state, or they avoid the connection between the Arabs in Israel and in the West Bank and Gaza Strip. In addition, most encounter program operate on an interpersonal level rather than on a group or community level.

## ARAB-JEWISH ENCOUNTER PROGRAMS AND EDUCATIONAL CONFLICT RESOLUTION MODELS

In order to address the application of conflict resolution in educational Arab-Jewish encounter programs, there is a need to identify the basic principles of the conflict resolution approach to educational encounters.

Conflict resolution intervention is defined in this research as those intervention models that relate equally and symmetrically to the parties of the conflict. The design of the intervention is based on equal rights for individuals, groups, and nations. The approach does not have any axioms that will serve the interest of the majority or the powerful groups. Such a setting, by its very nature, will empower the minority group participants.

It is a method that focuses on teaching participants encounter skills to analyze their conflict, understand basic components and issues, and  address the differences and similarities between the parties or participants. A conflict resolution encounter should incorporate a long and careful examination of the groups before they come to the encounter. Such intensive preparation will ensure that the encounter can address the different and shared needs of the different national groups. The conflict resolution encounter approach will teach the skills that enable participants to analyze structural aspects of their national or ethnic conflict and to apply these conflict resolution skills to their personal environment.

The analytical skills of this approach will enable participants to approach their conflict environments from a macro-level of analysis perspective. Participants will be encouraged to examine and comprehend the different actions and policies generated by the parties involved in the conflict in order to pursue their differential interests. Participants also will be trained to analyze and identify their behaviors and beliefs (on an individual level) and understand their function in dealing with the conflict.

To reach such an analytical mood, participants' emotions and feelings should be continually facilitated and expressed. This is an important component in reconstructing the participants' practical behavior and cognitive processes. The expression of the mutual negative and positive emotions of participants in the setting is a continuing and integral strategy that should be followed by the third party incorporated in the analytical process. It is not a two-hour session in which participants will air their anger and blame each other, then move automatically (i.e., in some cases artificially) to the next stage. In addition, each educational conflict resolution model should incorporate in its program practical methods and alternatives to implement positive attitude changes that occur during the program. The practical and action-proposed activities can be used as follow-up or as "tasks" to be completed by participants who are willing to increase their individual involvement in the conflict resolution.

Integrating the intergroup and collective identity of the participants as an integral part of the encounter is another essential conflict resolution principle. It balances the process of personalization of the interethnic ethnic conflict relations. Members of both encounter communities realize the meaning of the other side's collective identity—a realization that is often clouded and prevented by their isolated and one-sided socialization processes.

Through this approach participants will be educated to perceive conflict relations as a natural component of their lives. Thus, conflict will be presented as having potential for both negative and positive consequences. A main emphasis should be on the ability to transform the conflict relationship from adversarial and confrontational into cooperative and least coercive. Thus, teaching participants skills of controlling and shifting the course of conflicts becomes an important aspect of this approach.

The joint collaborative principle is another principle of conflict resolution approach that helps participants realize the benefit of cooperative relations and the advantages of taking ownership of their conflict relations.

Searching for creative solutions is a process that requires participants to evaluate and understand the limitations of black-and-white solutions or approaches to their conflict. The engagement in searching for new accepted and mutually agreed-upon solutions to the conflict is enriching and enlightening to participants from both sides of the conflict. Thus, solutions and future vision that should be developed in these encounters will not be based on current power relations or a minority–majority context, but take into consideration both ethnic groups' members' needs.

This outline of the proposed conflict resolution educational encounter incorporates goals not only on individual and interpersonal levels, but on group and structural macro-levels. The approach is designed to create individuals who are personally, socially, and politically involved in the conflict, and at the same time understand the complexity and interdependence of conflict relations. These participants will not be alienated from their conflict and aspire to live in a reality with no conflict, but they will be engaged in a process of transforming their conflict from its destructive course into a productive one. Therefore, a system and macro-analytical approach is what individuals and groups will be learning and practicing throughout the encounter.

The major focus is on producing participants who are more capable in their ability to critique, analyze, and understand the complexity of a conflict situation. Such participants will be more aware of the conflict caused by asymmetric power relations and be more able to challenge them theoretically and practically (on both levels of attitudes and behavior).

## CONFLICT RESOLUTION APPROACH
## IN ARAB-JEWISH ENCOUNTER

Having examined the Arab-Jewish intervention models in light of the proposed educational conflict resolution approach, it is clear that these programs do not fall under the definition of conflict resolution programs. Most of them operate without questioning the status quo, and some partially address core conflict issues. Their main output is to improve individual relationships, and those among them that do address conflict issues approach them on an individual or personal basis. In addition, these programs are very restricted by the access that the Ministry of Education provides to the school system. It is obvious that the Ministry of Education would not reconsider the basic assumption of the state as a Jewish state. The Ministry of Education's past and present policy has been to avoid political conflicts. Therefore, intervention programs that operate under the auspices, protection, and cover of the Ministry of Education are limited in the issues and content that they can address; therefore, they are also limited in the impact that they can produce.

Such an outcome is also clearly identified when comparing in the following two columns, the intervention programs' models with the conflict resolution approach. When the objectives of the educational conflict resolution approach are achieved, both Arab and Jewish participants will be more aware of the complexity of the conflict, more involved in the conflict, and more analytical and critical in their perception of the conflict.

| **Education for Coexistence** | **Educational Conflict Resolution Approach** |
| --- | --- |
| • Avoiding conflict | • Identifying and recognizing conflicts |
| • Focusing on similarities | |
| • Accepting minority–majority asymmetric power relations | • Acknowledging and respecting similarities and differences |
| • Preserving the status quo | • Questioning existing power relations, based on total equality |
| • Avoiding political involvement | • Empowering the participants |
| | • Encouraging social and political awareness and involvement |

Based on the above comparisons, it is obvious that none of the coexistence programs is designed and implemented to directly and intentionally influence the macro-level of Arab-Jewish relations (and some people argue that these programs do not have the intention to do so).

Nevertheless, several intervenors expressed their hope that their intervention has potential implications for the macro-level of Arab-Jewish relations in Israel. However, their main focus and primary goal remains on the interpersonal and educational level of contact.

The examined Arab-Jewish intervention programs are reform or status quo models and fall far short of the transformational conflict resolution educational approach. However, these organizations are fulfilling a certain need among both Arabs and Jews in Israel. In addition, they are functioning as a reminder, particularly to the Jewish majority, of the existence of a conflict and an asymmetrical relationship. It is ironic that, on the one hand, a main impact and function of these programs is the political statement that they reflect: the pressing need for the Ministry of Education to address Arab-Jewish relations and the need to place the Arab-Jewish relations on the national agenda of the state. On the other hand, the same organizations attempt to avoid being political or even dealing with political issues (see table 10.1).

There is no doubt that Arab-Jewish encounters and the education for equality, intercultural sensitivity and communication, and critical thinking

**Table 10.1. Arab-Jewish Encounter Programs and Conflict Resolution Approaches**[13]

| Intervention Model/ Change Attribute | Current Arab-Jewish Encounter Program | Conflict Resolution Approach |
|---|---|---|
| Cause | Change in individual | Change in individual |
| Change | Perceptions of other individuals | Perceptions of other individuals and system |
| Rate | Gradual | Gradual |
| Magnitude | Small-scale | Small- and large-scale |
| Process (Agent) | Individual | Group and individual |
| Time Span | Short-term | Long-term |
| Direction | Accept and maintain existing power relations | Question and change power relations |
| Outcome | Potential for attitudinal and perceptional changes on interpersonal level | Potential for attitudinal, perceptional, and behavioral changes on group and interpersonal levels |

are important and essential to the Arab-Jewish conflict, especially in a context where negative and destructive interaction overwhelms day-to-day interactions.

Because of this essential necessity of the encounters, there is a need to improve their design and implementation. The following part includes a general set of principles which if included in any Arab-Jewish intervention program, can contribute to its effectiveness and applicability to both Arabs and Jews in Israel.

## MAJOR RECOMMENDATIONS

Several principles should be followed by intervenors in designing an Arab-Jewish intervention model. First, the main goal of intervention ethics must be the empowerment of both parties. Empowering the Arab participants can be achieved by recognizing the fact that they are oppressed and that they, as other citizens in the state, should receive and demand equal rights.

Empowerment of Arab participants means increasing their ability to criticize their environment and issues in their internal community and their relation to the Jewish community. Empowerment of the Jewish group means increasing their awareness of and involvement in the state and governmental policies and raising more awareness of political and social responsibility.

Second, institutionalization of the concept of improving Arab-Jewish relations on equal bases can be the most effective condition on this field. This means that governmental offices in Israel, particularly the Ministry of Education, must recognize the importance and urgency of addressing Arab-Jewish relations from an early age in the school system. This can become a vital tool in legitimizing the necessity of dealing with Arab-Jewish relations among the Jewish majority. (Gaining legitimacy is a main concern and obstacle that intervenors face in addressing Arab-Jewish relations among members of the Jewish community.)

Third, an Arab-Jewish program must include education for democratic values, particularly adopting education for total equality as being the central value of the model. It should not be education for limited equality (i.e., advantages for one national group over those of the other group).

Fourth, symmetric and differential design and implementation of the intervention model should be incorporated in the program's projects. These models must be based on the different needs of the two groups. The program should reflect clearly the fact that the two groups of participants have two sets of different and similar needs and motivations for attending the program. If encounters are not beneficial or necessary to the needs of both groups, they should not be included in the program. An intervention program might be more effective—in specific stages and under certain conditions—without encounter or face-to-face interaction.

Fifth, an intervention program must be based on the fact that there are conflicts between Arabs and Jews in Israel, and that facing and discussing these conflicts is a constructive rather than a destructive act. Currently, by avoiding the discussion of the political issues and power relations issues in Arab-Jewish programs, Arabs and Jews are contributing to the escalation of the conflict in the future.

Sixth, on an organizational level the program sponsors must invest more resources (time, staff, and programs) because training their intervenors professionally qualifies them to conduct such a mission.

Finally, a program must be based on the notion that the application of these recommendations does not reduce the urgency of the structural changes needed to improve Arab-Jewish relations in Israel because any Arab-Jewish program cannot and should not substitute the need for such structural and institutional changes.

# Appendix 1

# Participants and the Intifada's Impacts

**Jews**
a. No impact of the Intifada.
b. Every time Arabs said "our brothers in the territories," they had an internal power that motivated them to change things; we could not deal with their strong argument on the occupied territories.
c. I did not expect them to be so influenced by the Intifada, since they live in Israel and receive the benefits of being israeli citizens. If I knew that before, I would have changed my strategy and thinking.

**Arabs**
d. The Intifada did not help us find solutions and it increased the tension, especially when a Jewish student left the discussion because her father was killed by the Intifada.

**Program MA:**
a. There was no impact because "I made a distinction between Arabs from the territories and those from Israel."
b. We did not discuss political issues at all.

**Program GH:**

**Jews**
a. The Intifada was used as a source for accusing each other, and it was confusing because first we were against them, then we understood that they are not involved. It is difficult to distinguish Israeli Arabs from those in the territories.
b. No need to talk about conflicts.
c. It was discussed with Arab students when they came to our rooms. It was very tense, and I was very afraid.

**Arabs**
d. It was a content issue with some tension.
e. The Intifada motivated "us" to attend the encounter and find solutions.
f. It caused anger and accusations during the discussion.

169

**Program BH:**

a. Did not discuss it.

**Program VL: Arabs and Jews**

a. It was always in the background of our discussion. It was a source of anger and "stuck" on our positions.

b. Only discussed it in the binational meetings.

**Program UFD: Arab and Jews**

a. Because of the Intifada's incidents, some participants left the group. But through the three years in the same group we learned to listen even in most difficult killing incidents.

b. The issue was always there, but we got used to it; therefore, people do not care.

# Appendix 2

# Participants and the Gulf War's Impact

**Program NS**

a. They did not speak about the Gulf War, but somebody drew Sadam's picture and since they supported Sadam, this added tension.

b. Did not discuss the issue.

c. Some students were against Sadam, but most Arabs supported him.

d. Sometimes we were on the same side.

e. It was an issue of accusation between Arabs and Jews.

f. An Arab student said: "Yes I am pleased when missiles reach Israel because they were pleased by the missiles falling on Baghdad."

**Program MA**

a. No impact since the war was in Iraq and it has nothing to do with us here.

b. No impact.

**Program GH**

a. There was no impact, because after we spoke we realized that this will affect both if Sadam attacks.

b. Did not address it.

c. Did not discuss it, but a student asked me personally.

d. Discussed it and speculated if Sadam has the capabilities.

**Program BH**

a. Discussed it only with friends informally.

b. Did not address it.

**Program VL**

a. Stopped the programs' meetings and changed the content: "Jews were talking about existential fear, therefore no time for encounters."

b. Increased mistrust between Arabs and Jews: "They dance on the roofs, you can not rely on them, cannot trust them."

c. Prevented the program from continuing, but did not influence, it was not on the agenda even.

171

**Program UFD**

a. Jews were afraid of the war; meetings after the war were sensitive and had to talk carefully.
b. It was a crisis that "broke something in Jews"; reduced sympathy and trust in Arabs, a sort of disappointment.
c. It was not a permanent content issue.

# Appendix 3

## Examples of Success in Arab-Jewish Intervention

**Jews:**
- A student that became active on the immigration issue.
- Class is continuing for the third year.
- A Jewish student who supported Kahana's movement decided to fight against it after the workshop.
- Participants of the program decided to meet with Palestinians from the West Bank and Gaza while their community leaders tried to prevent them.
- Students who are not afraid to enter an Arab village and enjoy the interaction.
- A group that refused to come, but then they thanked us.
- Group of teachers who decided to continue and work on joint curriculum.
- Group who stated their willingness to continue.
- Jewish teacher said that encounter helps her deal with her right-wing family.
- Teachers complement the encounter.
- Positive feedback at the end of the workshop: students are tired but happy something happened to them.
- A group tried to accuse the other side, but learned about themselves.

**Arabs:**
- During a lecture, a former participant responded positively to a question whether it was worth it or not to continue in our work.
- Soldiers who keep coming to show their friends the encounter place.
- Students demonstrate and organize petitions.
- Students of two schools wrote a letter jointly to the defense minister.

- Student who stood up against his parents and visitors when they accused Arabs as killers (wrote a letter).
- Participants calling me at home.
- Soldiers meet me at the street and salute me (2).
- Jewish group who decided to do national service in the program.
- Jewish female who agreed to equal rights for women but not for Arabs, but she realized her contradictions.
- An Arab teacher who stood up against her principal and challenged the teachers on their double standard.
- Success of two to three encounters out of ten.
- Group that resisted coming, then thanked them.
- Jewish principal who rejected the encounter with Arabs during the war and then agreed after the war, when the program director spoke to her.
- A teacher who understands that she should deal with the concept conflict and not coexistence.
- Jewish teachers who sympathize.

# Notes

## 1. INTERGROUP RELATIONS APPROACH

1. According to this theory, there are three principles of human perceptions: (1) there is a need to explain the cause of overt behavior; (2) overt behavior is explained as caused by either external or internal dispositions; and (3) in order to attribute an internal disposition to a person, the perceiver must know that the latter has the ability to choose an alternative response.

## 2. CONFLICT RESOLUTION PRINCIPLES IN INTERGROUP CONFLICT

1. For further information on the emergence of the field, see Abu-Nimer, 1993.

2. Based on the Creative Conflict Resolution for Children, Fairfax, VA, 1993, and Conflict Resolution Clinic, George Mason University, 1992.

## 3. ARAB-JEWISH CONFLICT IN ISRAEL

1. These figures do not include the inhabitants of East Jerusalem, and based on statistical abstract of Israel 1990.

2. At least those parts that were occupied in the 1948 war, and were not included in the Jewish area based on the 1947 partition plan.

3. One of the previous advisors of the Israeli prime minister for Arab affairs.

4. No integration of Arabs (even those who serve in the army) in high-ranking governmental or economic positions.

5. These statistics are based on a report by the committee of the heads of Arab councils in Israel, 1991.

6. This is a new instruction by the Ministry of Education that is not followed by all schools—only 42 percent of secular public schools.

7. This notion was expressed in 45 Arab schools during seminars on Arab-Jewish relations conducted by the Institute for Education and Coexistence between Arabs and Jews in Israel in 1986–89.

## 4. THE ARAB-JEWISH COEXISTENCE PROGRAMS

1. The Unit for Democracy operates as a coordinating office for the different Arab-Jewish activities in the school system. The Unit is one of the case studies in this research because its staff also conducts activities in many schools.

2. See the religious department's response to this plan. In addition, the Unit for Democracy shifted its focus from Arab-Jewish relations to democracy in general, and in 1990–91, the focus was shifted to the new Soviet Jewish immigrants to Israel.

3. Shutfoot was established after the failure to implement a Supreme Court decision to return parts of Ekrit and Bera'am (two Arab villages that were controlled by the Jewish Kibbutz while the original inhabitants were refugees in surrounding villages). Youth Sing Different Song was established in 1984, after Jewish masses attacked Arabs in the Afula Town to avenge the deaths of two Jewish teachers who had been killed in the area. Several other organizations were established after the Intifada and the Gulf War.

4. A Jewish religious newspaper published in Jerusalem.

5. Based on a statement of Tawfeek Asalia, Haaretz, July 19, 1985.

6. This is used by Hall-Cathala in his 1990 book to describe Arab-Jewish contact programs.

7. Since 1993, Neve Shalom/Wahat Al Salam's team and some faculty from the social psychology department at Tel-Aviv University, began a course that focuses on Arab-Jewish encounters. Such a course is currently being replicated at Ben Gorion University, David Yaleen College, and other academic institutions.

8. Rzael & A. Katz. "Education for Coexistence at Schools between Arab and Jewish Israeli Citizens," report ordered by the Ministry of Education, Unit for Democracy, 1990.

9. These are five of the six organizations, which are included in this research (Neve Shalom/Wahat El Salam is the sixth case study).

10. The Partnership ended its Arab-Jewish encounters in 1990 as a result of political and organizational problems. Based on interviews with staff members of Shutfoot, the argument is that the Ministry of Education

did not approve their encounter's program; therefore, the Ministry blocked the activity of Shutfoot in the schools and lobbied to prevent foreign funds from supporting Shutfoot activities.

11. Beit Hagefen is one of the six case studies that this research is examining.

12. Based on the reports of 1985–89 on Neve Shalom/Wahat El Salam's Project to the Ford Foundation, 1989.

13. Based on the Bar et al. (1989) report.

14. Such an argument does not apply to the Bar, Bargal, and Asaqla reports and research because they used the term "Palestinian Arabs," as their participants and facilitator preferred.

## 5. MOTHODOLOGICAL CONSIDERATIONS AND THE ARAB-JEWISH PROGRAMS

1. There were several Parliament members who refused to be interviewed for the study (all of them belong to the Likud Party). One Arab interviewee was not a Parliament member, but he is the leader of the Islamic movement in Israel. Also, I conducted an interview with an official of the Ministry of Education, who is inspecting and coordinating all the organizations' intervention in Jewish-Arab relations in Israel.

2. The facilitators explained the reasons for initiating Arab-Jewish encounters and other programs.

## 6. THE ENCOUNTER PROGRAMS' DESIGNS

1. The analysis of the data on conflict assumptions is according to both dimensions: subject role and organization are presented in the chapter on conflict perceptions.

2. This figure is based on the content issues described in chapter 4: Content of Intervention Models: Intervenors' Perspective.

3. Based on Katz and Khanov, 1990.

4. But GH has returned to the co-facilitation model with the recruitment of new staff after 1993.

5. A similar finding was indicated in Katz and Khanov's 1990 report. However, they did not provide an explanation for this tendency.

6. See chapter 3, on Arab and Jewish micro level of attitudes and perceptions.

7. The relations between Palestinians and Jews in Israel after the 1967 war and Land Day in 1976 influenced the minority members' identity and status.

8. Land Day, March 31, 1976, commemorates the day that six Arabs from Israel were killed in a confrontation with Israeli security forces. This marks the rise and the explicit expression of the Palestinian identity among the Arabs in Israel (Lustick, 1980).

## 7. PERCEPTIONS OF THE ARAB-JEWISH CONFLICT IN ISRAEL

1. The numbers in each of the following tables indicate how many responses were classified in each category.

## 8. PERCEPTION OF SUCCESS

1. Numbers represent frequency of responses among intervenors only.
2. Numbers represent frequency of responses among participants only.

## 9. IMPACTS OF THE POLITICAL CONTEXT
## ON THE ENCOUNTER MODELS

1. In 1992, the Arab-Jewish encounter program at Van Leer Institute was terminated and its one permanent staff member was moved to the Arab-Jewish center at Haifa, which agreed to host the program for an additional year during which its remaining funds were utilized in completing ongoing encounter projects.

2. This Arab-Jewish project in Van Leer ended its activities in August 1996.

3. The update on the political changes since Oslo agreement is based on chronology of events in the *Journal of Palestine Studes*, 1992–1997.

4. Based on interviewes conducted in November, 1995, and summer 1996, with a select group of intervenors in Arab-Jewish relations.

5. Support for this finding is reported in the lack of involvement of Arab parents in their children's schools activities or for school in general (see chapter 3).

6. The "Dome of the Rock" incident refers to the killing of nineteen Palestinians who were in the Jerusalem mosque for Friday prayer. the "Reshion Le Tzion" incident refers to the killing of seven Palestinian workers from Gaza by an Israeli soldier while they were waiting for a bus. The "stabbing knives" period refers to several killings and attacks on Jews by Palestinians from the West Bank and Gaza.

7. For example, in one of the observations, six months after the Gulf War, in a two-day encounter the issue of the Gulf War was not raised by either the facilitator or participants.

## 10. ARAB-JEWISH ENCOUNTER PROGRAMS

1. The list of limitations and problems with the programs was also provided based on interviews conducted during the second phase of the fieldwork (February, 1992) with a group of Arab and Jewish experienced facilitators. These facilitators work with many organizations and use different models of intervention.

2. This is a term they used to describe the Arab-Jewish intervention models implemented by the different organizations.

3. They based their argument on the UFD director's remarks during a May 27, 1991 conference in Tel-Aviv, in which the Unit for Democracy (the Ministry of Education office that inspects Arab-Jewish programs in the schools) instructed organizations to avoid political issues and focus on the cultural and professional aspects.

4. These Arab intervenors' goals, according to my hypothesis, function as an explanation and argument that enables them to justify their work in that field as national interest. This is their way of adjusting to the fact that they work in such a field.

5. The Ministry of Education and other governmental offices established a separate school system and curriculum for the Druze community in an attempt to separate the Druze from the Arab community in Israel (Halabi, 1989).

6. These arguments were presented by political activists and intervenors who were interviewed for Hall-Cathala's book.

7. According to one survey, 20 percent of Jewish teachers actually supported the extreme antidemocratic movement of Khana (Hall-Cathala 1990:138).

8. A clinical psychologist who criticizes one of the promising projects of Arab-Jewish relations, in which Arab students teach Jewish students and vice versa.

9. Peace Now is a liberal Jewish political movement that opposes the occupation of the West Bank and Gaza Strip.

10. The Israeli identity is mainly a composition of Jewish identity, symbols, values, and culture. It has no content that represents the Arab or Palestinian culture and identity. Therefore, during many of the encounters and workshops, when participants are asked to list components of their Israeli identity, they present mainly Jewish components. Arabs in Israel, according to research (see Rouhana, 1988; Mari'i, 1988; Lustick, 1980), are also alienated and excluded from the general Israeli consensus.

11. It was described by Lustick (1980) as one of the three components of the control system that the various Israeli governments imposed on Arabs in Israel.

12. It is important to mention that the purpose of this is only to illustrate the context in which Arab-Jewish programs operate. Obviously, there are many other components that are included in each category of the control analysis approach (for more detail see Lustick, 1980).

13. Some consistent differences were reported in the findings section, at least between the design and implementation of program NS and the other programs. Therefore, it is important to indicate that this typology represents at least five of the six examined intervention programs.

# Bibliography

Able, R. (Ed.). (1982). *The politics of informal justice.* Vol. 1. New York: Academic.

Abu-Nimer, M. (1993). *Conflict resolution between Arabs and Jews in Israel: A study of six intervention models.* Dissertation research, George Mason University, Fairfax, VA.

Adler, P. (1987). Is ADR a social movement? *Negotiation Journal, 3,* 1, 32–39.

Al-Haj, M. (1995). *Education and empowerment.* Albany, NY: State University of New York Press.

Al-Haj, M. (1991). *Arab local government in Israel: Development, problems, and needs.* Paper presented at the Leonard Davis Institute conference, Hebrew University, Jerusalem.

Al-Haj, M. (1991). *Education and social transformation among Arabs in Israel.* Tel-Aviv: International Center for Peace in the Middle East. (Hebrew)

Al-Haj, M. (1989). *Education for democracy in the Arab schools in Israel: Problems and tasks.* Giva'at Haviva. (Hebrew)

Al-Haj, M. (1987). *Social change and family processes: Arab communities in Shefar-Am.* Boulder, CO: Westview.

Allen, P. T. (1986). Contact and conflict in industry. In M. Hewstone & R. Brown (Eds.), *Control and conflict in intergroup encounters* (pp. 137–151). Oxford: Basil Black well.

Allport, G. W. (1954). *The nature of prejudice.* Reading, MA: Addison-Wesley.

Amir, Y. (1976). The role of intergroup contact in change of prejudice and ethnic relations. In P. A. Katz (Ed.), *Towards the elimination of racism.* New York: Pergamon.

Amir, Y. (1969). Contact hypothesis in ethnic relations. *Psychological Bulletin, 71,* 319-342.

Amir, Y., & Ben-Ari, R. (1989). Enhancing intergroup relations in Israel: A different approach. In Stereotyping and Jewish youth in Israel: Reality and potential. *Megamot, 30,* 306–315. (Hebrew)

Amir, Y., & Ben-Ari, R. (1987). Encounters between Arabs and Jews. In Bar-Tal, D. Graumann, Kruglanski, A. & Wolfgang, S. (Eds.), *Stereotyping and prejudice.* London: Springer-Verlag.

Amir, Y., Rivner, M., Bizman, A. & Ben-Ari, R. (1980). The contact between Arabs of the West Bank and Gaza and Israelis and its consequences: Theoretical and empirical evaluations. *Megamot, 26,* 179-192. (Hebrew)

Ashmore, R. D. (1970). The problem of intergroup prejudice. In B. E. Collins (Ed.), *Social psychology* (pp. 246–339). Reading, MA: Addison-Wesley.

Ashmore, R. D., & Del Boca, F. K. (1976). Psychological approaches to understanding intergroup conflicts. In P. A. Katz (Ed.), *Towards the elimination of racism* (pp. 73–123). New York: Pergamon.

Avruch, K., Black, P., & Scimecca, J. (Eds.). (1991). *Conflict resolution: Cross-cultural perspectives.* Westport, CT: Greenwood.

Avruch, K., & Black, P. (1990). Ideas of human nature in contemporary conflict resolution theory. *Negotiation Journal, 6,* 221–228.

Avruch, K., & Black, P. (1991). The culture question and conflict resolution. *Peace and Change, 16,* 22–45.

Avruch, K., & Black, P. (1987). A generic theory of conflict resolution: A critique. *Negotiation Journal, 3,* 87–96, 99–100.

Azar, E. (1979). Peace amidst development: A conceptual agenda for conflict and peace research. *International Interaction, 6* (2), 123–143.

Azar, E., & Burton, J. (Eds.). (1986). *International conflict resolution: Theory and practice.* Boulder, CO: Lynne Reiner.

Bacow, L., & Wheeler, M. (1983). *Environmental dispute resolution.* New York: Plenum.

Bandler, K. (1991). *Jewish-Arab relations in Israel.* New York: American Jewish Committee, International Perspective.

Bank, M. (Ed.). (1984). *Conflict in world society: A new perspective on international relations.* New York: St. Martin's.

Bank, M. (1987). Four concepts of peace. In D. Sandole & I. Sandole (Eds.), *Conflict management and problem solving* (pp. 259-274). New York: University Press.

Bar, H., & Asaqla, G. (1988a). *Encounter staff in Giva'at Haviva: Group profile April 1988.* Jerusalem: Institute for Applied Social Research. (Hebrew)

Bar, H., & Asaqla, G. (1988b). *Arab-Jewish youth encounter in Giva'at Haviva: Evaluation of attitudes "before" and "after."* Jerusalem: Institute for Applied Social Research. (Hebrew)

Bar, H., & Bargal, D. (1995). *Living with the conflict.* Jerusalem: Jerusalem Institute for Israeli Studies. (Hebrew)

Bar, H., & Bargal, D. (1987). *The school for peace at Neve Shalom, 1985: Description and assessment of a longitudinal intervention among trainees and staff.* Jerusalem: Israeli Institute of Applied Social Research.

Bar, H., & Bargal, D. (1985). *The school of peace at Neve Shalom: Description and analysis of an action research.* Jerusalem: Institute of Applied Social Research.

Bar, H., Bargal, D., & Asaqla, G. (1989). *The school for peace at Neve Shalom, 1985–1989: A preliminary integrative summary of the findings of an evaluation and action research.* Jerusalem: Israeli Institute of Applied Social Research.

Bar, H. Bargal, D. & Asaqla, G. (1988). *The school for peace at Neve Shalom,— 1988.* Jerusalem: Israeli Institute of Applied Social Research.

Bargal, D. (1990). Contact is not enough—the contribution of Lewinian theory to intergroup workshops involving Arab Palestinians and Jewish youth in Israel. *International Journal of Group Tension, 20* (2), 179–192.

Bargal, D., & Bar, H. (1992). A Lewinian approach to intergroup workshops for Arab-Palestinian and Jewish youth. *Journal of Social Issues, 48* (2), 139–154.

Bargal, D., & Bar, H. (1990a). Role problems of trainers in an Arab-Jewish conflict management workshop. *Small Group Research, 21,* 5–27.

Bargal, D., & Bar, H. (1990b). Strategies for Arab-Jewish conflict management workshops. In S. Wheelan, E. Pepitone, & V. Abt (Eds.), *Advances in field theory* (pp. 210–229). Beverly Hills, CA: Sage.

Bargal, D., & Peled, T. (1986). A practical theory for Arab-Jewish intergroup initiated encounters. In E. Stivers & S. Wheelan (Eds.), *The Lewinian legacy: Field theory in current practice* (pp. 213–220). Berlin: Springer-Verlag.

Bar-Tal, D. Graumann, C. T. Kruglanski, A. & Wolfgang, S. (Eds.). (1989). *Stereotyping and prejudice.* London: Springer-Verlag.

Bayley, J. C. (1973). Conflict research: The case against. *Community Forum, 3.*

Been, Y. (1991). *Eshkolot program—the vision, goal, process, and lessons, 1987–1990.* Kfar Masarik. (Hebrew)

Been, Y. (1976). *The Arab school: Examination of its human problems.* Giva'at Haviva. (Hebrew)

Ben-Ari, R., & Amir, Y. (1988a). Promoting relations between Arabs and Jewish youth. In J. E. Hofman (Ed.), *Arab-Jewish relations in Israel: A quest for human understanding.* Bristol, IN: Wyndham Hall.

Ben-Ari, R., & Amir, Y. (1988b). Intergroup conflicts in Israel: Evaluation and paths for change. *Psychology, A,* 49–57. (Hebrew)

Ben-Ari, R., & Amir, Y. (1986). Contact between Arab and Jewish youth in Israel: Reality and potential. In M. Hewstone & R. Brown (Eds.),

*Contact and conflict in intergroup encounters* (pp. 45–58). Oxford: Basil Blackwell.

Bengham, G. (1985). *Resolving environmental disputes: A decade of experience.* Washington, DC: The Conservation Foundation.

Benjamin, A., & Levi, A. M. (1979). Before Camp David: An experiment of peace education in Jewish-Arab workshops. *Havat Da'at, 11,* 83–99. (Hebrew)

Benjamin, A. (1970). *Report on sensitivity training workshop for Arab and Jewish students.* Haifa: American Jewish Committee and B'ni B'rith Foundation.

Benjamini, K. (1980). The image of the Arab in the eyes of Israeli youth: Changes over the past 15 years. *Studies in Education, 27,* 65–74. (Hebrew)

Bercovitch, J. (1984). *Social conflict and third parties.* Boulder, CO: Westview.

Bieran, H. (1990). *Superiority and inferiority feelings: Obstacles to dialogue between Arabs and Jews.* Unpublished paper.

Bizman, A. (1978). *Status similarity, status level and the reduction of prejudice following contact between national groups.* Unpublished doctoral dissertation, Bar-Ilan University, Ramat Gan, Israel. (Hebrew)

Blake, R., Shepard, H. A., & Mouton, J. (1964). *Managing intergroup conflict in industry.* Houston: Gulf.

Bligh, A. (1991). *Government policies towards the Arab sector in Israel.* Paper presented at the Leonard Davis Institute conference, Hebrew University, Jerusalem. (Hebrew)

Brim, O., & Wheeler, S. (1966). *Socialization after childhood: Two essays.* New York: Wiley.

Brimm, M. (1972). When a change is not a change. *Journal of Applied Behavioral Science, 8* (1).

Brislin, R. W. (1986). A cultural general assimilator. *International Journal of International Relations, 10,* 215–234.

Brislin, R. W. (1981). *Cross cultural encounters.* New York: Pergamon.

Burton, J. (1990a). *Conflict resolution and provention.* New York: St. Martin's.

Burton, J. (Ed.). (1990b). *Conflict: Human needs theory.* New York: St. Martin's.

Burton, J. (1988). *Conflict resolution as a political system.* Working Paper No. 1, Center for Conflict Analysis and Resolution, George Mason University.

Burton, J. (1986). *Resolving deep-rooted conflict: A handbook.* New York: University Press of America.

Burton, J. (1984). *Global conflict: The domestic sources of international conflict.* Brighton, Sussex: Weatscheaf.

Burton, J. (1969). *Conflict and communication: The use of controlled communication in international relations.* London: Macmillan.

Burton, J., & Dukes, F. (Eds.). (1990a). *Conflict: Readings in management and resolution.* New York: St. Martin's.

Burton, J., & Dukes, F. (Eds.). (1990b). *Conflict: Practice in management, settlement and resolution.* New York: St. Martin's.

Carpenter, S., & Kennedy, J. (1988). *Managing public disputes: A practical guide to handling conflict and reaching agreements.* San Francisco: Jossey-Bass.

Cohen, S. P., & Azar, E. (1981). From war to peace: The transition between Egypt and Israel. *Journal of Conflict Resolution, 25,* 87–114.

Cohen, S. P., Kelman, H., Miller, F. D., & Smith, B. L. (1977). Evolving intergroup techniques for conflict resolution: An Israeli-Palestinian pilot workshop. *Journal of Social Issues, 33* (1), 165–188.

Colosi, T. R., & Brekly, A. E. (1986). *Collective bargaining: How it works and why.* New York: American Arbitration Association.

Committee of Arab Local Councils. (1986). Memorandum to the minister of education in regard of the Arab education in Israel. (Arabic and Hebrew)

Committee of Arab Local Councils. (1991). The Committee for Social Conditions of the Arab Community. Nazareth. (Arabic and Hebrew)

Coogler, O. J. (1978). *Structured mediation in divorce settlement: A handbook for marital mediators.* Lexington, MA: Lexington.

Cook, S. W. (1979). Social science and school desegregation: Did we mislead the Supreme Court? *Personality and Social Psychology Bulletin, 5,* 420–437.

Cook, S. W. (1978). Interpersonal and attitudinal outcomes in cooperating interracial groups. *Journal of Research and Development in Education, 12,* 97–113.

Cook, S. W. (1962). The systematic analysis of socially significant events: A strategy of social research. *Journal of Social Issues, 18,* 66–84.

Coser, L. (1956). *The function of social conflict.* New York: The Free Press.

Curle, A. (1986). *In the middle: Non-official mediation in violent situations.* New York: St. Martin's.

Curle, A. (1971). *Making peace.* London: Tavistock.

De Reuck, A. (1983). A theory of conflict resolution by problem solving. *Man, Environment, Space, and Time, 3* (1).

De Reuck, A. (1974). Controlled communication: Rationale and dynamics. *Human Context, 4* (1), 64–80.

Dollard, J., et al. (1939). *Frustration and aggression.* New Haven, CT: Yale University Press.

Doob, L., & Fotz, W. (1973). The Belfast Workshop: An application of group techniques to destructive conflict. *Journal of Conflict Resolution, 17,* 489–512.

Doob, L., (1970). *Resolving conflict in Africa: The Fermeda Workshop.* New Haven, CT: Yale University Press.

Duke, J. (1976). *Conflict and power in social life.* Salt Lake City, UT: Brigham Young University Press.

Dunn, S., & Smith, A. (1989). *Inter school links.* Center for Study of Conflict, University of Ulster, Northern Ireland.

Egan, G. (1976). *Interpersonal living: A skills contract approach to human relations training in groups.* Monterey, CA: Brooks/Cole.

Egan, G. (1970). *Encounter group processes for interpersonal growth.* Monterey, CA: Brooks/Cole.

Ehrlich, H. J. (1973). *The social psychology of prejudice: A systematic theoretical review and propositional inventory of American social psychology study of prejudice.* New York: John Wiley & Sons.

Fisher, Ronald J. (1989). *The social psychology of intergroup and international conflict.* New York: Springer-Verlag.

Fisher, Ronald J. (1981). A third party consultation workshop on the Indian-Pakistani conflict. *Journal of Social Psychology, 112.*

Fisher, Roger, & Ury, W. (1981). *Negotiation agreement without giving in.* New York: Penguin.

Ganim, A., & Ausitsky, S. (1990). *Autonomy for Arabs in Israel: An initial discussion.* Review on Arabs in Israel, No. 5. Giva'at Haviva: Institute for Arab Studies.

Gordon, H., & Gordon, R. (1991). *Israel/Palestine: The quest for dialogue.* Maryknoll, NY: Orbis.

Gordon, H. (1986). *Dance, dialogue, and despair: Existentialist philosophy and education for peace in Israel.* Tuscaloosa: University of Alabama Press.

Gordon, H. (1980). Buberian learning groups: A response to the challenge of education for peace in the Middle East. *Teachers College Record, 82,* 291–310.

Greenbaum, C., & Abdul Razak, A. (1972). *An Arab-Jewish student workshop.* Unpublished manuscript.

Greer, C. (Ed.). *Divided society: The ethnic experience in America.* New York: Basic.

Gudyknust, W., Hammer, M., & Wiserman, R. (1977). An analysis of an integrated approach to cross cultural training. *International Journal of Intercultural Relations, 1,* 99–110.

Haidar, A. (1991). *The Arab population in the Israeli economy.* Tel-Aviv: International Center for Peace in the Middle East. (Hebrew)

Halabi, O. (1989). *The Druze in Israel: From religion to people!* Golan Heights: University Graduate Committee. (Arabic)

Hall-Cathala, D. (1990). *The peace movement in Israel, 1967–1987.* New York: St. Martin's.

Haraeven, A. (1989). *Arab-Jewish project: Evaluation report.* Jerusalem: Van Leer Institute. (Hebrew)

Haraeven, A. (1981). *One of every six Israelis: Mutual relations between the Arab minority and the Jewish majority.* Jerusalem: Van Leer Institute.

Harrington, C. (1982). Delegalization reform movements: A historical analysis. In R. Able (Ed.), *The politics of informal justice,* vol. 1. New York: Academic.

Haynes, J. M. (1981). *Divorce mediation: A practical guide for therapists and counselors.* New York: Springer.

Hertz-Lazarovitch, R. (1989). *Report on continual participation in encounters of Beit Hagefen—1989.* Haifa: Beit Hagefen. (Hebrew)

Hewstone, M., & Brown, R. (Eds.). (1986). *Control and conflict in intergroup encounters.* Oxford: Basil Blackwell.

Hofman, J. E. (Ed.). (1988). *Arab-Jewish relations in Israel: A quest for human understanding.* Bristol, IN: Wyndham Hall.

Hofman, J. E. (1987). *Project of meetings between Jewish and Arab high school pupils: A progress report, 1984–1987.* Haifa: Beit Hagefen.

Hofman, J. E. (1986). *Social psychological research on Arab and Jewish high school students in Beit Hagefen, Haifa, 1985/1986.* Haifa: Beit Hagefen.

Hofman, J. E. (1982). Social identity and readiness for social relations between Arabs and Jews in Israel. *Human Relations, 35,* 727–741.

Hofman, J. E. (1977). Identity and intergroup perception in Israel. *International Journal of Inter-Cultural Relations, 1* (3), 79–102.

Hofman, J. E. (1972). Readiness for social relations between Arabs and Jews in Israel. *Journal of Conflict Resolution, 16,* 241–251.

Hurwitz, D. (Ed.). (1992). *Walking the red line: Israelis in search of justice for Palestine.* Philadelphia: New Society.

Katz, I., & Khanov, M. (1990). Review of the dilemma in facilitating Arab-Jewish encounter groups in Israel. *Megamot, 73* (1), 29–47. (Hebrew)

Kaufman, E. (1988). An exchange on dialogue. *Journal of Palestine Studies, 17* (2), 84–108.

Kelly, H. (1968). The two functions of reference groups. In H. Proshansky & Seidenberg, H. (Eds.), *Basic studies in social psychology* (pp. 210–214). New York: Holt, Rinehart & Winston.

Kelman, H., & Cohn, S. (1986). Resolution of international conflict: An interactional approach. In S. Worchel & W. G. Austin (Eds.), *Psychology of intergroup relations* (pp. 323–342). Chicago: Hall.

Kelman, H. (1986). *Interactive problem solving: A social-psychological approach to conflict resolution.* Unpublished paper.

Kelman, H., & Cohen, S. (1976). The problem-solving workshop: A social psychological contribution to the resolution of international relations. *Journal of Peace Research, 13* (2).

Kelman, H., & Warwick, D. (1973). Bridging micro and macro approaches to social change: A social-psychological perspective. In G. Zaltman (Ed.), *Process and phenomena of social change.* New York: Wiley-Interscience.

Kelman, H. (1972). The problem-solving workshop in conflict resolution. In R. Merritt (Ed.), *Communication in international politics.* Champaigne: University of Illinois Press.

Kolb, D. (1983). *The mediators.* London: MIT.

Kretzmer, D. (1991). *The legal status of Israel's Arab citizens.* Paper presented at the Leonard Davis Institute conference, Hebrew University, Jerusalem.

Kriesberg, L. (1991). Conflict resolution applications to peace studies. *Peace and Change, 16* (4), 400–417.

Kriesberg, L., & Thorson, S. (Eds.). (1991). *Timing the deescalation of international conflict.* Syracuse, NY: Syracuse University Press.

Krussel, K., & Pruitt, D. (Eds.). (1989). Mediation research: The process and effectiveness of third-party intervention. San Francisco: Jossey-Bass.

Kuttab, J. (1988). An exchange on dialogue. *Journal of Palestine Studies, 17* (2), 84–108.

Lakin, M., Lomranz, J., & Lieberman, M. (1969). *Arabs and Jews in Israel: A case study in human relations training approach to conflict.* New York: American Academic Association for Peace in the Middle East.

Laue, J. (1990). The emergence and institutionalization of third party roles in conflict. In J. Burton & F. Dukes (Eds.), *Conflict: Readings in management and resolution* (pp. 256–274). New York: St. Martin's.

Laue, J. (1988). Getting to the table: Three paths. *Mediation Quarterly, 20,* 2–15.

Laue, J. (1987). The emergence and institutionalization of third party roles in conflict. In D. Sandole & I. Sandole (Eds.), *Conflict management and problem solving* (pp. 17–29). New York: University Press.

Laue, J. (1982). Ethical consideration in choosing intervention roles. *Peace and Change, 7* (2–3), 29–41.

Laue, J., & Cormick, G. (1978). The ethics of intervention in community disputes. In G. Bermant, H. Kelman, & D. Warwick (Eds.), *The ethics of social intervention* (pp. 205–232). Washington, DC: Halsted.

Lederer, K., Galtung, J., & Antal, D. (1980). *Human needs: A contribution to the current debate.* Cambridge, MA: Oelgeschlager, Gunn & Hain.

Lemish, P. (1989). *Cultural conflict and curriculum.* Paper presented at the conference of the American Educational Research Association, San Francisco.

Lemish, P., Mula, W., & Rubin, A. (1989). *Cultural and educational struggle: A model for curriculum development.* Nazareth: Arab-Jewish Facilitator Conference.

Lemish, P., Mula, W., Sonnenschein, N., Gur-ziv, H., & Zaretsky, E. (1991). *Power relationships in divided societies: The case of education for coexistence in Israel.* Unpublished paper.

Levi, A. M., & Benjamin, A. (1977). Focus and flexibility in a model of conflict resolution. *Journal of Conflict Resolution, 21* (3), 405–424.

Levi, A. M., & Benjamin, A. (1976). Jews and Arabs rehearse Geneva: A model of conflict resolution. *Human Relations, 20* (11), 1035–1044.

Levi, A. M., & Benjamin, A. (1975). High school attempt to resolve the conflict: The Nachsholim Workshop. *Iyumin B'hinuch, 9,* 131–146. (Hebrew)

Lewin, K. (1958). Group decision and social change. In E. Maccoby, T. Newcomb, & E. Hartley (Eds.), *Readings in social psychology* (3rd ed., pp. 197–211). New York: Holt, Rinehart & Winston.

Lewin, K. (1948). Conduct, knowledge, and acceptance of new values. In G. W. Lewin (Ed.), *Resolving social conflicts* (pp. 560–570). New York: Harper & Row.

Lewin, K. (1947). Frontiers in group dynamics. *Human Relations, 1,* 143–153.

Liberman, M. A., Yalom, I. D., & Miles, M. B. (1973). *Encounter groups: First facts.* New York: Basic.

Lustick, I. (1980). *Arabs in the Jewish state: Israel control of a national minority.* Austin: University of Texas Press.

Mahameed, H., & Gootman, Y. (1983). Autostereotyping and heterostereotyping of Arabs and Jews in different contact conditions. *Havat Da'at, 15,* 90–108. (Hebrew)

Mari'i, S. (1988). Sources of conflict in Arab-Jewish relations in Israel. In J. Hofman (Ed.), *Arab-Jewish relations in Israel.* Bristol, IN: Wyndham Hall.

Mari'i, S. (1978). *Arab education in Israel.* Syracuse, NY: Syracuse University Press.

Maslow, A. H. (1954). *Motivations and personality.* New York: Harper.

McDonald, J. (1991). Further exploration of track two diplomacy. In L. Kriesberg & S. Thorson (Eds.), *Timing the de-escalation of international conflicts* (pp. 201–221). Syracuse, NY: Syracuse University Press.

McDonald, J., & Bendahmane, D. 1987 (Eds.). *Conflict resolution: Track two diplomacy.* Washington, DC: U.S. Government Printing Office.

McDowall, D. (1989). *Palestine and Israel: The uprising and beyond.* London: I. B. Tauris.

Merry, S. (1989). Mediation in nonindustrial societies. In K. Kressel & D. Pruitt (Eds.), *Mediation research* (pp. 68–90). San Francisco: Jossey-Bass.

Ministry of Education & Hebrew University. (1990). *Democracy and coexistence: Identification and evaluation.* Bibliography Guide, Jerusalem.

Ministry of Education. (1985). General managers' report to examine alternative, Arab education situation.

Ministry of Education. (1984). *Hozer mankal meohad.*

Ministry of Education. (1975). A special committee on education in the Arab sector.

Mitchell, C. (1990). necropolis man and conflict resolution: More questions about basic human needs theory. In J. Burton (Ed.), *Conflict: Human needs theory* (pp. 149–176). New York: St. Martin's.

Mitchell, C. (1981). *Peace making and the consultant's role.* New York: Nichols.

Montville, J. (1987). The arrow and the olive branch: A case for track two diplomacy. In Bendahmane, D. & McDonald, J. (Eds.), *Conflict resolution: Track two diplomacy* (pp. 161–175). Washington, DC: U.S. Government Printing Office.

Mortimer, J. T., & Simons, R. G. (1978). Adult socialization. *Annual Review of Sociology, 4,* 421–454.

Moore, C. (1987). *The mediation process: Practical strategies for resolving conflict.* London: Jossey-Bass.

Murray, J. (1984). Third party intervention: Successful entry for the uninvited. *Albany Law Review, 48* (3), 573–615.

Nader, L., & Todd, H. (Eds.). (1978). *The dispute process—law in ten societies.* New York: Columbia University Press.

Peled, T., & Bargal, D. (1983). *Intervention activities in Arab-Jewish relations: Conceptualization, classification, and evaluation.* Jerusalem: Israeli Institute for Applied Social Research.

Peres, Y., Ehrlich, A., & Yuval Davis, N. (1970). National education for Arab youth in Israel: A comparative analysis of curricula. *Jewish Journal of Sociology, 12* (2), 147–164.

Pettigrew, T. (1986). The intergroup contact hypothesis reconsidered. In M. Hewstone & R. Brown (Eds.), *Control and conflict in intergroup encounters* (pp. 169–195). Oxford: Basil Blackwell.

Pettigrew, T. (1971). *Racially separate or together?* New York: McGraw-Hill.

Pompa, G. G. (1987). The community relations service. In D. Sandole & I. Sandole (Eds.), *Conflict management and problem solving* (pp. 130–134). New York: University Press.

Reicher, S. (1986). Contact and racialization: Some British evidence. In M. Hewstone & R. Brown (Eds.), *Control and conflict in intergroup encounters* (pp. 152–168). Oxford: Basil Blackwell.

Rogers, C. R. (1957). The necessary and sufficient conditions of therapeutic personality change. *Journal of Consulting Psychology, 22,* 95–103.

Rokeach, M. (1968). *Beliefs, attitudes, values.* San Francisco: Jossey-Bass.

Rokeach, M. (Ed.). (1960). *The open and closed mind.* New York: Basic.

Rosen, H. (1970). *The Arabs and Jews in Israel: The reality, the dilemma, the promise.* New York: American Jewish Committee.

Rosenfeld, H. (1980). Men and women in Arab peasant to proletariat transformation. In D. Stanley (Ed.), *Theory and practice* (pp. 195–219). The Hague: Mouton.

Rouhana, N. (1988). The civic and national subidentities of the Arabs in Israel: A psychopolitical approach. In J. E. Hofman (Ed.), *Arab-Jewish relations in Israel: A quest for human understanding.* Bristol, IN: Wyndham Hall.

Rouhana, N. (1987). Arab-Jewish relations as educational issue: Social psychological approach. *Psychology and Counseling in Education, 9* (8), 188–206. (Hebrew)

Rubenstein, R. (1990). Basic human needs theory: Beyond natural law. In J. Burton (Ed.), *Conflict human needs theory* (pp. 336–356). New York: St. Martin's.

Rzael, C., & Katz, A. (1991). *Education for coexistence at schools between Arab and Jewish Israeli citizens.* Jerusalem: Salid Institute. (Hebrew).

Said, E., & Hitchers, C. (Eds.). (1988). *Blaming the victim: Spurious scholarship and the Palestinian question.* London: Verso.

Salem, R. A. (1982). Community dispute resolution through outside intervention. *Peace and Change, 8* (2–3), 91–104.

Sarsour, S. (1991). *The structure and content of education in the Arab sector.* Paper presented at the Leonard Davis Institute for International Relations conference, Hebrew University. (Hebrew)

Scheillenberg, J. (1982). *The science of conflict.* New York: Oxford University Press.

Scimecca, J. (1991). Conflict resolution: The emergence of the field. In K. Avruch, P. Black, & J. Scimecca (Eds.), *Conflict resolution: Cross cultural perspectives* (pp. 19–35). Westport, CT: Greenwood.

Scimecca, J. (1988). Conflict resolution: Not just for children. *Peace and Change, 4* (1), 20–23.

Scimecca, J. (1987). Conflict resolution the basis for social control or social change? In D. Sandole & I. Sandole (Eds.), *Conflict management and problem solving* (pp. 30–34). New York: University Press.

Shammas, A. (1981). Diary. In A. Haraeven, *One of every six Israelis: Mutual relations between the Arab minority and the Jewish majority.* Jerusalem: Van Leer Institute.

Sherif, M. (1958). Superordinate goals in the reduction of intergroup conflict. *American Journal of Sociology, 43,* 349–356.

Shipler, D. (1986). *Arabs and Jews: Wounded Spirit in a Promised Land.* London: Bloomsbury.

Simon, B. (1985). *Stereotyping and homogenization of ingroup and outgroup in majority-minority contexts.* Doctoral dissertation, University of Munster.

Sites, P. (1973) *Control of the basis of social order.* New York: Dunellen.

Smith, M. W. (1981). *Improving intergroup relations: The impact of two types of small group encounters between Israeli Arab and Jewish youth.* Unpublished doctoral dissertation, Temple University, Philadelphia.

Smith, M. (1987). Findings from the field: Peace studies in practice. In Chetkow-Yanoov, B., (Ed.), *Dealing with conflict and extremism* (pp. 119–125). Jerusalem: JDC.

Smooha, S. (1992). *Arabs and Jews in Israel: Change and continuity in mutual intolerance.* Boulder, CO: Westview.

Smooha, S. (1989). *Arabs and Jews in Israel: Conflict and shared attitudes in a divided society.* Boulder, CO: Westview.

Smooha, S. (1984). *The orientation and politicization of the Arab minority in Israel.* Haifa: University of Haifa Arab-Jewish Center.

Smooha, S., & Peretz, D. (1982). The Arabs in Israel. *Journal of Conflict Resolution, 26,* 451–484.

Stephan, W. G. (1987). The contact hypothesis in intergroup relations. In Hendrick, C. (Ed.), *Group process and intergroup relations* (pp. 7–40). Beverly Hills, CA: Sage.

Stephan, W. G. (1985). Intergroup relations. In G. Lindzey & E. Aronson (Eds.), *The handbook of social psychology* (3rd ed., vol. 3, pp. 599–658). New York: Random House.

Stephan, W. G., & Stephan, C. W. (1984). The role of ignorance in intergroup relations. In N. Miller & M. B. Brewer (Eds.), *Groups in contact: The psychology of desegregation* (pp. 229–255). San Diego: Academic.

Stiles, J. & Robinson, B. (1973). Change in education. In G. Zaltman (Ed.), *Process and phenomena of social change.* New York: Wiley-Interscience.

Stock, E. (1968). *From conflict to understanding: Relations between Jews and Arabs since 1948.* New York: Institute for Human Relations.

Susskind, L. E., & Cruishank, J. (1987). *Breaking the impasse: Consensual approach to resolving public disputes.* New York: Basic.

Susskind, L. E., & Wheeler, M. (1983). *Resolving environmental regulatory disputes.* Cambridge: Schenkman.

Susskind, L. E. (1981). Environmental mediation and accountability problems. *Vermont Law Review, 6* (1), 1–47.

Tajfel, H., & Turner, J. C. (1986). The social identity theory of intergroup behavior. In S. Worchell & W. G. Austin (Eds.), *Psychology of intergroup relations* (pp. 7–24). Chicago: Hall.

Tajfel, H. (1982). *Human groups and social categories: Studies in social psychology.* Cambridge: Cambridge University Press.

Tajfel, H. (1970). *Experiments in intergroup discrimination. Scientific American,* *223,* 96–102.

Taylor, S. E. (1981). A categorization approach to stereotyping. In D. L. Hamilton (Ed.), *Cognitive processes in stereotyping and intergroup behavior.* Hillsdale, NJ: Erlbaum.

Tessler, M. (1980). *Arabs in Israel.* American University Staff Field Report, Asia, No. 1, 1–25.

Tilly, C. (1978). *From mobilization to revolution.* Reading, MA: Addison-Wesley.

Toval, S., & Zartman, W. (1985). *International mediation in theory and practice.* Boulder, Colo.: Westview.

Triandis, H. C. (1975). Cultural training, cognitive complexity, and inter-personal attitudes. In S. Brislin, S. Bochner, & W. Lonner (Eds.), *Cross-cultural perspective on learning.* Beverly Hills, CA: Sage.

Triandis, H. C. (1972). *The analysis of subjective culture.* New York: Wiley.

Tzimah, M. (1984). *Attitudes of youth in Israel toward democratic values.* Jerusalem: Van Leer Institute. (Hebrew)

Tzimah, M. (1980). *Attitudes of youth to democratic values.* Jerusalem: Van Leer Jerusalem Foundation. (Hebrew)

Van Leer Institute. (1990). *A report on Arab-Jewish encounters project-pairs.* Jerusalem: Van Leer Institute. (Hebrew)

Van Leer Institute. (1986). *A report on Arab-Jewish encounters project.* Jerusalem: Van Leer Institute. (Hebrew)

Walton, R. E. (1970). A problem solving workshop on border conflict in eastern Africa. *Journal of Applied Behavioral Science, 6,* 453–489.

Weiner, A., Bar-On, A., & Weiner, E. (1992). *The Abraham Fund directory of institutes and organizations fostering coexistence between Jews and Arabs in Israel.* Baltimore: Port City.

Wilmot, W., & Hocker, J. (1978). *Interpersonal conflict.* IA: William C. Brown. Dubuque, Ia.: Wm. C. Brown Communication.

Zureik, E. (1979). *The Palestinian in Israel: A study in internal colonialism.* London: Routledge & Kegan Paul.

# Index